Political and Economic Migrants in America

CUBANS AND MEXICANS

I took my Power in my Hand—
And went against the World—
'Twas not so much as David had—
But I—was twice as bold—

I aimed my Pebble—but Myself
Was all the one that fell—
Was it Goliath—was too large—
Or was myself—too small?

EMILY DICKINSON

Political and Economic Migrants in America

CUBANS AND MEXICANS

by Silvia Pedraza-Bailey

 University of Texas Press, Austin

First edition, 1985

Requests for permission to reproduce material
from this work should be sent to:
  Permissions
  University of Texas Press
  Box 7819
  Austin, Texas 78713

Library of Congress Cataloging in Publication Data
Pedraza-Bailey, Silvia, 1946–
  Political and economic migrants in America.

  Bibliography: p.
  Includes index.
    1. Mexicans—United States. 2. Cubans—United States. 3. United
  States—Emigration and immigration. I. Title.
  JV6895.M48P43   1985   325.2'72'0973   84-19648
  ISBN 0-292-76492-8

Poem on page ii reprinted by permission of the publishers and the Trustees
of Amherst College from *The Poems of Emily Dickinson*, edited by
Thomas H. Johnson, Cambridge, Mass.: The Belknap Press of Harvard University Press, Copyright 1951, © 1955, 1979, 1983 by the President and
Fellows of Harvard College.

Contents

Acknowledgments

The idea that underlies this work grew out of a personal experience. A friend once asked me to accompany him to the north side of Chicago to meet a Chilean political immigrant with whom he wanted to speak. I was to serve as the Spanish translator. Although I was a child of the Cuban political migration and had long known its details in my bones, it was on this meeting that it first acquired for me a significance that lifted it beyond that of my own life. As C. Wright Mills formulated more than twenty years ago, the sociological imagination lies at the intersection of troubles and history.

Like any life, this work now has but a dim memory of its first. Yet, with their encouragement, my dissertation committee assisted its first birth. My largest debt is to my chairman, Arthur Stinchcombe, because he believes that what we do has value, provided we have something to say. What is of value here is very much thanks to him. I also wish to thank Teresa Sullivan, William J. Wilson, Adam Przeworski, John Coatsworth, and Dennis Hogan. Altogether, during the years of my graduate study at the University of Chicago, they influenced me the most. Without being complacent I am content, so I owe them the largest thanks.

The American Sociological Association Minority Fellowship Program provided a Sydney S. Spivack dissertation fellowship and a National Institute of Mental Health grant, both of which enabled me to complete the first version of this work. The U.S. Department of Labor awarded Teresa Sullivan and me a research grant that provided the initial computer funds. Faculty research grants from Washington University helped me to deepen and broaden the research. Those years of effort are reflected in this second birth. The staff at the University of Texas Press responsibly guided me through the review process. These various supports proved essential. I remain grateful to all of them.

Without their being responsible for any of my faults, the comments of many opened me to new questions: Aristide Zolberg, Alvin Gouldner, Timothy Anna, Charles Hirschman, Gastón Fernández, Pedro Cavalcanti, Sergio Díaz-Briquets, and anonymous reviewers. I sincerely thank them. Beyond the academic community, by simply living their lives in decency, Marina López and Gilberto Suárez influenced my vision. We must provide bread with liberty.

Many friends also collaborated in typing numerous drafts: Mary Peters, Marcia Jones, Elsie Glickert, Opal Barbour, and Doris Suits. The skills of Earline Franklin and Karen Coleman are responsible for two full drafts. I especially thank them for the reliance and confidence they generated in me. With enthusiasm, Carol Dudziak and Stephen De Long also aided me.

David Pittman, my chairman at Washington University, kept asking me for the book. I need to thank him.

I dedicate this book to my husband, Lee E. Bailey. He tried to help me in every way he could.

For many Cubans such as myself, revolution and exile pruned the years of youth. Our Cuban childhood, the revolution, and our American adolescence generated a revolution of self. While our adolescence was never carefree, nor our adult years unerring, satisfaction still abides in commitment and change.

The meaning of this work lies for me in what Hemingway captured in *The Old Man and the Sea*: an old Cuban fisherman, born to be a fisherman, struggling with the biggest and strongest fish he had ever reckoned with. Perhaps, like Santiago, I have only his skeleton left to show for the long struggle. But I feel I have now returned ashore.

Political and Economic Migrants in America
CUBANS AND MEXICANS

1. Immigrant Assimilation

Popular Images of Cubans and Mexicans

In popular perception, Cuban immigrants in America seem a "success story," while Mexican immigrants remain a "silent invasion." For twenty years, the media celebrated Cubans for their economic success, particularly for making "faster progress in their adopted country than has any other group of immigrants in this century."[1] Depicted as "resourceful, aggressive, and energetic," Cubans emerged "almost overnight" from the deprived, refugee state and moved into the middle class, "skipping lightly over—or never even touching—the lowest rung of the economic ladder" that was a necessary first step for the immigrants of yesterday.[2] Cubans were celebrated not only for their remarkable assimilation and the "intangible resources" they brought with them—a vast capacity for hard work, faith in God, respect for American laws, united families—but also for fleeing communism: above all else, for their "unquenchable thirst for liberty."[3]

The "Cuban Success Story," as one account labelled it, abounds with individual stories of success. Those who started on shoestrings and in a few years grew to million-dollar businesses epitomized Cuban entrepreneurial success.[4] Among others, International Boats, Wajay Crackers, Calmaquip Engineering, and Suave Shoe Company bore testimony to the "innumerable rags-to-riches stories" so dear to American culture.[5] The Cuban success story was written not only by these prosperous business executives but also by the less obtrusive architects, builders, bankers, doctors, and teachers who launched new careers all over the United States, a result of the exodus called "the greatest brain-drain of the century."[6]

Few other nationality groups have "taken root so quickly or progressed so rapidly," observers stressed. The applause for their achievements generated faith in their future: "The Cuban bus boy in the restaurant, the record suggests, may soon be running that restaurant."[7] With this stress on the contributions of the Cuban immigrants, until the Mariel exodus the conclusion stood plain: "Castro's loss is U.S. gain."[8]

During those same twenty years, the media depicted Mexican immigrants as *bracero* farm workers who accepted wages and working conditions domestic workers refused, thereby contributing to the "worsening plight" of domestic farm workers.[9] They were also depicted as a source of despair for American labor organizers;[10] as a "legitimate and sensible source of seasonal labor" for growers horrified by the very thought of unionism;[11] and as unhappy "wetbacks" subject to the caprice of both smugglers and the American Dream.[12]

With the need for temporary farm labor to harvest perishable crops, American agriculture rejoiced in workers who could be obtained in large numbers on short notice and "just as quickly sent home" at harvest's end. The *braceros* were praised for being "skilled, highly motivated workers who obey orders, work quickly, and don't complain."[13] At the end of the *bracero* program, growers cried for Mexican "stoop labor": the harvest, they said, needed people conditioned to "hard and dirty" work often done under a "blazing sun."[14] When the United States "bid *adiós*" to the *braceros*, their replacements, domestic farmhands, often fled after a couple of days of bending over vegetables.[15]

When in the late sixties César Chávez spun La Causa, the movement that aimed to organize farm workers and change the lives of all Mexican Americans, illegal Mexican immigrants became "a special curse."[16] Hired as strikebreakers, illegal Mexican immigrants often impaired the strikes of farm workers.[17] As the number of apprehensions of illegal Mexicans rose in the seventies, they became "the nation's least clamorous but fastest growing minority," and the concern to "dam the alien tide" mounted.[18] As Mexican immigrants increasingly went to work not only on farms but also in cities, doing menial jobs in industry and service, the concern became alarm over their torrent. The conclusion stood plain: the "silent invasion" takes "millions of American jobs."[19]

What have been the processes of assimilation of Cuban and Mexican immigrants that they gave rise to such contrasting images? To understand the difference in the assimilation of these two groups of immigrants, we must first clarify what assimilation is.

Assimilation Theory: Cultural and Structural Emphases

In a nation of immigrants, American social scientists have long been concerned with the outcomes to the process of integrating those who arrived at its shores. The oldest and most persistent theory expected a process of assimilation. Yet from the outset there was an ambiguity in the idea. "It is not always clear," wrote Robert Ezra Park in 1913, "what assimilation means. Historically the word has had two distinct significations. According to earlier usage it meant 'to compare' or 'to make like'. According to later usage it signifies 'to take up and incorporate'."[20] Park himself later evolved the race relations cycle, stages of interaction through which racial groups progressed irreversibly: contact, competition, accommodation, and eventual assimilation.[21] The ambiguity remained until, in 1964, Milton Gordon distinguished among types of assimilation. But the fundamental characteristic of assimilation theory was already evident: assimilation was expected to be a natural evolutionary process that as time passed would yield an inevitable outcome.[22]

Gordon's concern was with the larger social structure. Social structure, he pointed out, is logically prior to and as important as individual attitudes and personality for understanding prejudice and discrimination.[23] Assimilation, he declared, is "a blanket term" that in reality covers a multitude of processes.[24] To untangle the idea, first he described the competing ideologies of assimilation that had taken root in American soil: Anglo-conformity, the melting pot, and cultural pluralism.

Of the three, Anglo-conformity was the most prevalent. Present already in colonial times, the prescription to conform to the ways of the dominant Anglo Saxons underlay the attitudes toward the hordes of European immigrants arriving in the nineteenth century. It culminated during World War I with the "one hundred percent American" movement, whose intent was to rapidly strip immigrants of their native culture and make them over into Americans along Anglo Saxon lines. The movement waned after the war, but its assumption of the "rightful dominance" of Anglo Saxon patterns in the nation became embedded in the laws that established the first immigrant quotas. Based on national origins, the quotas of the Immigration and Nationality Act of 1924 discriminated against southern and eastern Europeans.[25]

A more humane but less pervasive ideology of assimilation was that of the melting pot. Beginning in the eighteenth century, it conceived of the emerging nation as being a new blend of European cultures and types into something distinct and new: the American. The generosity of the melting-pot ideal was initially extended only to the immigrants from northern and western Europe. The arrival of the vast streams of immigrants from southern and eastern Europe posed the question of whether they could also be successfully "melted." The answer, said Gordon, came from Israel Zangwill's drama, *The Melting Pot* (1908). In the soaring oratory of the time, God's crucible, America, was extended to all.[26] From then on, the melting-pot theory of assimilation also became rooted.

Cultural pluralism was "a fact in American society before it became a theory."[27] The immigrants created ethnic enclaves where they could live with the familiarity of their own language and customs, attempting to provide mutual help and preserve some of their past. The theory of cultural pluralism rested on an appreciation of the value of the cultural heritage of immigrants—both to themselves and to America. It came as a protest to the Americanization as dissolution implicit in both the Anglo-conformity and melting-pot ideologies. In the work of Horace Kallen, who coined the term, cultural pluralism became an ideal that, if achieved, would make possible a truly democratic commonwealth. The distinctive nationalities would be preserved and form the basis for a "multiplicity in a unity" of mankind.[28]

Different as the theories of Anglo-conformity, the melting-pot, and cultural pluralism were, they were alike in one fundamental respect: all were more prescriptive of what immigrant assimilation should be rather than descriptive of what it actually was.[29] To understand what the assimilation process was actually like, Gordon argued that it is crucial to distinguish between cultural behavior and social structure.[30] Based on Park's awareness of the difference, Gordon set apart cultural and structural assimilation. To this day, that distinction typifies the contrasting emphases of social science research on race and ethnic relations: the emphasis on ethnic identification (its absence or strength) or the emphasis on tangible outcomes (such as occupation, education, and income). This study delves into the structural assimilation of Cuban and Mexican immigrants.

In the adaptation of a group to the core society, Gordon in fact distinguished seven different types or stages of assimilation: cultural assimilation, structural assimilation, marital assimilation, identification assimilation, attitude receptional assimilation, behavior receptional assimilation, and civic assimilation. But for Gordon the critical distinction was between cultural and structural assimilation. Once structural assimilation at the primary group level had occurred, at the same time or subsequent to acculturation, all the other types of assimilation would follow "like a row of tenpins bowled over in rapid succession by a well placed strike."[31]

To Gordon, cultural assimilation entailed a process of acculturation on the part of the immigrants, of becoming "like" in cultural patterns such as language, behavior, and values. While this process takes place only partially in the immigrant generation itself, Gordon expected that the American-born children of the immigrants, educated in the public school system and using English as their native tongue, would acculturate rapidly.[32] But, he stressed, the success of their acculturation in no way guaranteed their structural assimilation. A decade after Gordon, Andrew Greeley challenged the expectation of pervasive acculturation to the contours of Anglo-Saxon culture. Greeley proposed a more complex model of cultural assimilation, the "ethnogenesis" perspective.[33] In brief, the ethnogenesis model entailed the rediscovery of diversity—the diversity of different cultural heritages produced both by carry-overs from Old World cultures and by experiences over the course of time in American society. Still, Greeley focused on ethnic identification, an issue in cultural assimilation.

Structural assimilation, as Gordon defined it, resulted only when the immigrants had been "taken up and incorporated." Specifically, structural assimilation entailed the full integration of the immigrants and their descendants into the social cliques, clubs, and institutions of the core society that lead to "warm, intimate, and personal" primary relationships. Gordon expected that if this process took place on a scale large enough, it would result in a substantial amount of intermarriage: "If children of different ethnic backgrounds belong to the same play-group, later the same adolescent cliques, and at college the same fraternities and sororities; if the parents belong to the same country club and invite each other to their homes for dinner; it is completely unrealistic not to expect these children, now grown, to love and to marry each other, blithely oblivious to previous ethnic extraction."[34] This distinction aimed to provide a more exact conceptual tool to gauge the reality of immigrant assimilation in America. That reality, Gordon underlined, was this: while acculturation had taken place in America to a large extent, structural assimilation, with a couple of exceptions, had not been extensive.

The exceptions were of two sorts. Different ethnic groups merging through marriage but within the religious boundaries of Protestant, Catholic, and Jew had fashioned the "triple melting pot."[35] And the intellectuals, argued Gordon, formed a separate social world where a true mingling among persons of various ethnicities and religions had taken place.

Overall, Gordon stressed, structural assimilation in America had been retarded by religious and racial lines. White Protestant America had never really extended "a firm and cordial invitation" to its minorities; with the racial minorities, such as blacks, "there was not even the pretense of an invitation," resulting in the separate social worlds and parallel institutions that constituted a nation within a nation.[36] Hence, the lack of structural assimilation of minorities in America denied both the prospect of Anglo-conformity and the ideal of the melting pot. And the existing pluralism expressed not respect for other cultures but patterned social inequality.[37]

For the immigrant generation itself, structural assimilation at the primary group level was neither to be expected nor hoped. As Gordon explained, "With regard to the immigrant, in his characteristic numbers and socio-economic background, structural assimilation was out of the question. He did not want it, and he had a positive need for the comfort of his own communal institutions. The native American, moreover, whatever the implications of his public pronouncements, had no intention of opening up his primary group life to entrance by these hordes of alien newcomers. The situation was a functionally complementary standoff."[38] Instead, the necessary goal was the adjustment of the immigrants to American life, their penetration of secondary group institutions—in the occupational, educational, and political life of the core society.[39] Therefore, I will compare the assimilation of Cuban and Mexican immigrants into secondary group institutions. As Joe Feagin underscored, it is necessary to distinguish between primary and secondary structural assimilation because penetration of the society's secondary organizations, as in employment, does not necessarily mean penetration of the primary groups, such as friendship cliques. Even those descended from the white European immigrants, most of whom reached near equality in employment, education, and politics, succeeded in only limited primary structural assimilation, particularly the non-Protestants.[40]

The Structural Assimilation of Cubans and Mexicans

Let us now look at the contrast in the secondary structural assimilation of Cuban and Mexican immigrants. The Cuban political immigration began in 1960 and then halted in 1973, followed by a recent exodus from Mariel Harbor in 1980. The U.S. Bureau of the Census, in its 1976 Survey of Income and Education, provides adequate data to evaluate the first-decade immigrants. However, the immigrants of the Mariel exodus in 1980 still lie outside the national data surveys.[41] In addition, they are just beginning to enter American social life, and it is too early to assess their assimilation.

They will, however, be discussed when I portray the different waves of Cuban migration. To demonstrate the significance of the contrast between the Cuban political migration and the Mexican economic migration in America, this study will analyze national data for Cubans and Mexicans who immigrated from 1945 to 1970: the arrivals of a quarter of a century that embraced Cubans both as economic and political immigrants. But first we need to consider the different labor force outcomes of Cuban and Mexican immigrants, a difference I will seek to explain.

The contrasting popular images of Cuban and Mexican immigrants denote that the structural assimilation of Cubans proceeded farther than that of Mexicans. To see the penetration of these two groups at the secondary group level, we need only compare their average income, education, occupation, and rate of unemployment in 1976 against the yardstick of the average for white Americans.

The following data from the 1976 Survey of Income and Education pertain to Cubans and Mexicans who immigrated from 1960 to 1973, when Cubans were political immigrants and the Cuban Refugee Program was in full force.[42] In 1975, the average earnings of majority whites (not of Hispanic origin) were $11,427 for men and $5,122 for women.[43] While the earnings of neither Cubans nor Mexicans came close to this level, the earnings of Mexicans were lower than those of Cubans. The average earnings of Mexican men, $6,594, were only two-thirds as high as the average for Cuban men, $9,152. Cuban women earned $5,313 on the average, on a par with majority white women. But on the average, Mexican women earned only $2,961.

As earnings rise with increasing age, these income differences partly reflect the differences in age composition. On the whole, Mexican immigrants are younger than Cubans. Compared with a median age for the total population of 29 years,[44] the median age of Mexican immigrant men was 26.0 years and that of Mexican immigrant women 26.7. Cuban immigrants are much older: the median age of the Cuban men was 38.2 years and that of the Cuban women 36.9. But if we take into account only adults, the patterns of educational attainment and occupational distribution also confirm the greater penetration of Cubans into secondary group institutions.

Among adults (25 years and over), white men completed a median 12.5 years of school, white women a median 12.4.[45] As political immigrants, Cuban men had more formal schooling, a median 12.7 years, while Cuban women came close, a median 10.5 years. As economic immigrants, Mexicans lagged far behind. Mexican men completed a median 7.1 years of school, Mexican women, 7.0.

Compared to the 19.6 percent of white men who completed college or additional education,[46] 18.8 percent of Cuban men graduated from college, but as few as 1.9 percent of Mexican men did. Overall, 11.6 percent of white women graduated from college. As a group, Cuban women are more highly educated: 16.7 percent of them completed at least four years of college, while only 2.7 percent of Mexican women had that much education. While only 3 percent of adult whites in the United States had completed fewer than five years of school,[47] more than one-third of Mexican men, 38.2 percent, had only an elementary education, in contrast to one-tenth of Cuban men, 10.7 percent.

When the unemployment rate for all white workers hovered around 6 percent, the unemployment rate of both Cubans and Mexicans was substantially higher. Yet the differences between them were marked. The unemployment rate of Mexican men, 10 percent, was actually lower than that of Cuban men, 12.2 percent. But the women redressed this: only 9.3 percent of Cuban women were unemployed, half the unemployment rate of Mexican women, 17.5 percent. In addition, Cuban women participated in the labor force at a much higher rate than Mexican women. Among those 14 years and older, 51.8 percent of Cuban women were in the labor force, in contrast to only 35.9 percent of Mexican women.

In 1976 the distribution of occupations of all white workers showed that 51.8 percent worked in white-collar jobs.[48] So did 42.0 percent of Cubans, but only 10.8 percent of Mexicans. Among white-collar workers, professionals, administrators, and managers accounted for 27.1 percent of whites in the labor force. As many as 19.9 percent of the Cubans also held professional, administrative, and managerial jobs, but only a meager 3.1 percent of the Mexicans were in these more highly paid occupations. A third of all whites, 32.6 percent, were blue-collar workers. Nearly half of the Cubans were blue-collar workers, 46.8 percent, as were more than half of the Mexicans, 53.8 percent. But Mexicans were more concentrated in service and farm work, where Cubans remained underrepresented. The proportion of white workers in service occupations was 12.3, where almost as many Cubans worked, 10.7 percent, but twice as many Mexicans, 23.2 percent. And while only 3.3 percent of whites were farm workers, 12.2 percent of Mexicans worked on farms, but virtually no Cubans, 0.4 percent. Moreover, as Morris Newman noted, the proportion of Mexican workers who work on farms might be significantly understated. Undocumented workers, fearing deportation, might refuse to be interviewed. In addition, the migratory nature of farm work might itself prevent their being found by surveys.[49]

Thus we see that Cuban immigrants are more successful, having progressed much farther in structural assimilation at the secondary group level than Mexican immigrants in America. Why?

Assimilation theory has no answer. Assimilation theory is useful for defining the problem and distinguishing among types of assimilation. But it assumes that assimilation is a natural evolutionary process that takes place over the course of generations rather than one that can be helped or curbed.[50] I contend that the different outcomes of Cubans and Mexicans are partly due to state intervention. Since Cubans were political immigrants, the state lent them a firm hand; since Mexicans were economic immigrants, the state largely ignored them. This treatment reinforced the difference in their social class origins. The individual outcomes of Cubans and Mexicans hinge on the role of political and economic migration in America.

Migration Theory: Individual and Structural Perspectives

Traditionally migration theory proposed the "push" of diminishing opportunities and the "pull" of new ones to explain the flow of migrants from one place to another. Most fully expressed by Everett S. Lee, the theory focused on the individual migrant and his or her reasons for migration: the factors that "hold and attract or repel people."[51] Unlike many economists, Lee went beyond a simple cost-benefit calculus of perceived advantages and disadvantages at the origin and destination. Instead, he stressed both the role of intervening obstacles that prove more of an impediment to some individuals than to others—such as distance, physical barriers, immigration laws, and cost—and the influence of personal traits—such as stage in the life cycle, information, contact with earlier migrants, personality, and the effect of such transitions as marriage or retirement. Still, the decision to migrate was the focus of this theory, although, as Lee said, "Indeed, not all persons who migrate reach that decision themselves. Children are carried along by their parents, willy-nilly, and wives accompany their husbands though it tears them away from environments they love."[52] Subsequent studies concentrated on the individual characteristics of the migrants.[53]

In addition, the "push-pull" framework did not contrast political and economic migration, except as different negative factors pushing the migrants at the origin and selecting different personal traits.

Yet, as more recent immigration theories have proposed, we cannot fully understand migration without considering the functions of political and economic migration.

Immigrants are a distinct social category. Alejandro Portes reminded us that the study of immigrants was closely wedded with the beginnings of social science in America.[54] Immigrants and their plight in this country were the focus of vivid studies from the early days of American social science until the early sixties.[55] But, Portes stressed, with the arrival of racial demands and the militancy of the civil rights movement and black nationalism, "the decline of studies of immigrant groups coincided with a topical shift toward an alternative framework—ethnicity and ethnic relations."[56] All-encompassing, these analytic perspectives arrived at general theories of race and ethnic relations. For example, in Donald Noel's theory, ethnocentric groups with differential power competing for the same scarce resources were at the origin of ethnic inequality.[57] Or, according to Edna Bonacich, labor markets of higher-priced and lower-priced labor split along ethnic lines led to ethnic antagonism and efforts to control lower-priced labor through exclusion or caste.[58] Even more generally, R. A. Schermerhorn defined ethnic groups as all those who shared "a real or putative common ancestry."[59] And in the process what is really distinctive about immigrants was lost.

What is really distinctive about immigrants? To be sure, immigrants have their own ethnic identity and culture, as do Cubans, Puerto Ricans, Mexicans, Vietnamese, and Koreans.[60] But new immigrants are a distinct social category in two senses: at the micro level of the individual and at the macro level of the societies they exit and enter.

At the micro level the immigrants' preparation for adult roles in society took place in their country of origin, although they will live these roles (in whole or in part, depending on their age and circumstances) in the new society to which they migrated.[61] Furthermore, as Portes maintained, contrary to the case of ethnic minorities, immigrants "are decisively influenced not only by events in the United States but by experiences of a whole life in a different country. While the point was evident in classic studies of immigration, the tendency at present has been towards de facto fusion of new immigrants with native-born ethnic Americans."[62]

At the macro level the state in two societies permits the immigrants to exit and enter. As gatekeeper, the state regulates and directs migration through a body of law. Those laws can establish quotas for different countries or areas (for example, the Western

Hemisphere quota) and preference criteria for categories of persons (for example, occupational restrictions or family reunification preferences), depending on national purposes.[63] For Cubans and Mexicans, the state went further, not only acting as the gatekeeper to America but also involving itself in the process of assimilation, by helping Cuban political immigrants and ignoring Mexican economic immigrants.

All societies are simultaneously political and economic. Hence, in individuals' perceptions, political and economic conditions are entangled, particularly in the attitudes that lead to the consequential decision to emigrate from the land of birth. Lack of job opportunities easily results in lack of trust for public leaders; government policies that dislocate people can foster political disaffection.[64] Despite the inextricable relation of the political and economic, the analytical distinction between the Cuban and Mexican migrations as political versus economic migrations is necessary. The distinction rests on two criteria: first, the decisions they made to emigrate rested on the weight of their political disaffection or on a mere economic search;[65] second, the state granted them that very classification.[66] In so doing, it treated them very differently.

In the portraits of the Cuban political immigrants and the Mexican economic immigrants that follow, we will see that substantial differences exist in their social characteristics. Cuban immigrants of the sixties came from a higher social background than Mexicans. Cubans began migrating to the United States in large numbers as a result of the social transformations wrought by the Cuban revolution. In the early years of the exodus (1960–1962), the bulk of the refugees came from the upper classes: those most immediately affected by the changes in social and economic allocation wrought by the Agrarian Reform land expropriations and the nationalization of American industry.[67] Swiftly the educated professionals, managers, and middle classes left, but few skilled or semiskilled workers and peasants.[68] That immigration ended in 1962 in the aftermath of the Cuban Missile Crisis. In time, the social class level of the migration dropped. With the second major wave of immigration that began in 1965 in response to President Johnson's "open door" policy, the Cuban migration became largely working class.

In 1960, 54 percent of the Cuban immigrants who arrived in the United States were white-collar, with professionals, managers, and administrators accounting for 32 percent. In 1970, only 32 percent of the arrivals were white-collar, and only 16 percent were professionals, managers, and administrators. More than half the arrivals, 57 percent, were blue-collar workers.[69] As the 1980 Mariel émigrés demonstrated, the social transformations of the Cuban revolution were so pervasive as to be all encompassing. Poor relatives also followed the wealthier kin who had come earlier. With the passage of time, Cuban immigrants in the United States came to vary widely in social class. Still, as a group they are more educated and skilled than Mexicans.

Mexican immigration to the United States is much older, going back to the middle of the nineteenth century. At present, they also vary in social class. Mexicans of higher social class represent "brain drain." Alejandro Portes argued that "brain drain" is not a phenomenon different from the labor migration of the unskilled.[70] Working within a world-system approach (core versus periphery nations), he argued that the articulation of peripheral societies to core ones causes a structural imbalancing of peripheral nations that induces labor migration—both of the unskilled and the highly skilled.[71] Most Mexican immigrants, however, have always been the poor and unskilled in search of a better life. In 1970, only 12 percent of the Mexican immigrants that were admitted to the United States were white-collar, with professionals, managers, and administrators accounting for only 7 percent. Nearly two-thirds of the immigrants, 64 percent, were blue-collar workers, and 23 percent were either service or farm workers.[72] As a group, they are less educated and skilled than Cubans.

Since the structural assimilation of Cubans advanced farther than that of Mexicans, and since Cubans also came from a higher social background, some could easily argue that in this initial social class advantage lies the reason for the Cuban success story in America. Yet my argument is that without the help of the state this social class advantage would have been inadequate. Social class is a "place" in a society not necessarily transferable to another, not even for the higher classes. What was attained in one society needs to be "translated" to another. Let us clarify this point.

An immigrant encounters barriers along the way. The most obvious is the language barrier. Even for those who master the language other hurdles remain: citizenship (until very recently U.S. citizenship was required for those who wanted to teach in public schools); certification and licensing (a certified M.D. from another country is not qualified to practice medicine in the United States without undergoing the years of internship); training (the Cuban legal system was based on Napoleonic code, that of the United States is based on English common law); and the loss of personal career networks that assist in securing jobs and promotions. Because immigrants discover barriers to transferring their social class credentials, the type of migration, political versus economic, is important, for the state treated the two groups very differently.

Not only were Cubans more educated and skilled upon arrival, but also explicit state policy helped them to convert, or "translate," their Cuban credentials into valuable American credentials. Government policy created a many-faceted and generous Cuban Refugee Program, which included special programs for learning English, vocational traning, professional retraining, and job placement; financial assistance for higher education; and relaxed citizenship requirements. By contrast, despite their long history of immigration to the United States, Mexicans have always suffered from a lack of government policy to facilitate their structural assimilation. To this day, the state has never welcomed them as settlers.

Hence, the definition of political and economic immigrants depends, first, on the nature of the decision they made to emigrate and, second, on the state that defined them and treated them very differently. The firm hand the state lent resulted in a process of *cumulative advantage* for Cubans, whose higher social class was "translated," made valuable in America. For Mexicans, the lack of state policy to facilitate and support their structural assimilation amounted to *cumulative disadvantage*, reinforcing their social class disadvantage. The sharp contrast in their structural assimilation resulted. Figure 1 represents this argument.

Seeking to demonstrate this argument, I will bring to bear several methodologies throughout this book. Part of the methodology will consist of a quantitative analysis of the influence the varying social characteristics of Cuban and Mexican immigrants hold for the occupations and earnings they attained. The influence of those characteristics will be examined from both the competing theoretical viewpoints of human capital and segmented labor markets. Furthermore, the research design that underlies the data analysis will also seek to provide evidence for the impact of the Cuban Refugee Program in facilitating the structural assimilation of Cuban refugees.

Still another methodology, however, sets the stage for this research: a historical and comparative method. The historical perspective is necessary to understand the difference that time and place make in presenting particular social groups with different possibilities and alternatives. From this point of view, this nation of immigrants holds many varied ethnic histories—in the plural. The comparative perspective serves to illuminate one experience by comparing and contrasting it to another. Both the Cubans and Mexicans reflect contemporary Latin American migrations to the United

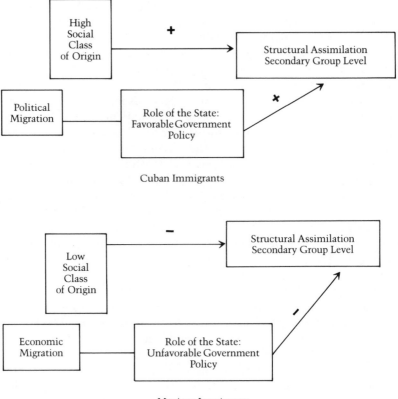

Figure 1. **Cumulative Advantage and Cumulative Disadvantage Process**

States. Yet the comparison rests on the contrasts, as political versus economic migrations. That difference implies not only sharp contrasts in the social characteristics of the immigrants, but also a sharp contrast in their processes of incorporation into American society.

I have argued that the state facilitated the structural assimilation of Cubans while it ignored that of Mexicans. Neither traditional migration theory nor assimilation theory can explain that varying attention. Traditional migration theory largely ignored the role of the state; assimilation theory expected the process of assimilation to be natural and evolutionary. As Joe Feagin argued, race and ethnic theorizing needs to develop a more comprehensive *incorporation theory* that takes into account that "in the process of incorporation there has been considerable variation in group access to social resources and rewards," by paying attention to "the initial and continuing placement and access of various groups" within the economic, political, and educational institutions of the society.[73] The processes of incorporation of Cuban and Mexican immigrants contrasted sharply.

The cumulative disadvantage of Mexican immigrants that retarded their structural assimilation resulted from the process of incorporation of migrant labor for many decades. Recently migration theory has stressed the increased significance of immigrant workers in developed capitalist societies. To counteract the traditional perspective of studies of labor migration that focused on the individual migrant's reasons for migration and its personal consequences, a structural perspective developed. In essence this perspective argued that a system of economic migration had developed from the flow of labor between developed and underdeveloped nations. What functions did the system of economic migration perform for Mexico and the United States?

Arguing independently but in a similar vein, Michael Burawoy, Manuel Castells, and Alejandro Portes reformulated the problem by examining the structural sources and social and economic implications of labor migration.[74] In a nutshell, they agreed that migrant labor—as immigrant, and as labor—had structural causes and that it performed important functions for the developed capitalist nation that received them.

Burawoy defined migrant labor institutionally: as a system that separates the functions of renewal and maintenance of the labor force physically and institutionally. The function of renewal takes place in the less-developed society, such as Mexico, while only the function of maintenance takes place in the more developed country, such as the United States. Both Castells and Portes defined migrant labor as cheap labor, whose function in capitalism is to maintain the rate of profit. As a Marxist, Castells judged that migrant labor serves to counteract the tendency of capitalism toward a falling rate of profit. Not a Marxist, Portes saw migrant labor as less necessary but more vital to small and medium-sized enterprises for whom alternatives (such as the overseas relocation of multinationals) do not exist.

While the Mexican migration provided the United States with a dependable source of cheap labor, it provided Mexico with a "safety valve."[75] Migration became the solution to Mexico's incapacity to satisfy the needs of its poor and lower-middle classes.

These new structural perspectives add a necessary component to the study of migration. The danger of the structural emphasis, however, lies in its tendency to obliterate people, to lose sight of the individual migrants who do make decisions. The theoretical and empirical challenge now facing immigration research lies in its capacity to capture both individuals and structure. We need to consider the plight of individuals, their propensity to move, and the nature of the decisions they make. We also need to consider the larger social structures within which that plight exists and those decisions are made. When the immigrants live in our midst, we ought to heed the part the government plays in promoting or ignoring their assimilation.

The cumulative advantage of Cuban immigrants, which promoted their structural assimilation, resulted from the process of incorporation of political immigrants in the sixties. State policy aided tremendously in their success story. The government created the Cuban Refugee Emergency Center in Miami, supported by the national Cuban Refugee Program. Acting in concert, they helped the refugees resettle all over the country and find jobs while providing the immigrants with support services. In addition, they instituted numerous bilingual education programs not only to teach the refugees English but also to retrain and certify former doctors, teachers, lawyers, and social workers so that they could practice their professions in the United States. Moreover, they supported the needs of the school systems that instituted the retraining programs, provided college loans to the students, and relaxed citizenship requirements.

Unlike the majority of exile movements, the Cuban exodus to the United States was often coordinated and organized, based on special arrangements between the two governments. Like economic migration, political migration can also constitute a system when, in certain historical periods, it performs beneficial functions for the two societies involved. What functions did the system of political migration perform for Cuba and the United States?

To be sure, the loss of such large numbers of the professional and skilled classes eroded the Cuban revolution. But the exodus also performed an important political function: it lessened the capacity of those politically disaffected by the revolution to undermine it. In externalizing dissent, the Cuban government in effect controlled it. As a result, the revolution grew stronger.

In America, all the political migrations that took place during the peak years of the Cold War—the Hungarians, Berliners, and Cubans—served an important symbolic function. In this historical period of the Cold War, West and East contested the superiority of their political and economic systems. Political immigrants who succeeded in the flight to freedom became touching symbols around which to weave the legitimacy needed for foreign policy.

Cuban and Mexican immigrants in America have undergone very different processes of incorporation. Their assimilation and its outcomes contrast sharply. To understand it, we must understand the different functions of political and economic migration. The role of migrant labor is economic; the role of political migration is symbolic.

2. Lending Cuban Political Immigrants a Hand

Portrait of the Cuban Exiles: Waves of Migration

In the sixteen years from 1960 to 1976, the United States admitted over 750,000 Cuban refugees. In the spring of 1980 arrived 125,000 more, whose immigration status remains one of "entrants."[1] Twenty years of political migration that brought close to a million persons to American soil harbor distinct waves of immigrants, alike only in their final rejection of Cuba. This portrait of the Cuban exiles will encompass all the different waves of immigration. To understand the varying characteristics of the exiles over time, we need to pay attention to the changing phases of the Cuban revolution.

Nelson Amaro and Alejandro Portes portrayed the different phases of the Cuban political immigration as changing over time with the exiles' principal motivation for their decision to leave. With the unfolding of the Cuban revolution, over the years "those who wait" gave way to "those who escape," and they to "those who search." Overall, the Cuban migration is characterized by an inverse correlation between date of departure and social class of the immigrants.[2] To the demographic portrayal of Cubans in the United States, Lourdes Casal added their changing political attitudes.[3] Based on the collected life stories of hundreds of Cubans, José Llanes drew fifty-eight composite characters.[4] These composite oral histories serve to preserve the human dramas of the personal histories.

On the Heels of the Revolutionary Transformation

Typical of the first phase of the immigration were "those who wait." Beginning with the success of the Cuban revolution in 1959 and the exit of the *Batistianos*,[5] the exodus of political immigrants really gained force with Cuba's nationalization of industries in the summer and fall of 1960. In this first phase, those who left were Cuba's elite. These upper and upper-middle classes were not tied to Batista's government, but were bound to a political and economic structure that, Amaro and Portes underlined, was completely inter-penetrated by the demands and initiative of American capital: "These executives and owners of firms, big merchants, sugarmill owners, manufacturers, cattlemen, representatives of foreign com-panies and established professionals, were those most acquainted with the United States' political and economic guardianship of Cuba, under which they had created or maintained their position, and thus were the least given to believe that the American govern-ment would permit the consolidation of a socialist regime in the Island."[6]

Hence, amid the economic and diplomatic war that ensued be-tween Cuba and the United States in 1960, they decided to leave.[7] Maximiliano Pons, a successful business executive who was one of Llanes' characters, expressed it thus: "I came to the United States in 1960. After Fidel nationalized the American company I was working for, I decided to leave. My family left with me. The com-pany's U.S. base offered me a job in New Orleans. I took it, and after a short while I was moved to Caracas. I have never worked for any-one else in my life except when I worked for my father."[8] Like many members of Cuba's elite, he had attended college in the United States and become "an American aspirant." The experience of exile returned him his Cuban identity—"Fidel turned me back into a Cuban."

The immigrants of this first phase came imagining that exile would be temporary—waiting for the "inevitable" American reac-tion and help to overthrow Cuba's new government. In this first stage, the exile's political activity was intensely militant, support-ing military counterrevolution against Cuba. Of these, the Bay of Pigs invasion was only the largest; certainly, also the most tragic. Some of Llanes' representative characters fought in the Bay of Pigs invasion. Manolo Llerena explained their motivation, the hope to make their country free again: "We weren't a bunch of mercenaries. We had a solemn purpose and the backing of the U.S. government. We didn't want Marines in Cuba. We wanted our own *soldados* [soldiers] returning to claim their freedom in glory and for the good of the people."[9]

Amaro and Portes judged that this first phase of the Cuban exile ended with the fiasco of the "freedom fighters," the April 1961 invasion of Cuba. Those who waited inside the Bay of Pigs itself for the United States' promised air cover waited in vain. The failure of the invasion further consolidated the revolution; Castro announced for the first time that he was a Marxist-Leninist. The exodus doubled.

"Those who escape" constituted the second phase. It lasted from April 1961 to October 1962, when the regular flights that had brought the immigrants from Havana to Miami ceased due to the threat of nuclear war the Cuban Missile Crisis posed. As Amaro and Portes noted, the inverse relationship between date of emigration and social class in Cuba began to show. Still largely a middle-class exodus, it now became more middle class than upper-middle class: middle merchants and middle management, landlords, middle-level professionals, and a considerable number of skilled, unionized workers. Members of the economic elite that had earlier been reluctant to leave also departed. Their decision to leave, stressed Amaro and Portes, corresponded not to an attitude of patiently waiting the overthrow of Castro, but of wanting to escape a new order they were increasingly convinced was stable, whose end was neither certain nor immediate.[10]

The immigrants of the first two phases, they stressed, were not so much "pulled" by the attractiveness of the new society as "pushed" by the internal political process of the old. Increasingly, the Cuban government restricted the conditions surrounding exit. For example, capital restrictions rapidly escalated. At the end of 1959, an émigré could take $150 out of the country; in the middle of 1960, the allowance dropped to only $60; at the end of 1961, to only $5; and in 1962, to none. Most Cubans arrived in the United States with little or no money. Moreover, from 1961 on, the government confiscated all the personal property of those who hoped to emigrate.[11] Yet the exodus quickened.

When the private universities and schools began to close in 1961, the fear of having the children educated by the state became prevalent. Llanes' interview with Miranda Martín revealed that, at the outset, her father had tried to help the revolution by donating his medical research services: "We became gradually aware of the shift in Fidel's policies to the left, but *papi* didn't want to leave Havana, not if there was any chance that he could survive there. My mother, on the other hand, was panicked. What will they do to the children in school? Will they force them to go to communist schools? Finally in August we left."[12] Over 14,000 children arrived alone, sent by parents who feared their loss of parental authority to the state.[13] "What began as a trickle," wrote Richard Fagen, Richard Brody, and

Thomas O'Leary, was "by the middle of 1962, a small flood."[14] By this time 153,534 Cubans had registered with the Cuban Refugee Center.[15]

Table 1 shows the higher social class origin of Cuban refugees in the early years of the exodus. Fagen, Brody, and O'Leary, using a sample of Cuban refugees aided by the Cuban Refugee Emergency Center in Miami from 1961 to 1962, showed that, in comparison with the overall occupational distribution of Cuba as reflected by the Cuban Census of 1953, the occupational distribution of Cuban refugees in these early years was top-heavy. The exodus overrepresented the professional, managerial, and middle classes (31 percent), as well as clerical and sales workers (33 percent); it underrepresented the skilled, semiskilled, service, and agricultural workers.[16] Likewise, the educational level of the Cuban refugees was much higher than that of the Cuban population. While only 1 percent of Cuban adults had a college education, over 12 percent of the early exiles did.[17]

With breathtaking speed and in response to myriad exigencies, in a couple of years the Cuban revolution moved through distinct phases. Nelson Amaro captured them in flight: democracy, humanism, nationalism, socialism, and Marxist-Leninism.[18] The punitive policy of the United States at this time probably aided the rapidity of this transition: cutting the sugar quota, instituting a trade embargo, breaking diplomatic relations, and backing the exiles' invasion of Cuba. Amidst this swift progression, some dissented at one point, some at others: all who left were labelled "counterrevolutionaries." In these early phases of the Cuban migration the Cuban Refugee Program, which will be described later, was initiated and institutionalized. In two years alone, the program assisted over 68,000 persons—58 percent of the refugees in Miami.[19]

Casal judged that after the massive failure of the organized invasion, exile political activity fragmented into "uncoordinated acts" of hostility against the Cuban government: infiltrating, sabotaging, and fostering internal dissent. After the Cuban Missile Crisis, the role of the U.S. Coast Guard turned to stern prevention of these raids.[20] Casal observed that, although the "highly belligerent" counterrevolutionary movements of the first two phases never actively engaged all exiles, they did draw on the financial or moral support of most. Cubans in exile hoped for Castro's overthrow and for their own return to Cuba. But according to Casal, "As these organizations failed to reach their goal—and the international situation plus the internal consolidation of the Cuban regime made it pro-

Table 1. Occupational Distribution of Cuban Immigrants at the Time of Arrival in the United States Compared with the Cuban Population in 1953 (in Percentages)

Pre-Exile Occupations	1953 Cuban Census	Years of Arrival							
		1959–1962[a]	1962–1965[b]	1965–1966[a]	1967[a]	1970[c]	1971[c]	1973–1974[d]	1980[e]
Professional, semiprofessional, managerial	9.2	31.0	18.1	21.0	18.0	12.4	13.1	10.1	11.2
Clerical, sales	13.7	33.0	11.7	31.5	35.5	30.2	27.0	24.6	6.6
Skilled	27.2[f]	17.0	49.0[f]	22.0	26.0	25.2	23.2	22.3	25.5
Semiskilled, unskilled		8.0		11.5	8.0	16.0	18.6	12.3	45.4
Services	8.3	7.0	10.5	9.0	8.5	9.0	8.9	26.4	4.8
Agriculture, fishing	41.6	4.0	10.7	5.0	4.0	7.2	9.2	4.3	6.5
Total percentage	100.0	100.0	100.0	100.0	100.0	100.0	100.0	100.0	100.0
N	1,938,228	27,419	10,632	17,124	14,867	14,755	12,350	586	5,809

Note: Data are for those in the labor force, excluding students, housewives, retired, unemployed.

[a] Fagen et al., *Cubans in Exile*, Table 7.1.
[b] In Casal, "Cubans in the United States," Table 1.
[c] In Aguirre, "Differential Migration of Cuban Social Races," Table 2.
[d] Adapted from Portes et al., "The New Wave," Table 6.
[e] Adapted from Bach, "The New Cuban Immigrants," Table 1, and Bach et al., "The Flotilla 'Entrants,'" Table 6.
[f] Skilled, semiskilled, and unskilled workers.

gressively more unlikely that they would—the Cuban communities became disenchanted with such activities and withdrew their support."[21]

Escape as Escape Can

After the October missile crisis, the flights ceased, slowing down the migration rate. The United States provided direct transportation only for the more than 1,000 prisoners from the Bay of Pigs fiasco and their relatives. The Cuban government exchanged the prisoners for vital needs: medicine, medical and surgical equipment, food, and money. During this period, other Cubans who arrived had either previously stayed in other countries or had escaped Cuba illegally in boats and rafts to the shores of Key West. Francisco Mateo crossed the ninety miles between Cuba and Key West in a small rowboat: "Some of the people who left from Mariel [in 1980] took twenty hours to cross the distance in a motorboat. We took twenty days in 1962, my family and me, in a boat with three oars and holes . . . You tell me how eight people could leave on an eight-foot rowboat and expect to get anywhere. Across the Miami Causeway maybe, but not those stinking, treacherous ninety miles. God was with us. There is no other answer."[22]

During this phase of the exodus, as Table 1 shows, the proportion of professionals nearly halved, to 18.1 percent, and that of clerical and sales workers more than halved, to 11.7 percent. Close to half of the arrivals, 49.0 percent, were blue-collar workers, skilled and unskilled. And for the only time in what was to become twenty years of migration, agricultural workers and fishermen constituted over 10 percent. Cuba's introduction of food rationing in 1962 and compulsory military service in 1963 probably accounts for the change in the exodus.[23] Altogether, from October 1962 to November 1965, the Cuban Refugee Emergency Center registered 29,962 Cubans.

Freedom Flights and the Revolutionary Offensive

In the fall of 1965, a chaotic period ensued that previewed the 1980 wave of immigrants. From Miami hundreds of boats left for the Cuban port of Camarioca, where they picked up relatives to come to the United States. In two months, this flotilla exodus brought about 4,993 Cubans to the United States, until the U.S. and Cuban governments completed the negotiations for the orderly air bridge that began in December 1965.[24]

In Amaro and Portes' view, "those who search" characterized the next major wave of the Cuban migration that resumed in 1965. In response to President Lyndon Johnson's "open door" policy, the Cuban exodus was organized and executed. The "freedom flights" from Varadero to Miami brought Cubans that the Cuban Refugee Program swiftly processed and relocated throughout the United States. Excluding the newcomers of 1980, 40 percent of the Cubans in the United States arrived through this air bridge. After eight years, in 1973, both the flights and the refugee program were phased out. When the refugee airlift closed, over 2,800 flights had brought nearly a quarter million persons.[25] Throughout the years of the freedom flights, the Cuban Refugee Emergency Center registered 264,297 Cubans.[26]

Throughout this period, the Memorandum of Understanding regulated the immigrants' departure. This joint agreement of the U.S. and Cuban governments decided that relatives of exiles already living in the United States should have priority: first husbands and wives, next parents, and then siblings.[27] Both governments compiled master lists of those who claimed and who were claimed, and jointly decided who would emigrate. Cuba barred from exit young men of military service age (15 to 26), as well as professional, technical, and skilled workers whose exit would cause "a serious disturbance" in delivering social services or in production.[28] To the Cuban Revolution, initially the exodus proved erosive.

With this phase of the migration, the exodus of the upper and upper-middle classes largely came to an end. This wave of immigration was largely working class and petit bourgeois: employees, independent craftsmen, small merchants, and skilled and semiskilled workers. Over time, Amaro and Portes judged, the political exile increasingly became an economic exile as "those who search" sought greater economic opportunities than were provided in a socialist society that substituted a new ethic of sacrificing consumption to achieve collective goals for the older ethic of individual consumption goals.[29]

Without doubt, these were the leanest years of the Cuban revolution. The impact of the hemispheric trade embargo imposed by the Organization of American States in 1964 resulted in a spare parts crisis and other economic dislocations.[30] The exodus amounted to a drainage of technical and administrative skills. And Cuba failed in its attempts to cease being a sugar monoculture, industrialize, and diversify.[31] Amaro and Portes judged that the impossibility of realizing economic aspirations characterized this phase of the migration: "Increasingly, the emigration ceases to be a political act and be-

comes an economic act."[32] Although de jure the new immigrants
were considered political immigrants, Amaro and Portes affirmed
that de facto they increasingly came to resemble "the classic immigrant," whose origins are in the lower social classes of the native
country and who is seeking better economic opportunities overseas
in a developed country. Contrary to the earlier immigrants, who
were "pushed" by the Cuban revolutionary transformation, Amaro
and Portes considered that the legendary attraction of American opportunity "pulled" the immigrants of this phase. Yet Amaro and
Portes' distinction misses the reality that while life in Cuba grew
harsh for all, it turned bitter for those who had announced their
dissent by declaring their desire to leave. Antonio Chacón had sent
his children to the United States in the beginning of the exodus
and applied to leave Cuba in 1962. When he finally arrived in
1966, he was suffering from malnutrition, diabetes, and high blood
pressure:

> We had applied for an exit permit. This meant that I would lose
> my job at the newspaper. We had planned for a few months of
> unemployment. It was unavoidable . . . Then, slam. The door
> closed and I was inside. Unemployed. We finally left in 1966. Can
> you imagine that? Four years knocking around doing "volunteer
> work" on weekends in order to get the food allowance. We lost
> our belongings. Everything we owned was sold or traded for food.
> We ended up living with my friend Jacobo, who took us in at
> great risk. I lost eighty pounds in those four years.[33]

The political and economic transformation the Cuban revolution
effected was so pervasive that it always "pushed" Cubans. America,
in facilitating the migration, always "pulled" them. Moreover, the
Cuban migration is unique in that both the U.S. and Cuban governments organized and facilitated the exodus.[34] Together, I argue,
they set in motion a system of political migration.

Within the Cuban community in the United States during this
period the immigrants gradually depoliticized. As Casal noted, the
militant anti-Castro organizations drew progressively fewer participants, and "among the majority of exiles, private issues such as job
training and improvement of living standards took precedence over
participation in political activities."[35] Indeed, the immigrants became American: they sought to acculturate and to compete successfully. For many, the myth of the return gradually lost its compelling force.

Now Cubans came to be a heterogeneous group, varying widely

in their social class origin. The former social distinctions were perpetrated and reenacted in exile, often with little bearing to their
life in America. Those who had belonged to the five most exclusive
yacht and country clubs in Havana founded another in Miami, in
nostalgia dubbed the Big Five. Cubans of working-class origin remain outsiders to these attempts to recreate once-enviable social
positions: a golden past that was not theirs but which, with increased distance and time, seems to grow only more golden.

At the start of the migration in the early 1960s, 31 percent of the
Cubans who arrived in the United States were professionals or
managers. By 1970, as Table 1 shows, only 12 percent were professionals or managers. More than half the arrivals, 57 percent, were
blue-collar, service, or agricultural workers. While Cuban exiles are
clearly heterogeneous, their celebrated "success story" obscures it.
It particularly serves to obscure the many Cuban poor.

Casal emphasized the costs of the "success story": it prevents
Cubans from getting a clear picture of their true situation; it desen-
sitizes them and others to the hidden costs of "success"; and it
isolates Cubans from other American minorities.[36] She went on to
add: "Other information, gleaned from the 1970 Census and the
U.S. Budget, documents the darker side of the story. For instance,
one out of five metropolitan Cubans lives in an area designated as
"low-income" by the Census Bureau. Again, there are wide regional
variations; more than half the Cubans in Newark and Boston in-
habit such areas. As another instance, at the end of 1972, 90,700
persons were receiving financial or medical assistance under the
Cuban Refugee Program."[37]

The Cuban poor are also evident in many neighborhoods of southwest Miami. But not only are they hidden from the view of Americans, Cubans also tend to hide them from themselves. Thus Jorge
Domínguez concluded that "although there seems to be a certain
correlation between those who are less hostile in their attitudes
toward the revolution and those who are concerned about social
inequality among Cubans, there is a great deal more of the former
than the latter. Social action groups aimed at helping Black Cubans,
elderly Cubans, and, in general, those Cubans that look upon the
success of their co-immigrants with a sigh, are extremely limited.
This cleavage is very real and too latent."[38]

Spain's refugees arrived next. With the end of the "freedom
flights" from Cuba to the United States, the next wave of immigrants that arrived from 1973 to 1975 consisted of refugees who
had first lived in Spain. Hoping to join their relatives in America,
they had waited in Spain for immigrant visas to the United States.

Their arrival was delayed because the 1965 amendments to the Immigration and Nationality Act imposed a ceiling of 120,000 immigrants from all countries of the Western Hemisphere, a quota that went into effect in 1968. From 1968 to 1974, therefore, Cubans who wished to leave the island increasingly went to Spain. Finally, in October 1973, special family reunification provisions allowed Cubans from Spain to enter the United States.

Alejandro Portes, Juan Clark, and Robert Bach interviewed a sample of 590 male heads of family from this migration soon after their arrival.[39] They found, as Table 1 shows, a different occupational distribution from that of earlier exiles. These émigrés represented Cuba's "middling service sectors."[40] Throughout the 1960s, the proportion of émigrés from the service sector had ranged from 7 to 10 percent. Now that rate more than doubled, as 26 percent of the immigrants came from the service occupations: cooks, gardeners, domestics, street vendors, shoe shiners, barbers, hairdressers, taxi drivers, and small retail merchants.

They had left Cuba during the period when, nearly a decade after the triumph of the revolution, Castro launched a new "revolutionary offensive" in Cuba, labeling them "parasites" and confiscating 55,636 small businesses that were still privately owned.[41] With this last wave of nationalization, all industrial, trade, and service activity passed into the hands of the state. Of all socialist countries, Cuba then held the highest percentage of state-owned property. Only the small farmer prevailed: to this day 30 percent of agricultural activity remains in private hands.[42]

The interviews of Portes, Clark, and Bach suggest that "concern with the long-term *continuation* of political and economic limitations rather than with short-term shortages was the decisive factor for many" as they left.[43] From 1968 on, both the émigrés who came directly to the United States on the freedom flights and the émigrés who first needed to go to Spain responded to the push of the "revolutionary offensive." This last wave of nationalization in Cuba pushed, in disproportionate numbers, the small entrepreneurs and their employees.

The Dialogue: A Brief Collaboration

The decade of the seventies witnessed the institutionalization of the revolution in Cuba and the assimilation of the exiles in America. In Cuba, with the economic transition to socialism effected, the government cast the shape of the political system.[44] Although created in 1965, the new Cuban Communist Party held its first

congress in 1975, the hallmark of the process of institutionalization. The new constitution of 1976 aimed to provide support for
the consolidated and expanded party structure and the new legal
codes. In many ways, the old idealism and romanticism of the
1960s gave way to what Carmelo Mesa-Lago called pragmatism.
The failure of the mobilization of workers to cut the 10 million
tons of sugar planned for 1970 caused the revolution to enter this
new phase. Cuba reintroduced material incentives, wage differ-
entials, and cost-benefit analysis in an effort to promote greater
productivity and capital accumulation—economic growth that
would deliver Cubans from scarcity. In the sixties, trade unions,
their role neglected, had virtually disappeared. Now unions were
restructured, garnering some vitality; other mass organizations,
such as the Organs of People's Power, took form.[45] With increasing
institutionalization, Cuba gradually took on the features of Eastern
European communism.

For the vast majority of Cubans in the United States throughout
these years the issue continued to be life in America. Yet that very
stability, and the cultural impact on the young who lived face to
face with "the sixties" in America, gave birth to an increased ideological pluralism, "denser" than that which had always existed,
though obscured by the uniform rejection of Cuba. As Casal observed, "The Cuban community is not monolithic now (if it ever
was)."[46]

Among other splits, such as social class and waves of migration,
the Cuban community is certainly cleft by age. Without doubt, a
generation gap exists among all generations. But this gap reflects
more than that; it is the difference between political generations.
Karl Mannheim conceived of generations as the common location
in the historical dimension of the social process that limits individuals to a specific range of potential experiences during their
youth—a stratification of experience that shapes a frame of reference for the future.[47] Among Cuban exiles, the gap between the
political generations which came of age during certain critical periods of Cuban history[48] and which came of age in America under the
impact of the civil rights and anti–Vietnam War movements is often
a chasm.[49]

It was fifty-five progressive young people who, in December 1977,
first broke through nineteen years of hostility, abuse, and isolation.
Known as the Antonio Maceo Brigade, this group visited throughout the island, leaving behind a profound mark. Cuba filmed it: *55
Hermanos* captured their search for cultural identity; for some, for
political identity.[50] Widely shown in Cuba, it proved heartrending in

its portrayal of the suffering that exile brought both for those who left and who were left behind.

In November of 1978 an unprecedented meeting took place. President Castro met with representatives of the Cuban community in exile, and engaged with them in a give-and-take of ideas and proposals that came to be known as the Dialogue. Whatever Castro's motives may have been, the importance of the Dialogue rests in that it bore multiple fruits. The Cuban government agreed to release 3,000 political prisoners plus 600 others caught trying to escape from Cuba illegally; to promote the reunification of families by allowing Cuban families rent apart in the early years of the revolution to reunite with their relatives in America; and to recognize the right of Cubans in the United States to visit their homeland.[51]

All at once the counterrevolutionaries, or *gusanos* (worms), of yesterday respectfully became "members of the Cuban community abroad." Immediately the release of political prisoners began. Gradually they arrived, until 3,600 political prisoners were released. In January 1979 the return visits of Cuban exiles commenced. Twenty years of revolution and twenty years of emigration issued a sincere common effort. Whatever the future may hold, that is already part of Cuban history.

The Cuban community split into the opposing camps of those who supported the Dialogue and those who opposed it; those who returned to Cuba and those who refused to. Maximiliano Pons refused to return: "Thousands of people ended up going to Cuba. I wanted to go myself. There is someone there I want to see before he dies. I'm afraid I will never see him again . . . But not until Fidel is gone."[52] Still, in the year 1979 alone, over 100,000 Cubans returned to Cuba.

The significance of the Dialogue was not lost on the right-wing Cuban terrorists. After some years of aimless violence, a fresh wave of terrorism surged with a clearer aim: two Cubans who endorsed the reopening of Cuba were murdered.[53] Yet this act of spite could not undo the reunification so many achieved. Those reunions were partly responsible for the next mass exodus.

The Mariel Exodus

After the refugees from Spain arrived, the flow of Cuban refugees halted for many years. Only the political prisoners released by the Cuban government gradually arrived. With the increasing institutionalization of the Cuban revolution and the increasing assimilation of Cuban immigrants in America, few expected the next turn. The chaotic flotilla exodus in the spring of 1980 belied many expectations.

Initiated in April by those who asked for political asylum at the Peruvian embassy, it grew massive within days. When the exodus ceased some months later, it had brought approximately 125,000 more Cubans to America. From Miami thousands of boats manned by relatives sped across the ninety miles of sea to Cuba's Mariel Harbor. At times they succeeded in bringing their families, other times they brought whomever angry officials put on the boats. Toward the end, this group included Cuba's social "undesirables," such as inmates of jails and mental hospitals, and homosexuals, irrespective of their desire to leave the country. Right from the start, therefore, this wave of refugees included two types of persons: those who left and those who were sent.

Unlike other waves of migration, this one lacked order and process. In Cuba these "antisocial elements," or "scum," as they were called, represented a large public slap in the face. They were no longer the immigrants of the transition from capitalism to communism, but of communism itself. In America they arrived in the throes of an ambivalent government policy that scarcely knew whether it wanted them and an antipathy toward the refugees that was solidly rooted in a declining economy. After twenty years of celebrating the achievements of Cuban exiles, the press contributed to their damaging portrayal. It focused on the criminals, the homosexuals, the many blacks—categories of people whom Americans accord too little respect. Who are the latest immigrants? Are they "scum?"

To dispel the more damaging and inaccurate portrayals, Robert Bach studied their characteristics.[54] Among the most salient was the visibly higher proportion of blacks. Approximately 40 percent of the Mariel refugees were black Cubans,[55] a sharp contrast with the previous immigrants.

Despite their differences, common to all waves of Cuban immigrants prior to this one was that they were predominantly white. With a Caribbean history of plantation slavery, Cuba is a multiracial society: the 1953 Cuban census listed the proportion of blacks as 27 percent.[56] Yet, while throughout the decade of the sixties the occupational distribution of Cuban refugees became more representative of Cuban society, "paradoxically," said Benigno Aguirre, Cuban blacks "participated less in it."[57]

In Cuba, as in much of the Caribbean, social class and race overlapped in the extreme. So Cubans valued whiteness as tantamount to beauty, status, and honor.[58] Contrary to American practice, color gradations had meaning, particularly when buttressed by income and authority.[59] Despite the coincidence of race and class while the social class level of the Cuban migration dropped, for fifteen years the immigrants remained overwhelmingly white. While information on race is not available for the early waves of migration, it can be inferred by the change in the proportion of black Cubans in the United States. The 1960 U.S. census showed that 6.5 percent of Cubans were black; the 1970 census showed only 2.6 percent. As Casal noted, "This suggests that almost all of the Cuban émigrés to the U.S. during this intercensal period—half a million—must have been white."[60] Data from the 1976 Survey of Income and Education show that 96 percent of Cubans who immigrated from 1960 to 1973 were white. In addition, 95 percent of the refugees who arrived from Spain between 1973 and 1975 were white.[61] Yet the differential migration of the Cuban races up to this time was quite explainable. Two different social processes, Aguirre concluded, were at work.

At the outset, the revolution pulled the power out from under the upper classes, which had deliberately excluded blacks from their midst. The immigration proceeded through the chain of extended family and friends, further selecting whites.[62] In addition, the migration policy of the United States and Cuba contributed to the exclusion of blacks. From 1965 on, the exodus was regulated by the Memorandum of Understanding between the two countries, both of which gave priority to close relatives of Cubans already in the United States. This policy unwittingly excluded Cuban blacks from the possibility of emigrating.

The Cuban revolution eradicated the old and blatant forms of racial discrimination in Cuba and actively sought to incorporate blacks into the mainstream of the revolution. Aguirre stressed that the ideological climate in Cuba accentuated two themes: that socialism, in promoting egalitarianism, eradicated racism, and that the United States is a racist society incapable of eradicating racial discrimination, tied as it is to capitalist exploitation.[63]

But not only revolutionary ideology prevented blacks from emigrating. Blacks in Cuba did benefit from the revolution. Cuba never had a body of law that explicitly condemned blacks to the denigrating inequality that Jim Crow laws perpetuated in the United States. Furthermore, Cuban culture was an amalgam of white and black cultural traditions, a "creolization" that Orlando Patterson notes is peculiar to Caribbean societies.[64] Yet prerevolutionary Cuba excluded blacks from the pinnacles of society: yacht and country

clubs, the best resort beaches, hotels, and private schools were re-
served for the elite. As Maurice Zeitlin observed, however, these
"were closed to the *poor* of Cuba—black and white alike."[65] Given
the overlap of class and race in Cuba, the normal operation of a
highly unequal class society perpetrated many a subtle act of racial
discrimination. But discrimination also was real.

One of the first acts of the revolution was to make these exclusive facilities public and available to all, regardless of color or
wealth. In addition to such palpable gestures, the Cuban government promoted new opportunities for blacks in employment and
education, filling administrative positions and providing scholarships to study at the university. The place of blacks in Cuban history was also recognized, honoring their contributions. Like many
others, Richard Fagen noted that the race problem in Cuba was "a
boon to Castro." The revolutionaries found it extremely useful for
discrediting the old social order. With the "instant liberation" of
blacks, "tens of thousands of disadvantaged Cubans were recruited
into the ranks of revolutionary enthusiasts."[66]

Given the confluence of migration policy, ideological themes, and
real benefits, the low proportion of blacks in the earlier exodus was
explainable. Why then was there such a large number in the last
wave?

At present we have no answer. But future research ought to consider several possibilities. As early as 1971 Geoffrey Fox remarked
that "almost all those emigrating today are from among the poorer
classes in Cuba, the very people in whose name the revolution was
made," blacks included.[67] To study "the defections of the sans-
culottes," Fox interviewed fifty working-class émigrés in Chicago.
Both for white and black workers he concluded that the salience
of race in the revolution predisposed them to leave, for it had created role strain: both felt unequal to the new expectations. White
workers perceived that the revolution displayed favoritism toward
blacks; blacks felt that the revolution suffered from tokenism.

Another possibility lies in the persistence of racial prejudice in
Cuba, despite the government's attempts to eradicate discrimination. Cuban blacks might have sensed these attitudes as real and
felt that they denied the changes effected.[68] In prerevolutionary
Cuba both individual and institutional forms of discrimination
were condoned.[69] Under the revolution, all institutional forms of
discrimination were abolished; all individual forms of discrimination were condemned. Access to the mainstream of society in educational and occupational opportunities, administrative posts, and
political participation was a reality. Yet at the same time, while dis-

crimination as a set of practices of individuals and institutions died, racism (and sexism) as a set of cultural beliefs, as an ideology that defines superiority, beauty, and worth, still lives.[70]

The twin concepts of prejudice and discrimination guide social science research on race and ethnic relations. Until very recently, as Joe Feagin and Douglas Eckberg pointed out, the underlying model was prejudice-causes-discrimination. With this assumption, "analysts seek to reduce bigotry as a means of reducing discrimination," thereby ignoring the economic and political context within which prejudice exists.[71] While this is certainly problematic, the Cuban experience presents us with another predicament. With discrimination eradicated why should prejudiced attitudes persist?

One answer is the "relative autonomy" of the superstructure because, as Casal said, "superstructural elements can be independently transmitted by various socializing agencies."[72] Although within the conceptual framework of structural Marxism, her answer is the same that Max Weber pointed to so long ago when he stated that, whatever their origins, attitudes, once established, take on "a life of their own." Both statements serve to explain the persistence of attitudes.

Another possibility is that while discrimination can be eliminated and equality promoted by government decree, only social movements initiated from below touch consciousness.[73] To those participating in a social movement politics is personal. People who constitute a movement are reaching for a goal of personal change for themselves in their own lives as well as social change. A successful social movement is the point of intersection between personal change and social change. Then attitudes change. There are limits to what can be achieved by fiat.

Last, it is also possible that the pattern of race relations changed so considerably in twenty years of revolution that the émigrés, overwhelmingly young, were hardly conscious of their race and that their motive for migration lay elsewhere. Mariano Medina, a black Cuban, arrived in 1980. An officer in the Cuban army who had fought in Angola, he explained his decision to leave in this way: "I decided to leave Cuba many years before I was able to leave. I had been sent to Angola. I was a military officer and volunteered for duty in Angola, hoping I could escape and live in a free country . . . My job for ten years had been to train guerrilla personnel, living in the mountains along with them, with one month's leave a year. The food was good, but the control was total. I felt like a beast of burden in someone's yoke."[74] Whatever role their race may have played in the decision to emigrate, black Cubans will find their steps uncertain in America. As blacks, they will not be fully accepted by whites; among blacks, they will be Cubans, still subject to all the skepticism that permeates bonds among minorities.

What else characterized the Mariel refugees? Most important are their former occupations. Based on Bach's studies, Table 1 shows the overall picture for the 1980 immigrants, both those processed in south Florida and in the military camps. As Bach et al. observed, "Most were from the mainstream of the Cuban economy."[75] They are hardly "scum."

The professionals who left numbered 11.2 percent, very similar to their proportion throughout the 1970s. Among them, teachers appeared most frequently. Accountants, entertainers, urban planners, architects, and nurses also arrived "at a greater than incidental rate."[76] Alejandro and Rosalia Pérez were both physicians in Cuba, he a respiratory and heart specialist, she an internist. Rosalia explained that they had been all over the Third World as envoys from Cuba: "There was always much need wherever we were sent." In explaining his reasons for leaving, Alejandro stressed that in Cuba they had lived much better than anyone else, as they had a big house and a car, the opportunity to travel, the respect of others. Yet he felt that there must be more to life than this: "What can I say to you that is new or that no one has said to you before about my reason—or reasons—for leaving Cuba? We were not free. We could not do as we wanted to, or say, or even think anything that was against Fidel or critical of his way of thinking."[77]

The 1973–1974 immigration from Spain was distinct in the high proportion of service workers (26.4 percent) that resulted from the nationalization of the small commercial sector in the late sixties, when most left Cuba. In 1980, by contrast, service workers as well as clerical and sales workers emigrated at the lowest proportions ever, 4.8 and 6.6 percent. These low figures, however, may reflect the decline in the commercial sector itself.[78] As nearly constant for twenty years of migration was the very small exodus of agricultural workers. Gastón Fernández interpreted this as reflecting the improvements in the rural areas during the revolution.[79]

Most salient is that this last exodus was overwhelmingly working class—70.9 percent were blue-collar workers. Of these, 25.5 percent were craft workers, skilled workers who left at approximately the same rate for fifteen years. The major difference lies in the large number of semiskilled and unskilled laborers, 45.4 percent. In comparison to the Cuban population, construction and transportation were overrepresented.[80] Fernández judged that their exodus may be partly due to the shifts in government investment patterns to industry, away from the expansion of education and medicine in the 1960s that created and maintained many professionals as well as construction workers. Coupled with the recent economic crises in Cuba that centered on the key industries of sugar and tobacco—"We are traveling through a sea of economic difficulties," said Castro seven months before the exodus—the discontent of urban workers ran high.

In addition, the return visits of Cuban exiles had an impact. They relinked family members whose ties had become loose from twenty years of disuse. These visits also made the scarcity of consumer goods and food less bearable in the face of the comfort their American relatives enjoyed.[81] Ramón Cisneros, a clinical psychologist, had been a member of the neighborhood Committee for the Defense of the Revolution. He explained the profound impact of his cousin Mario's visit: "The day my cousin Mario returned to the United States I cried the whole day. We had been like brothers . . . Then suddenly we had to say good-bye again . . . I couldn't make it happen in my mind. Before his visit, I could say to myself that I had a job to do in Cuba. I could see the reality of life in Cuba. The reality didn't bother me. Things *had* to be that way in order for Cuba to survive. Now I didn't know."[82] More than any of the previous migration waves, this one might be characterized as "those who hope."

In the United States, the press focused inordinately on the criminal element. Indeed there were many who had been in prison. The Cuban government, increasingly angry at the exodus, dumped prisoners and mental patients on the boats toward the end of the outflow. Overall, approximately 16 percent of the immigrants had spent some time in jail.[83] Of these, however, over half had served short sentences of one to three years for robbery, participating in the black market, drugs, vagrancy, refusing to serve in the military or to work for the state, or trying to escape to the United States. (The Cuban Ley de la Peligrosidad [law of dangerous people] made some forms of dissent "antisocial" behavior subject to prison terms.)[84] Others, some 20 percent, were political prisoners,[85] whom Cuba would have released and the United States taken, as in the previous years. Only a fraction could be considered serious criminals under any legal system.[86]

Also salient in the 1980 immigrants is their youth. Most of the immigrants were young male adults, single or heads of families who left their wives and children behind. Bach's studies showed that between 58 and 64 percent of those processed in the south Florida centers were 20 to 34 years old; at the military camps of the Midwest, the median age was 31.[87] At Fort Chaffee, Fernández's study showed nine times as many refugees in the age range 15 to 34 as in the range 45 to 64.[88] The disproportionate number of the young who left, stressed Fernández, suggests new generational strains. These generational strains may be the result of the more limited economic and political opportunities available to the young. The older generation of Cubans who brought about the revolution hold the key posts, and the young shoulder the burden of military service in Cuba and overseas.[89]

A year after the Bay of Pigs fiasco, with the revolution consolidated, Maurice Zeitlin studied the political generations in the Cuban working class. Different political generations formed among Cuban workers "as a result of the impact on them of distinct historical experiences," resulting in a differential support of the generations for the revolution.[90] Following Mannheim, Zeitlin found that individuals of approximately the same age who shared, in their coming of age, certain politically relevant experiences constituted a political generation: their political outlook had been shaped by a specific historical period. Operationalized as those 18 to 25 years of age during five critical periods of Cuban history, Zeitlin identified five political generations, whose attitudes toward the revolution differed. The stronger support for the revolution came from the generation of 1953, their consciousness marked by the anti-Batista struggle, the generation of the rebel leaders themselves. The two generations that came of age during the 1930s followed, the anti-Machado struggle and "the abortive revolution of the thirties" shaping them.[91] The lowest support for the revolution came, unexpectedly, from the then-current generation of 1959, followed by the republican generation of the 1940s. Hence, the historical period in which individuals came to adulthood "played a significant role in the formation of the political identities of succeeding generations of Cuban workers," affecting their response to the revolution.[92]

Because the young are overrepresented in the latest immigrants, we need to think of them also as a political generation—one whose coming of age occurred long after the early revolutionary struggle and sharp social cleavages that demanded great sacrifices but affirmed the loyalty of many. Those who were 18 to 30 in 1980, roughly half of the immigrants, came of age during the late 1960s or the 1970s. In these later stages of the Cuban revolution, issues surrounding freedom of expression, such as the Padilla affair, stood paramount. Deviance, particularly homosexuality, was scorned, and new political and social institutions were cemented. In addition, in the late seventies, Cuba turned to a decisive internationalism of military support for struggles in Africa. Mariano Medina, a black Cuban and former officer in the Cuban army, spoke of the distance that separated him from the earlier exiles: "I can now see that they feel no ill will toward me and may even want to help me, but they can't help me come to grips with the twenty years I've spent in Cuba. They don't understand how I feel . . ."[93]

What does the future hold for the Mariel immigrants? Although it is still too early to tell, the prospects look dim. Their arrival coincides with a recession, inflation, and particularly unemployment, conditions that sharply contrast with those in the land of plenty that welcomed the immigrants of the sixties and early seventies. In addition, the government assistance available to them as "entrants" pales beside the extensive support system found in the Cuban Refugee Program from 1961 to 1973.[94] In the Miami "ethnic enclave" Bach was optimistic that many would find jobs, often without the need to learn English, thereby cushioning their adjustment.[95] But, as he also stressed, the change in occupational and educational background in the successive waves of Cuban immigrants has affected the Cuban communities in the United States: "The later arrivals have, in a sense, become the working class— lower waged and skilled—for the golden exiles of the 1960's and early 1970's. Thus, there has been a total transplantation of the prerevolutionary Cuban social structure to Miami, with all the implications of unequal wealth, power, and prestige. The recent emigrants will add to the lower strata."[96] Despite the willing help of many in the Cuban community, many others exhibit a defensive prejudice against the newcomers, who are "not the same as we were" and who may tarnish the reputation of the established.

The insistence of press reports on the criminal element also has consequences for the vast majority, now resettled out of camps and trying to make a place for themselves in America. A young refugee from Mariel recounted his fruitless search for a decent job. Formerly he was a draftsman, skilled and educated. At the interviews, he said, employers demonstrated their interest by asking him many questions. After telling them he was Cuban, he was then asked: "How long have you been here?" When he replied "One year," there were no further questions.

For all the stress placed on the differences between the latest immigrants and the earlier ones, a gap remains unmentioned. Oscar

Handlin wrote of the immigrants who came from Europe at the turn of the century to fashion America. He caught the sadness, despair, and nostalgia of everyone who has ever been uprooted:

> Yesterday, by its distance, acquires a happy glow. The peasants look back . . . and their fancy rejoices in the better days that have passed, when they were on the land and the land was fertile, and they were young and strong, and virtues were fresh. And it was better yet in their fathers' days, who were wiser and stronger than they. And it was best of all in the golden past of their distant progenitors who were every one a king and did great deeds. Alas, those days are gone, that they believed existed, and now there is only the bitter present.[97]

So did Cuban immigrants in America for many years miss Cuba. But one night in Key West, while speaking with four refugees from Mariel, I was struck by the difference. While fishing, they listened on the radio to a baseball game being played right then in their hometown in Cuba. The early refugees' nostalgia attached them to the Cuba they once knew, the Cuba that was. The nostalgia of the Mariel refugees is for the Cuba that is.

Differences abound, yet the questions raised by this last wave of refugees are the same ones that for twenty years have framed the debate over the meaning of the Cuban migration. Interpretations of the meaning of the exodus once again became polarized. At one pole, the immigrants were said to be a manifestation of the loss of legitimacy of the Cuban revolution, discrediting it. At the other pole, the immigrants were said to be propelled by the scarcity of consumer goods.[98] Hence, at one pole the immigrants are political refugees; at the other, economic refugees. Twenty years, and close to a million persons: Are they political or economic immigrants?

Without doubt, the answer depends on the different ideological convictions that filter reality. But, in addition, the question is poor. For all societies are simultaneously and inextricably political and economic. Hence, in the perceptions of individuals, political and economic conditions are entangled; particularly in the attitudes that lead to the consequential decision to emigrate from the land of birth. In a society in transition, political disaffection easily results when government policies change the basic economic allocation and dislocate people; they lose their economic, social, and ideological "place." Even in a stable society, lack of economic opportunities easily results in lack of trust for public leaders.[99] In this sense,

Cuba's refugees are, and have always been, both political and economic. But when people grow politically disaffected, even for underlying economic reasons, they can no longer be disposed of as simply economic refugees. Cuba's refugees are, and have always been, fundamentally political. In addition, the governments that regulate their exit and arrival define immigrants as political or economic. In the United States, the 1980 Haitian immigrants, who face hearings and possible deportation, underscore the point. In Cuba, all who left were labelled counterrevolutionaries.

We ought, then, to change the question. The meaning of the Cuban exodus of nearly a million persons over a period of twenty years ought not to lie in whether they are political or economic refugees—discrediting the revolution or merely embarrassing it. The meaning of the Cuban exodus lies in the role of dissent in society. A society in which the only choice possible is to "love it or leave it" provides too few choices.

A truly democratic society is defined not only by its party structure, constitution, delegation of authority, or electoral representation, but principally by its capacity to tolerate and incorporate dissent. Democracy is not only a set of institutions; it is also a set of practices.[100] With applicable reasoning, in *Exit, Voice and Loyalty*, Albert Hirschman explained that two options exist for customers of a firm (or members of an organization, association, or party) when the quality of what these provide deteriorates: to attempt to change an objectionable state of affairs by using the "voice" of individual or collective actions or protests; or to "exit" by withdrawing. If you cannot express your "voice," you "exit." But after exiting, you have lost the opportunity to use your voice to promote recuperation.[101]

Writing of the very first wave of Cuban immigrants in the early 1960s, Richard Fagen et al. judged the exodus to be "one of the more humane solutions to the trauma of change in contemporary Cuba"[102] and issued the following prediction: "Dissatisfaction among certain groups in Cuba will continue, of course, and new sectors will come to view the revolutionary society as less than perfect. But this does not mean that disaffection sufficient to lead to self-imposed exile will result."[103] That prediction proved false—because for two decades the Cuban revolution's only solution to dissent was to externalize it.

When Cuba ceases to externalize its dissenters and begins to provide political channels to express and incorporate their voice, it will become a truly democratic society woven not only by mass mobilization, but also by the mass participation of both those who agree and who disagree. As Gonzalo Ponce said, "It was all because people have no rights in Cuba."[104]

The Cuban Refugee Program

Throughout the sixties and early seventies, the United States supported the exodus and facilitated the structural assimilation of Cuban immigrants. During this period, as we shall see, the refugees contributed to an important symbolic function. The program itself stands as a remarkable achievement that provided "a bridge between the old life in Cuba and a new life in the United States."[105] Government policy at the federal, state, and local levels aided the assimilation of Cuban refugees by lending them a hand.

As political refugees, most Cubans arrived in the United States with no personal belongings or currency. Initially, local public and voluntary agencies, such as churches, civic groups, and schools, provided emergency help to the arrivals in Miami. For these agencies, the assistance entailed an enormous drain on resources. Richard Ferree Smith stressed that two characteristics set the Cuban refugee problem apart from that of all other refugee groups. First, for the first time in history, the United States became a country of first asylum for refugees. Second, the U.S. government assumed a great deal of financial responsibility in assisting the Cubans.[106] Under the direction of the federal government, national, state, and local agencies conducted a concerted effort to aid them, help them become self-supporting, resettle them, and integrate them.[107] The program that evolved to receive them was vast in scope and imagination.

The first such effort was the creation, by President Eisenhower in December 1960, of the Cuban Refugee Emergency Center located in Freedom Tower in Miami, Florida. Known to Cubans as El Refugio, it received an allocation of $1 million to provide initial relief (food, clothing, health care), to help the refugees find jobs and to initiate a resettlement program for employable refugees that would distribute them to other areas. In addition, in February 1961, President Kennedy directed that a Cuban Refugee Program (receiving an initial $4 million allocation) be established under the U.S. Department of Health, Education, and Welfare. The program was a cooperative one involving the Public Health Service, the Employment Service of the U.S. Department of Labor, the Florida State Department of Public Welfare, the Dade County Health Department, the Dade County public schools, the University of Miami, and voluntary agencies in the Miami area and throughout the nation.

In the beginning, funds were allocated to the program from presidential discretionary funds. Permanent authority for the program was provided by the Migration and Refugee Assistance Act, which provided for transportation costs from Cuba; financial assistance to needy refugees; financial assistance to state and local public agencies that provided services for refugees; the costs of resettlement outside of Miami; and employment and professional training courses for refugees. From the beginning of the Cuban Refugee Program until the end of fiscal year 1973, about $957 million was spent on the program. Table 2 presents the yearly program expenditures.

The comprehensive nature of the program, outlined in the Migration and Refugee Assistance Act, was realized in its implementation. As Rafael Prohías and Lourdes Casal described the program, ultimately it would do all of the following:

1. Help voluntary agencies to provide daily necessities, to resettle, and to find jobs.

2. Gain private and government agency cooperation to provide job opportunities.

3. Provide funds for resettlement, including transportation and adjustment costs in the new community.

4. Furnish financial assistance for basic maintenance in Miami and communities of resettlement, administered through federal, state, and local channels based on standards used in the communities involved.

5. Provide essential health services.

6. Furnish federal assistance for local public school operating costs related to the Cuban impact.

7. Initiate measures to augment training and educational opportunities, particularly for physicians, teachers, and those with other professional backgrounds.

8. Provide financial aid for unaccompanied children.

9. Undertake surplus food distribution administered by the Dade County (Miami) Welfare Department.[108]

The program was vast in scope and reach. According to Juan Clark, only 27.9 percent of Cuban exiles did not register with the Cuban Refugee Emergency Center in Miami and did not receive any organized assistance. From 1960 to 1974, 461,373 Cubans received some form of assistance through the Cuban Refugee Emergency Center.[109] Cubans outside Miami often benefited from other aspects of the multifaceted program.

Table 2. Assistance to Cuban Refugees by the Cuban Refugee Program, 1961–1974 (in Millions of Dollars)

Fiscal Year	Program Administration Amount	%	Welfare Assistance[a] Amount	%	Resettlement Amount	%	Education Amount	%	Movement of Refugees Amount	%	Fiscal Year Total Amount
1961	0.2	4.9	2.3	56.1	0.5	12.2	1.0	24.4	...	...	4.1
1962	0.6	1.6	28.5	74.0	3.8	9.8	5.5	14.2	...	...	38.5
1963	1.0	1.8	41.9	75.0	3.7	6.5	9.5	16.9	...	...	56.0
1964	1.0	1.8	33.2	72.2	2.2	4.7	9.7	21.0	...	...	46.0
1965	0.9	2.9	20.7	63.6	1.3	4.0	9.6	29.5	...	...	32.5
1966	2.0	5.6	18.9	52.8	4.5	12.6	10.4	29.0	0.9	1.0	36.2
1967	2.0	4.3	23.5	49.5	5.8	12.7	14.3	31.3	0.6	1.3	46.2
1968	2.0	3.6	30.5	54.7	4.9	8.8	17.8	31.9	0.6	1.0	55.8
1969	1.9	2.7	44.5	63.0	4.8	6.7	18.8	26.9	0.6	0.9	70.6
1970	2.3	2.6	59.3	67.8	4.7	5.4	20.5	23.4	0.7	0.8	87.4
1971	2.6	2.3	81.5	72.7	5.5	4.9	21.6	19.2	0.9	0.8	112.1
1972	2.4	1.8	113.0	82.7	2.9	2.1	17.8	13.0	0.5	0.4	136.7
1973[b]	2.0	1.4	125.3	86.5	1.3	0.9	16.0	11.0	0.3	0.2	145.0
1974[b]	1.6	1.8	73.3	81.1	1.0	1.1	14.0	15.6	...	...	90.0
Total											$957.1

Source: U.S. budgets. In Prohías and Casal, *The Cuban Minority*, Table 45.
[a]Includes health services.
[b]Estimated.

The Resettlement Program

As John Thomas explained, it soon became evident that "the Miami/ Dade County area, magnificent as its people had been in welcoming the Cubans, could not support such a heavy increase in population." Hence, a top priority of the Cuban Refugee Program was the resettling of Cuban immigrants away from Miami.[110] Four voluntary agencies handled the resettlement: the United States Catholic Conference, the Church World Service, the United Hebrew Immigrant Aid Service, and the International Rescue Committee. They succeeded in resettling two out of every three registrations at the center, or 296,806 persons from 1961 to 1972.[111] The program paid their transportation expenses and provided a small transitional grant to assist in their adjustment.[112] Some of Llanes' characters who recounted their resettlement experiences included Sergio Espinosa, who went with his mother to live the harsh life of the poor in New York: "My mother came to the United States in January [1960]. We were relocated to New York, where we lived in the lower west side of Manhattan, in the garment industry. Everything there was grey or black or rusted . . . As far as I am concerned, I can rest in peace if I never see New York again. And you know, I am a product of New York. I can see it in many things I do now . . . It is a hard place, New York. Like me."[113]

Once in the new community, the network of family and friends helped the refugees find work and adjust to life there.[114] Prohías and Casal estimated that from 12 to 22 percent of the refugees resettled through 1971 returned to the Miami area.[115] Rosa Contreras and her family encountered a warm and supportive community in their resettlement to Michigan. Still, after three years, they returned to Miami. As she explained, "Everyone tried very hard to help us, and they made sure we had work and spiritual support. But the change was too severe for us. We could not adjust. We left as soon as we had saved enough money. Those three years in Coldwater are filled with happy memories."[116]

The resettlement agencies contacted the families of newly arrived refugees, made travel arrangements for the family reunion, developed a network of sponsors to resettle refugees without families, and handled emergencies and provided affidavits of support. But even outside of Miami, if the refugee lost a job, became seriously ill, or encountered other trials, public welfare was still available in the new community through funding by the Cuban Refugee Program. As Clark said, "In fact the Program's responsibility to the resettled exile ceased only when he became a citizen."[117]

Cuban refugees resettled to all fifty states, to more than 2,400 communities.[118] Their resettlement outside of Florida permitted them to find better opportunities in employment and income than would have been possible in Florida.[119] The Cuban refugee, said Thomas, "had to be persuaded that resettlement was his main hope for a new life."[120]

The Public Schools: Bilingual Education

The judicial mandate for bilingual education programs in the public schools did not come about until the 1974 *Lau vs. Nichols* case, which initiated the numerous efforts in bilingual education throughout the United States.[121] But bilingual education was in fact born in the school year of 1960, fourteen years before it was legally mandated. The federal government funded bilingual education programs for Cuban refugees that the Dade County public school system creatively designed in response to the sudden influx of non–English-speaking students.

Joe Hall, superintendent of the public schools of Dade County, recalled these problems:

> It was early in 1960 that the public schools of Dade County began to experience a problem which was unique not only to the local school system but probably in the entire history of education in the United States. This was the first time that thousands of persons, forced to flee from their native homeland because of political upheaval, had sought refuge in the United States and brought with them their children to enroll in the local school system . . . because of an accident of geography the citizens of Florida and of Dade County accepted responsibility for these refugees for the entire nation.[122]

Substantial federal aid was essential to educate the Cuban refugee children. Beginning with the school year 1960–1961, the Cuban Refugee Program allocated funds to the Dade County public schools through annual agreements signed by the Dade County School Board and the U.S. Office of Education. From 1960 to 1972, the federal government paid over $130 million dollars to the Dade County school system under the Cuban Refugee Program.[123]

At first, the federal government paid 60 percent of the cost of educating all Cuban refugee students. But in 1965 the second major wave of Cuban immigration began, bringing a new influx of Cuban students to the Dade County public schools. In addition, some of the refugees who had earlier resettled throughout the country began to filter back into Dade County. As the superintendent of the school system mourned, "There is no end in sight." Once again the federal government stepped in to help. For the refugees of this wave, the federal government paid 100 percent. In 1961, Cuban refugee pupils numbered 4,327; in 1970, 31,230.[124] The instructional program for these children became a prototype for later efforts in bilingual education, combining aspects of both models of bilingual education: "transition" to English and "maintenance" of the native language.

In addition to programs for children, the schools offered three kinds of adult programs: conversational English, vocational training, and English-language "retooling" courses for Cuban professionals. The English Institute Program for adults trained approximately 200 persons every ten weeks.[125] English-language classes often provided a transition to vocational education. The year-long adult and vocational programs added more English classes as well as classes in the areas of business education, shop, adult high school, reading, office work, home economics, and the like. In 1961, its first year of operation, 10,000 students participated in the program. As word spread that these classes were available, more and more refugees enrolled. By the school year 1962, over 20,000 students attended. In the school years of 1963 and 1964, the number of students reached 30,000 a year. The school year of 1966 it stabilized at about 20,000 a year, where it remained until 1972.[126] The federal government further assisted the education of Cuban adults by agreeing to partly subsidize the county school board for Cuban refugees attending Dade County Junior College.[127] The schools coordinated the vocational training given Cuban refugees with the Cuban Refugee Emergency Center so that the training could facilitate the adjustment of the refugees.[128]

Both the special programs for adults and the instructional programs for children also provided Cuban adults with employment. The schools employed former Cuban teachers to coordinate the programs, to serve as teacher aides, and to bridge the language barrier and provide a link between the Spanish-speaking community and the school.

From 1960 to 1972, the federal government spent over $130 million dollars for Cuban refugee pupils in the Dade County public school system. Of this total, $117 million supported the primary and secondary bilingual instruction, over $12 million went to the vocational and adult programs, and over $1 million provided funds for the summer programs.[129]

Without setting out to design a bilingual education program, the Cuban Refugee Program nevertheless provided, through federal funding and the cooperation of state and local agencies, a comprehensive program for receiving Cuban political immigrants. The program served both children and adults. It also provided employment opportunities for teachers as part of the retraining programs for professionals.

Retraining Programs for Professionals

The Cuban Refugee Program targeted the professionals. The retraining programs for Cuban professionals instituted with federal funds show the ways in which the state cleared the obstacles of language, training, certification, licensing, and citizenship for Cuban refugees. The role government played facilitated the "translation" of the refugees' social class into valuable American credentials.

John F. Thomas, first director of the Cuban Refugee Program, was keenly aware of the barriers to the structural assimilation of immigrants imposed by citizenship, training, and certification requirements, even for immigrants of higher social class origin:

> One common requirement affecting employability in certain professions is U.S. citizenship or a declaration of intent to become a citizen, a requirement which cannot be met by the vast majority of the refugees because of their immigration status. Data . . . show that citizenship or a declaration of intent is a requirement for licensing as follows:

Architects	24 states
Dentists	45 states and D.C.
Lawyers	most states
Professional nurses	22 states, Puerto Rico and V.I.
Practical nurses	28 states, Puerto Rico and V.I.
Physicians	41 states and Puerto Rico
Public school teachers	most states
Veterinarians	29 states

> Other requirements also affect certain professionals. Six states do not accept any foreign-trained physicians. Dental studies pursued in a foreign university receive virtually no recognition in the United States. The same is true of law studies pursued in countries such as Cuba that do not base their legal system on English common law.[130]

The Cuban Refugee Program helped to institute programs that retrained selected groups of skilled and professional Cubans—largely teachers, college professors, doctors, optometrists, and lawyers. While the professional retraining programs did not reach all Cuban professionals, it is certain that they did enable a great many to practice in the United States the professions for which they were trained. Hence, the state facilitated the secondary structural assimilation of Cuban refugees into American institutions. Omar Betancourt explained it thus:

> Back in the 1960s people who had been dentists in Cuba worked as hotel porters in Miami and, of course, no one expected any more than that. It was a means of keeping body and soul together. That was all that mattered, for a while. Then came the struggle for credentials and licenses—going to night school for three years so that you could get a license to enable you to do the thing you had done for ten years in Cuba. The protectionism of professions is still the most powerful barrier to complete social integration.[131]

In 1963, the University of Miami initiated the Cuban Teacher Retraining Program. The program met both the needs of the former teachers for Florida licensing and certification and the needs of students in Miami for bilingual teachers.[132] Ten years later, in 1973, nearly 500 Cuban teachers had completed the program and attained certification.

The advisory board of the Cuban Teacher Retraining Program was composed of personnel from the Dade County public school system, the Cuban Refugee Program, the Florida State Department of Education, and the University of Miami. The guiding philosophy of the program was to gradually immerse the Cuban teachers in the culture of the United States, especially in its educational system, to help them make the transition to teaching in this country. Its aim was to enable Cuban teachers to meet the licensing and certification requirements of their profession so that they could practice it. The Florida State Board of Education required teachers with university degrees from Cuba to validate their degrees through a North American institution. Another obstacle was that Florida required citizenship for teacher certification. After numerous negotiations, the state of Florida allowed Cuban refugee teachers to obtain provisional certification prior to obtaining citizenship.

In addition to the University of Miami, eight other colleges and universities sponsored similar programs to enable teachers from

Table 3. *Special Teacher Retraining Courses for Cuban Refugees*

Cooperating Institutions	Years Offered	Number Completing Courses
University of Iowa Iowa City, Iowa	1963–1965	62
Indiana State University Terre Haute, Indiana	1963–1964	93
College of Great Falls Great Falls, Montana	1964	30
Kutztown State Teachers College Kutztown, Pennsylvania	Summers of 1964, 1965	44
Pacific University Forest Grove, Oregon	1964	27
Fairleigh Dickinson University New Jersey	1965–1968	85
Kansas State Teachers College Emporia, Kansas	1964–1968	22
Mount St. Mary's College Los Angeles, California	Summers of 1965, 1966, 1967, 1968	57
University of Miami Miami, Florida	1963–1973	500
Total		920

Source: Adapted from Sevick, "A History and Evaluation of the Cuban Teacher Retraining Program," p. 20; and Moncarz, "Professional Adaptation of the Cuban Teachers," Table 2.

Cuba to become American teachers. These programs also enabled other professionals (such as lawyers, for whom the difference between the two legal systems was impossible to bridge) to become teachers. Table 3 lists the other institutions conducting these programs, the years of the programs, and the number who completed the programs. Thomas, the director of the Cuban Refugee Program, was very proud of its achievements: "Thousands of school teachers have escaped from Cuba, and HEW has sponsored more than 15 training projects at universities in various parts of the country leading to the employment of Spanish-language teachers in hundreds of communities previously not able to locate teachers of that skill.

Cuban lawyers have become teachers, insurance adjusters, abstract readers, librarians, and social workers as the result of retraining."[133]

Iowa was the first state outside of Florida to offer help. The Cuban Refugee Center in Miami selected the participants for the University of Iowa program. Already hired by school districts in Iowa before beginning their studies, the teachers were assured of employment after their studies. The director of the Institute for Cuban Refugee Teachers in Iowa expressed its aims: "We believed that our program would serve a dual purpose: it would be beneficial to the State of Iowa by facilitating the extension and enrichment of foreign language instruction in the public schools of Iowa; it would also help the Cuban refugees by giving them an opportunity to rebuild their lives and regain economic security."[134]

Kansas State Teachers College conducted both a teacher education program for Cuban teachers as well as courses in library education for other professionals, most of whom were Cuban lawyers. Lasting over four years, this program enabled over 100 persons to practice teaching or library work in the United States. Tom Alexander understood the plight of many Cuban professionals: "Of all the professional men, the Cuban lawyers have the hardest time obtaining employment that uses their talents, since they were trained in the Napoleonic Code, rather than the common law practice in the U.S. To help the lawyers, the refugee program has sponsored a special series of training programs aimed at turning lawyers into Spanish teachers, and by now several hundred of them are teaching in U.S. schools and colleges."[135]

The largest teacher retraining program was at the University of Miami.[136] Over the years it expanded to serve not only students with Cuban university degrees (who needed only to validate them and meet state certification), but also students who had not completed their university training or who had only an *escuela normal* degree and who thus needed to complete the bachelor's degree program.[137] Over the course of ten years at the University of Miami alone, nearly 500 participants obtained teacher certification.[138] Together, all the institutions retrained over 900 persons. As Sevick claimed, the program was "a unique educational experiment, for never before have so many teachers from a foreign country been 'retrained' as a group to teach in the United States."[139]

Professional "retooling" was especially important for professionals who needed to pass American licensing examinations. Cuban doctors provide an example of both the effort and success of the professional retraining programs. By 1966, about 2,000 of the 6,600

Cuban doctors had left Cuba; by 1972, 3,100.[140] Most of them came to the United States, "where they were free to do almost anything—except be doctors."[141] In the United States, Cuban doctors needed to be accredited before they could practice medicine and to obtain their licenses before they could practice privately. To assist them in preparing for the necessary exams, the University of Miami Medical School, with support from private agencies, initiated a postgraduate medical retraining program in 1961. Later, the federal government supported it through the Cuban Refugee Program, providing funds and tuition assistance for Cuban doctors.

The refresher course consisted of twelve weeks of instruction, with lectures simultaneously translated into Spanish, stressing medical English. In 1972, thirty members of the University of Miami School of Medicine were lecturing in the program. The principal goal of the retraining program was to enable Cuban doctors to pass the exam of the Educational Council for Foreign Medical Graduates, the basic entry to the American health care system.[142] By 1973, over 2,166 Cuban doctors had taken this course and about half had passed the exams and gone on to practice medicine in the United States. With the "big and insistent demand for them in doctor-starved public hospitals," an article praised, "Castro's loss is a U.S. gain."[143] Thomas also underscored the success of the medical retraining program: "It is purported that the cost to the taxpayer for the training of an American doctor from kindergarten to internship is over $40,000. HEW has placed nearly 1,700 Cuban doctors into public service at the cost of $300 per doctor; this represents quite a sizeable return on our investment!"[144]

College Tuition Loans

Beginning in 1961, as part of the Cuban Refugee Program, the federal government instituted a program of making loans available to Cuban exiles wishing to attend college. Undergraduates could borrow up to $1,000 a year, and graduate or professional students as much as $2,500. The money could pay for tuition, room and board, books, and related expenses. From 1962 to 1976, the government lent about $34 million to 16,100 persons.[145]

Thus, Cuban students could enter college and complete their studies if they wished to pursue professional retraining programs or a new career of their own. Besides, the college loans removed the economic burden for parents financing their children's college education. Without this financial assistance, Clark stressed, "the college education of many would have been severely compromised or impossible."[146]

Citizenship

Clearly, the lack of citizenship is a major obstacle for immigrants wanting to enter certain occupations, especially professional roles that require it. Thomas was keenly aware of its importance for professionals:

> As time went on it became obvious to those concerned with the assimilation of the Cuban refugees that the lack of permanent resident status was a handicap to many. Professional people found many avenues to licensing or certification closed due to this factor. Skilled persons encountered difficulties in meeting requirements in many states because of lack of permanent resident status. To meet this problem Congress passed the necessary legislation last session which enables many Cuban refugees to better their economic position.[147]

The government policy that facilitated the attainment of citizenship for all Cuban refugees was a very important component of the comprehensive package of aid.

In November 1966, Public Law 89-732 gave Cubans the chance to become citizens. This law allowed Cubans in the United States to apply for permanent residency without the expensive requirement of applying at a U.S. consulate. Even more important, the government allowed Cubans to claim up to two and a half years of their stay in the United States toward the five years of residence required for citizenship. Never before had the government relaxed citizenship requirements so.

Throughout the late 1950s, the number of Cubans who became naturalized remained fairly constant—about 1,200 every year. From 1961 to 1965, the average doubled to around 2,400 naturalizations a year. Beginning in 1966, they increased steadily until 1970, when a dramatic jump took place: 20,888 persons became U.S. citizens.[148] For many, citizenship opened the doors of opportunity.

The Cuban Refugee Program, in all its various facets, was an enormous effort to support Cubans and to facilitate the transference of their credentials, making their social class origin valuable in America. No wonder that Alexander, writing about "Those Amazing Cuban Emigrés," judged that "their ready absorption into the economy can be attributed, not only to their own considerable skills and energy, and to the enormous American manpower requirements of the past few years, but to an enlightened U.S. Government policy. Washington has worked hard to get the refugees established in homes and jobs all around the U.S."[149] A former Cuban teacher, for ten years regarded by U.S. public schools as a model teacher, expressed her gratitude by echoing that view: "They have helped us a lot."

Throughout the sixties and early seventies, the state, through the collaboration of federal and local agencies, played a substantial role in the structural assimilation of Cuban political immigrants in America. It lent Cubans a firm hand.

3. Ignoring Mexican Economic Immigrants

Portrait of the Mexican Immigrants: Prolonged Labor Migration

Longer, larger, and poorer than the Cuban immigration, Mexican immigration to the United States also proceeded over distinct waves. For over 150 years, the main "push" and "pull" factors that drove and lured Mexicans remained constant: a huge disparity in levels of living across a border. Hence, in comparison with the Cuban migration, the waves of Mexican migration vary less in the social and demographic characteristics of the immigrants. Rather, the waves of Mexican immigrants offer enormous contrasts in the number of immigrants at hand.[1] To understand the pattern of fluctuation in this immigration, we need to consider the social and historical context that conditioned the immigration flows.

Early Frontier Migration

From its beginning in the middle of the nineteenth century, as Arthur Corwin depicted it, Mexican immigration was more of "a seasonal labor trek" than an immigrant voyage across the ocean. Often undocumented, uncommitted, and unskilled, Mexican immigrants historically played the role of "a rural and industrial proletariat."[2] What is now the American Southwest was acquired through conquest. At the end of the Mexican-American War, in 1848, by the treaty of Guadalupe Hidalgo, Mexico relinquished its northern territories.[3] Immediately the California Gold Rush spurred the immigration of thousands of Mexicans, many of them miners. The Mexican miners were but one link in the chain of migrants that arrived after 1848, foreshadowing the *braceros* and wetbacks of the twentieth century.[4]

Thereafter, Mexicans from the poorest states in the north of Mexico continued to filter with ease into California and then into the mines of Nevada, Arizona, and even Colorado. But it was really the boom of the 1880s that prompted the continuous flow of emigration from the more populated center of Mexico. Technology, said Corwin, laid the groundwork: "The completion of a transborder railway system in the 1880s joined the heartland to the United States and practically eliminated historic barriers to Hispano-Mexican migration northward. The Iron Horse leaped over hostile deserts and barren plains."[5]

Yet even before the railway was completed, the seasonal labor supply was already established. Anglo ranchers in Texas increasingly employed Mexicans to help. Migrant families moved into the border towns; recruiters and agents sent them inland to work. Encouraging Mexicans to settle on or near their ranches, Texas Anglos practiced "a semifeudal agricultural pattern" that created many migrant labor colonies alongside towns. This pattern spread to other states as employers continued to search for a mobile and cheap supply of "stoop labor." The railroads functioned to spread this labor, as well as the pattern of cyclical seasonal work, throughout the border states. By 1900, Mexicans were working in agriculture nearly everywhere in the Southwest—as pickers, planters, and packers for the emerging vegetable and fruit industries.[6]

Despite the many incidents of racial discrimination and the hounding of the Texas and Arizona rangers, the Mexican population continued to increase in the border states. No accurate counts of Mexican immigrants exist for this period, but, using the decennial increases in the U.S. censuses, Corwin confirmed the remarkable growth of immigration in this settlement period.[7] According to the census of 1900, about 103,410 persons born in Mexico lived in the United States, about eight times the number reported by the 1850 census. While Mexican migration was not yet the mass migration it was to become in the twentieth century, the parameters that to this day define it were already evident. As Corwin underlined, Southwestern *patrones* "continued to welcome Mexican labor (so long as it wasn't unionized)" while native American and immigrant workers as well as labor organizations "continued to resent them."[8]

The mass migration of the twentieth century, observed Arthur Corwin and Lawrence Cardoso, can be "conveniently divided into two phenomenal waves": one lasted until 1930, when the Depression dammed it; the other, induced by World War II, is still with us today.[9]

An analysis of the causes of this mass migration reveals that at the root was the problem of land. As Ernesto Galarza said, "Migration is the failure of roots. Displaced men are ecological victims. Between them and the sustaining earth a wedge has been driven. Eviction by drouths or dispossession by landlords, the impoverishment of the soil or conquest by arms—nature and man, separately or together, lay down the choice: move or die. Those who are able to break away do so, leaving a hostile world behind to face an uncertain one ahead."[10] Cardoso underscored that, as the twentieth century opened, the Mexican peasantry found its land base disappearing. Intending to modernize the countryside, the government of Porfirio Díaz destroyed the community-owned *ejidos* where peasants lived. Most peasants came to suffer from peonage, particularly an insuperable, inherited peonage, which constituted a form of involuntary servitude.[11] Corwin and Cardoso stressed that, with almost all land in the hands of a small elite, the population explosion that took place about the turn of the century also contributed "to the deprivation and displacement of the peasantry,"[12] to an abject poverty which the peasant could not escape. Mass emigration ensued. Landless peons moved from the more populated states of the central plateau to the cities of Mexico and to the north of Mexico, where there was a rising demand for labor.

Typically, the early immigrant was from the peon labor class, but many of the early immigrants also came from the casual laborers of the *rancherías*, which predated Díaz's regime. These often became camps of squatters attracted by seasonal work. And the immigrants also included small peasant proprietors, small shopkeepers, artisans, and workers who—skilled in mining, ranching, and railway work—were hired in the more industrialized country to the north as gangs and ended up as common labor.[13] The Sonorans, from northern Mexico, were experienced miners. The discovery of gold in California beckoned them. In the latter half of the nineteenth century, western mining developed, as Carey McWilliams said, by "a series of 'waves': first gold, then silver, and finally copper."[14] Mexican immigrants contributed to its development.

Then, as well as now, the primary "pull" factor was higher wages. At that time, wages in the United States were six times higher than those for similar work in Mexico.[15] The railroads served to spread the labor. American companies set up recruiting centers along the border with *enganchistas*, whose task was to lure Mexicans across the border to sign up.[16] The railroads also served to fix the early settlement patterns of Mexican workers. The immigrants made their way to citrus groves in California, beet fields in Colorado, cotton plantations in Texas, and railway service centers, such as

Laramie, Kansas City, and Chicago.[17] "Wherever a railroad labor camp was established," pointed out McWilliams, "a Mexican *colonia* exists today."[18]

The economic development of the Southwest itself also pulled the immigration. Railroads not only facilitated the crossing of the border; they also linked the isolated Southwest to the nation's industrial economy. The halt to Chinese and Japanese immigration in 1882 and 1907 made the Mexican immigrants, with their temporary and intermittent patterns of work, all the more desirable: the "ideal solution" to cyclical labor needs. "It thus happened," Corwin and Cardoso stressed, "that the migratory habits of the Mexican *campesino* fit neatly with the needs of southwestern agribusiness."[19]

A link was soon established between the prosperity of agriculture and the availability of migrants, who cleared, levelled, planted, tended, and harvested, providing the impetus for the growth of agriculture. In mining, as in agriculture, Mexican workers took jobs that other groups refused—chopping, picking, shovelling, and cleaning.[20] From the railroad, workers also found access to jobs in industry, although after 1910 employers often used Mexicans as strikebreakers to forestall the unionization drives of American workers.[21] Thus they reached into the industrial cities of the Midwest, where they worked in tanneries, steel mills, foundries, and packing plants.[22]

Manuel Gamio interviewed Mexican immigrants throughout the 1920s and recorded their life stories. The autobiographical sketches demonstrate their seasonal and mobile work patterns. Gonzalo Galván, for example, first worked in a railroad camp, then at a copper foundry, then on a road crew, and last as a wood chopper:

> When we got to El Paso we put ourselves under contract to go to work in a railroad camp at Wiles, California. When we got to that place the foreman received us. There were a number of Mexicans at the station who turned out to be from the same town that we were from, and they told us not to go and work on the tracks because they paid little and would mistreat us. Nevertheless we went to the railroad camp, and there they gave us an old car in which to live . . . On the next day one of the boys took us to the *esmelda*, a copper foundry, and there they gave us work paying us $1.50 for 9 hours work. The work was hard there. I stayed about two weeks and as I didn't like the work I was waiting for a chance to leave.[23]

Francisco Gómez, over 50 years old in the mid-twenties, recalled his childhood:

> I lived in Chihuahua until I was five years of age. Then I came back with my parents to San Antonio and from there we went to Fort Worth and from there to El Paso and to Arizona. We were two boys and my father and mother. I never went to school, for since we kept going from one place to another it wasn't possible for me to do so but my parents taught me to read and write Spanish. From the time I was ten years old I helped my parents pick cotton, cultivate beets and do other work. When I was about fifteen I began work in the mines because my father also worked in them . . . Little by little I kept learning and later when I was older I worked many years in the mines in Texas and in Arizona. Coal and ore mines they were.[24]

In Mexico, lack of land, abject poverty, excess population, the railroads; in America, economic expansion, higher wages, lack of other sources of cheap labor—all these "pushed" and "pulled" the mass emigration that responded with *vamos al norte* (let's go north). With an apt image, McWilliams depicted the history of Spanish influence in the Southwest. Three hundred years apart, he said, Spanish-speaking people invaded the borderlands twice. The first invaders, the Spanish *conquistadores*, came "in search of gold and silver"; the second, the Mexican peons, came "in search of bread and a job."[25]

With the migrant labor flow already so well established, the Mexican Revolution (1910–1920) was but a catalyst to an exodus already underway. Corwin and Cardoso stressed that the revolution's impact was particularly felt in the rural areas, where the abolition of peonage and land redistribution "snapped" the semifeudal bonds between master and peon, often displacing them both.[26] Immigration to America jumped. From 1908 to 1925 "the whole border was aflame," said McWilliams.[27] Table 4 shows that in the first decade of this century, 49,642 legal immigrants arrived. During the decade of the revolution, immigration increased to 219,004.

For some immigrants, the United States became a base for revolutionary activity. Manuel Gamio's interviews of Mexican immigrants in the 1920s offer an illustration. Upon inheriting part of an hacienda from her grandparents, Flores de Andrade freed all the peons from their debts and divided part of her property among them. Eventually, she began to fight for liberal ideals, against the dictatorship of Porfirio Díaz. As a result, she grew poorer and poorer, until in 1906 she decided to leave Mexico:

> Finally after four years' stay in Chihuahua, I decided to come to El Paso, Texas. I came in the first place to see if I could better my economic condition and secondly to continue fighting in that region in favor of the Liberal ideals, that is to say, to plot against the dictatorship of Don Porfirio . . .
>
> In 1909 a group of comrades founded in El Paso a Liberal women's club. They made me president of that group, and soon afterwards I began to carry on the propaganda work in El Paso and in Ciudad Juarez. My house from about that time was turned into a conspiratory center against the dictatorship. Messengers came there from the Flores Magon band and from Madero bringing me instructions. I took charge of collecting money, clothes, medicines and even ammunition and arms to begin to prepare for the revolutionary movement, for the uprisings were already starting in some places.[28]

But it was really World War I in America that set off the first mass exodus as well as the first cries of a "silent invasion."

World War I: The First Silent Invasion

When World War I placed working-class Americans in the military, the demand for labor intensified. At the same time, the immigration and nationality acts of the 1920s closed the door on the huge waves of European immigration crossing the ocean. American employers turned to Mexican immigrant labor. And the increase in legal immigration spawned the "wetback invasion" of the 1920s.[29]

"Nowhere else on earth," remarked Vernon Briggs, "does a political border separate two nations with a greater economic disparity."[30] Until 1924, that border was open. Then the Border Patrol was established for control. Yet, the 1924 Immigration and Nationality Act, despite its national origins quotas, exempted all the Western Hemisphere countries from immigrant quotas. Arthur Corwin pointed out that American immigration policy toward Mexico has been "a story of ad hoc exemptions."[31] The growers lobbied successfully to keep Mexicans exempt from the quota restrictions.

Often recruited by the growers, Mexicans then arrived in great numbers until the Great Depression. This constituted an "informal" *bracero* program, as Ray and Gladys Gilmore called it, long before the formal program of the post–World War II period.[32]

Bonifacio Ortega, a young man from Jalisco, summed up his experience well: "We have never had any trouble here in this country. At least I don't have anything of which to complain. But as one might suppose I love my country more and more each day and I hope to go back to it; but I want to go back with some little money so as to start up in business again. Life is very hard here. One has to work hard and in whatever one finds first, for whoever doesn't do that suffers a lot."[33]

The growers' influence on immigration policy can be understood only within the broader context of the development of agriculture into an industry. Carey McWilliams traced the growth of California agriculture into agribusiness through the growers' monopolization of land and the use of successive waves of immigrants to tend the fields. By the end of the decade of the twenties, California agriculture had become an industry that yielded "factories in the field." As McWilliams said, "California agriculture is monopolistic in character; it is highly organized; it utilizes familiar price-fixing schemes; it is corporately owned; management and ownership are sharply differentiated; it is enormously profitable to the large growers."[34]

Starting around 1870, California agriculture underwent a great change: wheat production ended, and fruit and sugar beets became its mainstay. Intensive farming required a large supply of cheap, mobile, and temporary labor. Successive waves of immigrants provided the solution to recruiting and maintaining this labor. The Chinese were first. The Chinese Exclusion Act and the anti-Chinese riots during the depression of the 1890s drove them from the fields, so from 1900 to 1913 the Japanese filled the void.[35] The first two decades of the twentieth century saw what Linda Majka identified as the first two periods of farm labor unionism in California.[36] In the first, from 1900 to 1913, farm labor organized as ethnic associations. Japanese "clubs" supplied the labor for harvesting. The Japanese associations sought control over hiring and greater land ownership. When the Japanese sought to become landowners, anti-Japanese feeling mounted, culminating in the Alien Land Acts of 1913 and 1919 to prevent aliens from land ownership as well as the 1924 immigration restriction on further Japanese immigration.

In Majka's analysis, the efforts of the Industrial Workers of the World defined the second period of farm labor unionism, roughly from 1913 to 1920. The Wobblies were migratory workers themselves. As such, McWilliams pointed out, they naturally "moved with the workers and organized them, so to speak, in transit."[37] For many, McWilliams observed, the Wheatland Riot of 1913 and later actions brought a realization of the dismal conditions under which California farm workers lived and worked. But the arrival of World War I destroyed that recognition.[38] With the war came a demand for agricultural production and a labor shortage. The great flow of Mexican labor began. For a time, Hindus also worked the fields. But the national origins quotas turned the large growers to unorganized Filipino and Mexican labor.[39] When the Filipinos became organized in the Filipino Labor Union and struck for higher wages, they also ceased to be desirable.[40]

Throughout the 1920s, growers recruited and imported Mexicans. As McWilliams stated it, during this decade the farm industrialists were "enchanted" with the Mexicans. Despite the closed door on immigration, they fought to keep Mexican immigrants from being placed under a quota restriction. To this end, growers used the argument that the Mexican would not become a public charge because, like a homing pigeon, "he goes back to roost."[41] From 1914 to 1930, Mexicans became the main source of agricultural field labor. Table 4 shows that from 1921 to 1930, approximately 459,278 Mexicans immigrated legally.

The Depression: Repatriation

During the Depression the number of Mexican immigrants plummeted to only 22,319 for the whole decade of the 1930s. This sharp drop can best be seen in Figure 2. The decline, however, was due to more than the economy. Massive deportations took place. While Mexican immigrants usually took jobs that others refused, during the Depression even these jobs were wanted by native workers. Then the current allegation that they take jobs from American workers rang true. Corwin and Cardoso reminded us that "native workers eagerly grabbed for jobs previously held only by Mexicans."[42] Whites from the Dust Bowl areas of Oklahoma and Texas provided a new source of cheap labor for agriculture in California.[43]

Unlike the homing pigeon, after the harvest Mexicans had often remained in cities and towns on relief. In addition, in the late 1920s Mexicans became organized in Mexican labor unions. In the early thirties, even in the midst of those very hard times, Mexicans repeatedly struck in the fields.[44] In Majka's analysis, the Depression issued the third period of farm labor unionism. Central to the strikes of Mexicans, observed Majka, was the fight against the labor contractor.[45] But the collective bargaining efforts of farm workers foun-

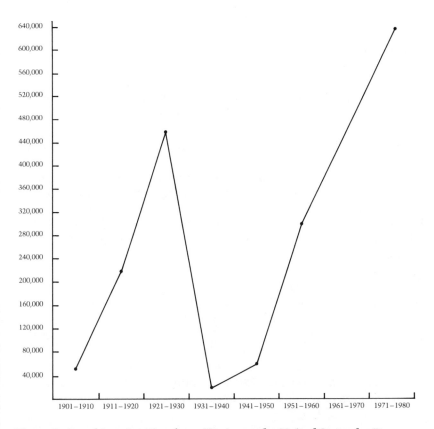

Figure 2. *Legal Immigration from Mexico to the United States by Decades, 1901–1980*

dered on the shoals of the Depression. Both the increasing organization of Mexican farm workers and the economic ruin caused by the Depression resulted in massive deportations. Abraham Hoffman's figures, based on the consulate general's reports of Mexicans returning at the time, show that from 1931 to 1935 over 288,000 Mexicans were repatriated.[46]

In the ten years from 1921 to 1930, legal Mexican immigration reached close to half a million; from 1931 to 1941, it fell to just over 22,000. The first major wave of Mexican immigration had ended. McWilliams stressed that the transformation of the Southwest, its economic development in the first forty years of this century, was largely due to the use of Mexican labor, unorganized and inexhaustible.[47]

World War II: The Bracero Program

Another war began the second massive wave. World War II made the Mexican immigrant workers again welcome. The manufacturing and military needs of the nation again led to a labor shortage in agriculture. Despite the bitterness Mexicans still felt over the re-patriation drives of the 1930s and their awareness of the discrimi-nation that they would encounter in the Southwest, a second exo-dus began, still lured by the magnet of higher wages.[48] But this time both the American and Mexican governments directed and regu-lated the migration through their joint *bracero* program. The name comes from the Spanish word for arms, *brazos*, for planting and picking. The conditions under which *braceros* worked were clearly below American standards. But the difference between American and Mexican wages for the same work was still large and inviting.

Despite Mexico's vast agrarian reform programs, Corwin and Car-doso observed, the aridity of the soil and lack of irrigation remained as obstacles to real changes in the lives of many peasants. In addi-tion, as elsewhere in the less developed world, the introduction of public health measures triggered a population explosion, many times larger than the one at the turn of the century. In the twenty years from 1940 to 1960, Mexico more than doubled its population: from 17 to 35 million. As the "push" factors intensified, the *bra-cero* program that recruited Mexican immigrants as temporary guest workers provided a new "pull."[49] Merchants of labor, Ernesto Galarza called them.

Initiated in 1942 by the joint agreement of the U.S. and Mexican governments, in 1951 Public Law 78 formalized the *bracero* pro-gram. Amended at various times, the Mexican farm labor agree-ment lasted until December 1964.[50] As Julian Samora pointed out, "it was a labor program that was planned, inexpensive, efficient, administered to benefit the employer, and mostly subsidized by the United States government."[51]

The emergence of the *bracero* program changed the character of Mexican immigration. As Ernesto Galarza expressed it, the migra-tion "by drift" of 1900 to 1940 turned into the "administered mi-gration" that began in 1942.[52] In the first phase, the migration was "pushed" by the vicissitudes of life in Mexico, both the uncer-tainty of economic opportunities and the dislocation occasioned by the revolution. In the second phase, with the emergence and con-solidation of the *bracero* program, the migration was also "pulled" by the collaboration of the U.S. and Mexican governments, which jointly institutionalized it.

Galarza detailed the rise and consolidation of the *bracero* program and its history in the state of California, the leading agricultural state and chief utilizer of the *braceros*.[53] Prior to the birth of this administered migration, employers had long relied on seasonal labor pools that farm labor associations recruited, distributed, and maintained. But the labor crisis that World War II generated spurred the institutionalization of the administered migration. As Galarza noted, "agriculture was being continuously drained of manual labor by manufacturing, transportation and the service trades. These offered opportunities for better jobs which alert farm workers bid for. Industry and the service trades were expanding, their draft on the farm labor bank threatening to keep pace with accelerating war demands."[54]

According to Galarza, fear of loss—loss of crops and loss of status—overcame the risks growers perceived in institutionalizing the *bracero* program. In addition, its advantages outweighed the risks. The risks involved allowing government interference as well as setting minimum standards for agricultural work. The advantages entailed orderly recruitment, a guaranteed supply of workers, unorganized workers, government subsidies to carry the financial burden, and workers who returned home at the end of the season.[55] Initiated in 1942, the *bracero* program was initially thought of as a war emergency measure. It lasted twenty-two years.

In the main, the agreement between the U.S. and Mexican governments provided that Mexican workers were not to be used to displace domestic workers, but only to fill shortages; that their transportation would be paid for; that a written contract between the worker and the employer would regulate the hiring; that workers could only work in agriculture; that work was guaranteed for three-quarters of the duration of the contract; and that wages were to be equal to those prevailing in the area of employment.[56] In 1942 within the United States responsibility for the program was placed under the Farm Security Administration. A year later, it passed to the War Manpower Commission. From 1948 to the end, it rested with the Department of Labor and its Bureau of Employment Security. The bureau, in turn, utilized the services of the Farm Placement Service in the various states.[57] In California alone, the Farm Placement Service spread over forty-five counties in over ninety permanent field offices. Its original aim was to assist workers by directing them to employment opportunities, eliminating farm labor contractors, stabilizing employment opportunities, and reducing unnecessary travel in seeking jobs. But, as Galarza pointed out, ultimately its aim became to guarantee the labor supply for growers. Its chief function became need determination. In determining the supply of *braceros* that growers needed, the agency set about making available large labor pools.[58] As Table 4 shows, in the decade of the 1940s close to half a million *braceros* were contracted. The program was not only renewed; it was expanded. It attained its massive proportions in the 1950s when, from 1955 on, close to half a million *braceros* were contracted a year. That decade brought approximately 3.5 million new recruits. With the official termination of the program in 1964, the *braceros* declined to less than a million in the 1960s. Altogether, under the *bracero* program, more than 4.8 million temporary workers were admitted to the United States. Most worked in agriculture, where their *brazos* (arms) were needed most. For the growers, as Briggs said, the *bracero* program proved to be a "bonanza."[59]

Twice, therefore, growers wielded enormous influence on immigration policy: the Western Hemisphere exemption in the twenties, and the *bracero* program in the forties. Both of these shaped the flows of Mexican immigration to the United States.[60] The state ignored Mexicans, and did not promote their structural assimilation because it favored the interests of their employers.

Like all guest worker programs, the *bracero* program was intended to import a temporary worker. Instead, it brought a human being. Many *braceros* acquired immigrant visas and became permanent workers. As they sent for their relatives and friends, both legal and illegal immigration from Mexico rose. As Table 4 shows, throughout the 1940s, legal immigration from Mexico remained low, under 9,000 persons a year, totalling only 60,589 for the decade. Yet in the 1950s it surpassed a quarter of a million, and in the 1960s Mexican immigration attained the same height as in the 1920s: nearly half a million. This sharp increase can be seen in Figure 2. "Thus," Corwin and Cardoso concluded, "the bracero program helped prime a new current of legal immigration." Furthermore, it had "an even more significant impact on the emergence of wetbackism."[61] During the twenty-two years when 4.8 million *braceros* were contracted, over 5 million wetbacks were apprehended.[62] No doubt many of the apprehended were relatives and friends, but many were also former *braceros*. Sometimes employers encouraged them to return illegally; other times, they did so voluntarily, having learned the ropes. Thus, as Briggs observed, there is some truth to the allegation that the United States created the illegal alien problem.[63]

Illegal aliens are not only a problem, however. Like many other researchers, Samora contended that the presence of illegal aliens in the United States is directly related to the interests of employers in securing an ample supply of cheap labor. As Samora explained, "Wetback labor is even cheaper—no need for contracts, minimum wage, health benefits, housing, transportation, etc. Since the workers are illegal aliens, they have few rights before the law and can be dismissed at a moment's notice."[64]

Galarza also argued that to protect themselves from the drawbacks of the *bracero* program—the risk of U.S. government interference, the demands of the Mexican government for protection of workers, the contracting fees, and the transportation expenses—growers continued to rely on wetback labor.[65] Joan Moore pointed out that "'Braceros' and 'wetbacks' often worked on the same crews. Administrative processes reached the ultimate in absurdity: illegals could be transported back across the border and then readmitted as 'legally contracted' workers. It was a process aptly called 'drying out' the wetbacks."[66]

This reliance on the wetback led to Operation Wetback. At its peak, in 1954, the deportations reached over one million wetbacks. Thereafter they declined to fewer than 250,000 in 1955 and 72,442 in 1956, declining further until in 1960 there were fewer than 30,000.[67] The success of Operation Wetback, said Galarza, was partly due to the indignation that wetback strikes had caused, but especially to the change in attitude of farm employers, "hundreds of whom had come to accept the legal *braceros* as a practical and safe alternative and had joined associations to procure them."[68] Galarza argued that, in effect, the massive deportations marked the difficult transition from illegal to legal labor, at the lower wage rates made possible by the prevalent use of illegal labor.

The *bracero* program held consequences not only for the legal and illegal currents of Mexican immigration but also for American workers. Initially conceived as a response to the labor crises generated by World War II, the agreement of the U.S. and Mexican governments insisted that *braceros* were not to be used to displace domestic workers. But the progressive displacement of native workers ensued. Essentially, one kind of migrant seasonal labor force substituted another. Mexican workers came to dominate the production of many crops. Using California as an example, Galarza pointed out that in 1951 Mexicans picked only 25 percent of the tomato crop; in 1956, domestic workers constituted less than 5 percent of the pickers. In the sixteen counties where *bracero* employment was analyzed, domination ranged between 55 and 95 percent. For example, *braceros* represented 94.5 percent of the seasonal labor force harvesting lettuce; 97.6 percent of the labor force in tomatoes; and 81.1 percent in strawberries.[69] From being a supplementary labor force, the *braceros* became *the* labor force. Despite the costs of recruiting and transporting Mexicans, costs that the growers incessantly alluded to, the *braceros* made possible a decline in wages and savings in workers' benefits. In addition, *braceros* provided a reliable and dependable labor force, as gladly intermittent as the crops. Agribusiness benefited.

The initial agreement between the U.S. and Mexican governments sought to prevent such harm to domestic workers by insisting that *braceros* be paid the prevailing wages in the area of employment. But in practice, the employers—organized within farm employer associations to recruit, distribute, and supervise workers—set the prevailing wages. Farm work lay outside the boundary of the minimum wage laws and the right to collective bargaining. Hence, as Galarza pointed out, the wages prevailed only in that they were "set by the associations and accepted by employers."[70] The government supported these employer associations as the administrators of the administered migration. In so doing, Galarza stressed, their attitude of neutrality gave way to one of "deferment and deference,"[71] augmenting the power and influence of those who already had much. Despite the intention of the initial provisions to uphold the employment of American workers, domestic farm workers lost most—the higher wages of the past and their jobs in the fields. As Galarza expressed it, the *bracero* influx "was a massive current of alien manpower that cut squarely across the domestic seasonal market, which gave way at every point."[72]

Domination of crops by Mexican workers depressed wages; American workers disappeared from the fields as the yardstick for job offers and wages became the *bracero*, not the American worker. Had the American worker been the standard, that would have protected both domestic and foreign workers. When employers wanted to break strikes and used *braceros*, always isolated and under the threat of deportation, thousands of domestic workers roundly lost.[73]

The use of *braceros* to break strikes inaugurated another period of farm labor unionism. From 1947 to 1960, the National Agricultural Workers Union sought to find domestic farm labor a place in the American labor movement.[74] It aimed to achieve the markings of trade unionism—representation, negotiation, collective bargaining, a minimum-wage scale, and protective legislation. While not successful, the National Agricultural Workers Union documented and publicized the ill effects of the *bracero* program for both American and Mexican workers. With its efforts, it served to bring the program to a close.

The *bracero* program had to end before farm labor unionization became possible. Its termination, said Majka, was "the single most important factor leading to the creation of the United Farm Workers Union."[75] In their analysis of farm worker movements, Craig Jenkins and Charles Perrow attributed the success of the United Farm Workers from 1965 to 1972 not only to the termination of the *bracero* program, which indeed changed the social composition of the farm labor force, but especially to the changed societal response to the challenges.[76]

The protest of mobilized farm workers, ably led by the exemplary actions of César Chávez, became a political symbol that dramatized the cause. The success of the farm workers' protest, in their nonviolent struggle, also depended upon the cooperation of the liberal community—students, churches, labor unions, elected officials—which served to reinforce the national boycotts. As Chávez explained,

A lot has to do with respecting other groups. The best thing we have going for us is having all kinds of people help us in a variety of ways.

For example, we tell people, "If you don't eat lettuce today, you are really helping us." This is the key to successful organizing: letting people who want to help know what they can do.[77]

The political environment also changed because, with the *bracero* program ended, the federal government adopted a more neutral role toward farm workers, ceasing to support agribusiness at their expense. That neutrality, Jenkins and Perrow stressed, also depended on the support expressed by the broad coalition of liberal and labor organizations. Ultimately, the United Farm Workers succeeded in attaining union contracts, raising wages, changing the conditions of hiring and working, and providing an enduring form of organization.

Throughout the twenty-two years of its existence, as both Galarza and Craig showed, the *bracero* program was embroiled in conflict and controversy. The end of the *bracero* program arrived because, in Craig's analysis, the constellation of interest groups that supported it, domestically and internationally, changed.[78] The decline in the agricultural sector in the economy, at the same time that agriculture became increasingly mechanized, also rendered the need for such large labor pools of stoop field labor obsolete.

In the middle of the twentieth century, Craig showed, the machine "all but replaced the man" on the American farm. From 1949 to 1965, while the total U.S. population grew by 45 million, the farm population declined from 16.3 to 6.4 percent of the total population. During the decade of the 1950s, the total number of farm workers declined by the largest percentage in any decade, 41 percent.[79] At the same time, mechanization accelerated. Machines that dug, lifted, sorted, picked, delivered, and packed replaced human hands in harvesting potatoes, onions, corn, lettuce, lemons, and beets. "A 'hoe with a brain,'" explained Galarza, "could weed a beet field faster than twenty men, using an electronic eye to distinguish between wild grass and beet leaves." Machines could handle even very delicate fruits, such as peaches, pears, and plums, which were "poured gently" into bins, "cradled" onto trucks, and "wafted" into boxes.[80] Cotton was a leading crop that employed the majority of *braceros*. In 1950, only 8 percent of the cotton crop was machine-harvested. By 1964, the last year of *bracero* recruitment, machines harvested between 78 and 97 percent of the cotton crop, depending on the state.[81] Mechanization dealt a large blow to the *bracero* program. Supporters of the program lost one of their principal arguments.[82]

Despite the two extensions of the *bracero* program thereafter, already in 1960 it was apparent that the program was in peril. The root cause, judged Craig, lay in the U.S. Department of Labor's change in policy. From 1956 on, the Department of Labor increasingly regulated *bracero* housing, wages, and transportation with the goal of improving the lot of *braceros* as well as lessening the adverse effects of the program on American farm workers. Much to the dismay of agribusiness, James Mitchell, the Secretary of Labor, while not entirely anti-*bracero*, came to be regarded as "a friend of native farmworkers."[83] According to Craig, the critical turning point came when farm employers and their congressional spokesmen overextended themselves by proposing to curtail Mitchell's authority. As a result, anti-*bracero* groups augmented their ranks, both among national interest groups and in Congress. For the first time, supporters of *bracero* labor went on the defensive.[84]

Yet the program underwent two more extensions before its death. For it depended, Craig repeatedly pointed out, not only on domestic interests but also on international interests. President Kennedy was opposed to the *bracero* program due to the harm it demonstrably brought to domestic farm workers. Yet in 1961 he extended it again because Mexico opposed its sudden termination.[85] The *bracero* program provided Mexico both with foreign exchange and with a "safety valve" for the discontent of many.[86] But in 1962 when Secretary of Labor Arthur Goldberg sought to protect domestic farm workers by instituting statewide adverse-effect wage rates for the twenty-four states using *braceros*, the *bracero* program lost its allure. As Craig showed, both the accelerating mechanization and the adverse-effects policy impacted on *bracero* recruitment. In 1959, 437,543 *braceros* were imported. Two years later, in 1961, *braceros* declined to 67 percent of that number. Only a year later, in 1962, the first year of the new adverse-effect wage rates, the *braceros* declined another 67 percent, to 194,978.[87]

Mexico's continued opposition to the sudden termination of the program achieved a one-year extension, until the United States unilaterally terminated the program in December 1964.[88] Craig underscored that when domestic forces are balanced, or have reached a stalemate, "pressure from the international environment may prove decisive."[89] But the *bracero* program had lost its stake. For all the acknowledged harm the *bracero* program brought to American farm workers, it lasted twenty-two years. The reason, Craig uncovered, was that it rested on the "congruence" of domestic and foreign interests.[90] That congruence had finally come to an end.

A Delimited Flow

After the *bracero* program ended, the current period began. For the first time in a very long history, the U.S. government trimmed legal Mexican immigration. The McCarran-Walter Act of 1952 had established the principles that still guide immigration policy today: the reunification of families, the protection of domestic labor, and the immigration of persons with needed skills. But the national origins quotas remained intact, and immigration from the Western Hemisphere countries remained largely unrestricted. The 1965 amendments to the Immigration and Nationality Act, which went into effect in 1968, overturned the national origins quotas for the first time, imposing a Western Hemisphere quota of 120,000 immigrants a year. The law also developed a new system of seven preference categories based on the conditions of job certification or family reunification for legal entry, and exempted close relatives of U.S. citizens from the quota.[91] As Charles Keely explained, these preference categories reflected a compromise between the two competing philosophies of immigration that underlay congressional hearings and debates. One emphasized humanitarian values; it achieved the termination of the national origins quota system and the emphasis on family reunification. The other emphasized the maintenance of American society; it achieved the protection inherent in labor certification.[92]

As a result of these changes, the volume of legal immigration to the United States increased substantially, and the geographic origins of the newcomers changed. From 1960 to 1965, 75 percent of all immigrants to the United States came from Europe; after 1968, 62 percent came from Asia and Latin America.[93] In 1976, due to concern over the swelling tide of Mexican immigration, the Immigration and Nationality Act was amended to include a quota of 20,000 immigrants per country in the Western Hemisphere, close relatives still exempted.

Illegality also increased. The per-country limits had an effect. The legal migration flow created by the historical link between U.S. and Mexican migration stood at around 40,000 persons a year, their relatives exempted. The country limit of 20,000 cut Mexican immigration in half.[94] This created a potential for 20,000 illegal aliens plus their relatives, over and beyond those who already lived outside the pale of the law.

In addition, during the *bracero* era, as Corwin and Cardoso pointed out, "perhaps 2 million Mexican nationals, besides legal braceros, had acquired a taste for higher wages and adventure on the American side and had learned the tricks of getting around."[95] As we saw, alongside the *braceros* wetbacks asserted themselves. Both still inspire today's wetback. For example, in 1982 a young Mexican woman who had just crossed the Rio Grande to the United States told me her story. She needed to come and work, she said, because her husband had left her, and her child was quite ill. Her two older brothers had once come to the United States to work as *braceros*. When her child grew sick, they told her, "Now the time has come for you to make the trip."

The New Silent Invasion

In this new period, the apprehensions of illegals soared. In 1965, there were 48,948 apprehensions; in 1973, half a million, or 576,823; in 1979, apprehensions climbed to nearly a million, 998,830. Table 4, based on apprehensions, shows the increasing magnitude of illegality. From 1961 to 1970, apprehensions of illegals surpassed 1 million; from 1971 to 1980, over 7.4 million.[96] With the recession of the mid-seventies, recurrent alarms over the "silent invasion" of pernicious illegal aliens sounded.[97]

Since the mid-1960s, Corwin and McCain argued, a number of factors prevented the Immigration and Naturalization Service from effectively controlling the alien flow.[98] It is worth reviewing the most salient. First, the termination of the *bracero* program meant

**Table 4. *Immigration from Mexico to the United States,*
1820–1980: Legal Immigration, Braceros *Contracted, and*
*Illegal Aliens***

Period	Legal Immigration[a]	Braceros Contracted[b]	Illegal Aliens[c]
1820–1840	11,416		
1841–1860	6,349		
1861–1880	7,353		
1881–1900	2,884		
1901–1910	49,642		
1911–1920	219,004		
1921–1930	459,287		48,503
1931–1940	22,319		94,629
1941–1950	60,589	430,485	1,436,744
1951–1960	299,811	3,485,786	3,313,769
1961–1970	453,937	887,635	1,017,719
1971–1980	640,294		7,473,248
Total	2,232,885	4,803,906	13,384,612

[a]U.S. Department of Justice, Immigration and Naturalization Service, *1980 Statistical Yearbook of the Immigration and Naturalization Service,* Table 2. Since prior to 1900 immigration statistics are not accurate, they are reported in twenty-year periods. There is no record of immigration for the period 1886–1893.

[b]Data for 1942–1960 in Galarza, *Merchants of Labor,* pp. 53, 79; data for 1961–1967 in Portes, "Structural Causes of Illegal Immigration," Table 2.

[c]Data for 1924–1970 in Briggs, *Mexican Migration and the U.S. Labor Market,* Table 2. Since official definitions of illegal aliens have changed over time, the figures include illegal Mexican aliens apprehended and/or deported. As Briggs noted, however, they correctly reflect the order of magnitude. Data for 1971–1980 are for apprehensions; provided by the U.S. Immigration and Naturalization Service, Washington, D.C.

that former *braceros* and wetbacks resorted to illegal entry to regain the chance to work in the United States and also that Mexico halted its efforts to protect contract workers from illegals. Second, Mexico's border program created new industries and new jobs, but also generated a massing of jobless and subemployed millions at the border, craving the opportunity to become border commuters.[99] Third, while the Immigration and Naturalization Service suffers from insufficient staff and funds, Corwin and McCain rightly stressed that "the new wetback is not so wet."[100] For around the illegal traffic developed a sophisticated technology of smuggling in which the illegal invested for transportation, identification papers, false documents, and housing. Fourth, since the mid-sixties the costs of American labor also rose, due to the coupling of union wage demands and inflation with the floor on wages established by government welfare programs. Poverty programs, argued Corwin and McCain, created a "labor vacuum"; illegals filled the menial jobs of industry and service.[101] Fifth, the rise of ethnic protest, organization, and demands in the sixties made immigration an ethnic issue. In the forties and fifties, Corwin and McCain pointed out, Mexican-American organizations often demanded wetback control whereas more recently they embraced what they considered to be other members of *la raza*.[102] Sixth, initial trips as illegals provide Mexicans with the conditions for becoming legal, a process of "building up equity."[103] Building family ties allows future legal entry as an immediate relative; attaining the promise of a job from an employer confers future job certification.[104] Last, the Texas Proviso protects employers of illegals. While it is illegal to be an illegal alien as well as to import or harbor illegals, to date it has never been illegal to hire them. An alien who is caught is simply returned over the border; for the employer, there is no loss. Nor are there insurmountable penalties for being a wetback.[105] With these many "push" and "pull" factors, in addition to the ever-present lure of the rich, promised land to the north, it is scarcely surprising that since the mid-sixties the "silent invasion" of illegal aliens should have grown massive.

How many illegals are there? Their number is subject to considerable debate. Since a random sample cannot be drawn from an unknown population, all estimates derive from indirect methods.[106] In recent years, government officials clamored that 2 to 3 million illegal aliens entered the United States each year. They based their alarmist estimates on the number of apprehensions effected, together with the rule of thumb that, for every illegal caught, two to three successfully got away. As David Heer pointed out, however, these estimates failed to take into account the difference between gross and net flows of immigration.[107]

Many illegal aliens do return home. More important, the number of apprehensions cannot be used as an index of the number of illegal aliens, for repeaters, who risk little by trying again, inflate the number of apprehensions. Jorge Bustamante's participant observation study of the wetback problem led him to attempt the same trip across the river and fields. Bustamante may have been a novice wetback, hardly fit for the arduous crossing. But his agile companions were experienced repeaters.[108] In addition, because of the temporary and intermittent nature of much of the Mexican migration, legals and illegals may often be the same workers on different trips. Charles Hirschman's study of legal Mexican immigrants entering the United States in 1973 and 1974 at the border stations of Laredo and El Paso, Texas, lends this hypothesis support.[109] Nearly two-thirds of these immigrants reported previously residing in the United States often as their last permanent residence or for long stays of three or more years. This information indicates that formerly they may have been illegal aliens. And that very experience taught them the conditions for gaining legal entry: either building family ties or obtaining the promise of a job from a previous employer. As Hirschman observed, it appears that "the process of immigration is not a single step phenomenon."[110]

David Heer sought to estimate the annual net flow of undocumented Mexicans to the United States. To estimate it, he used the Current Population Survey's estimates of the Mexican-origin population in the United States in 1970 and 1975, varied the assumptions as to their undercount, and took into account two of the three components of growth—their natural increase in the absence of migration as well as the increase due to documented migration, gross and net. Thus Heer derived seven separate estimates of the third component of growth—the number of illegal immigrants entering the United States between 1970 and 1975. The resulting estimates of the annual net number of illegal aliens from Mexico ranged from 82,300 to 232,400. Even the highest of seven estimates is far below the number of apprehensions and but a fraction of the alarmist cries of millions.

While the actual magnitude of illegality may be much lower than public officials decry, the problem is still real and widespread. As Table 4 shows, in recent decades both legal and illegal immigration expanded. Illegals, indeed, are no longer found only in agriculture. Since the mid-sixties, they have gone directly to urban areas for jobs. Like legal Mexican immigrants, they are found in a wide variety of industries and occupations.[111] As agriculture became more mechanized, its labor demands declined. In addition, not only American agriculture benefited from the illegals but also industrial and service sectors lacking strong union organization. The lure of the north remained strong; its cities and industries became the new destination.

As ever, Mexico "pushed" its migrants due to wretched poverty and the population explosion. In the fifteen years from 1960 to 1975, the population of Mexico nearly doubled, to 61 million.[112] Yet for this recent period, Alejandro Portes' analysis of the causes of migration introduced an additional source. While mass poverty is real in Mexico, Portes argued, pressures for recent migration to the United States emerged not because Mexico was so underdeveloped and stagnant, but because it was undergoing a "rapid transition toward development."[113] Francisco Alba also underlined the interaction between migration and the development process.[114]

For the last three decades Mexico's gross national product grew at an annual rate of about 6 percent. Yet, at the same time, income inequality widened.[115] The development strategy pursued by the state favored the organized upper and middle classes to the detriment of the poor. In Portes' analysis, it was the combination of rapid economic development with a corporate capitalist strategy that created heavy pressures for migration, not only on the rural peasantry but also on the urban working class. Thus, Portes argued, "contrary to popular myths, if Mexico were at present at a stage of social and economic development similar to that of the less advanced countries in Latin America, wetback migration would tend to be of lower magnitude that it is now."[116]

In addition, Portes judged that the urban working classes were "most subject to the contradictions of the system": the contradictions between the spread of a consumer culture and the inability of urban workers to achieve such goods, between the growth of productivity engendered by foreign capital and the lack of growth of employment in manufacturing. Hence, illegal immigration resulted not from the failure of a development strategy but from its success.[117]

While the study of legal and illegal immigration cannot be meaningfully separated, as both Hirschman and Portes concluded, nonetheless there are consequences to the massive illegal flow. For illegal aliens themselves, the consequence lies in being wholly dependent on unscrupulous smugglers and arbitrary employers, both of whose exploitative excesses go unchecked. Illegal workers have no recourse to justice, no protection of civil rights. An unprotected life hangs by the thread of the good will of strangers and spells of luck. As Bustamante concluded from his personal experience as a wetback, the wetback role places a human being "in a position where he endangers his physical well-being, his human dignity, and even his life for a pittance."[118]

For American workers, the consequence is displacement. In their analysis of policy choices for this "intractable" issue, Sidney Weintraub and Stanley Ross underscored that "as a nation, we do not know the labor market impact, and this really is the crux of the issue." Yet they go on to add that illegal immigration "hits hardest" on the secondary labor market, on the poor people who can hardly compete or cope: "How much it is hurting them is in dispute, but that it does affect them is clear."[119] Briggs stressed, in particular, the consequences for Chicanos of a process "whereby poor Mexicans make poor Chicanos poorer."[120] Ironically, illegal Mexicans have displaced Chicanos, their *raza* kin, from agriculture. Roger Conner emphasized that those who pay the price are the black teenagers, the white laborers, and the enterprising children of maids and janitors, because for them unskilled jobs and low-skill entrepreneurial activities could represent the way out of poverty.[121] Not only do illegals give rise to job displacement, but they also serve to prevent reforms that would improve jobs for others. Jobs remain poorly paid and working conditions remain abysmal because immigrants will work at low-paid jobs under onerous conditions. If the rights to a minimum wage and to collective bargaining were extended to all sectors of the American labor force, in particular to the agricultural and service sectors, the migration of Mexicans would not give rise to job displacement and illegals would cease to hold an allure. Then the play of the marketplace would more fairly decide among contenders and excessive immigration would be checked. These rights remain to be achieved for all workers.

Looking back over the history of the Mexican immigration, we are struck by the very different processes of incorporation of Cuban political immigrants and Mexican economic immigrants. While the state facilitated and supported the structural assimilation of Cuban exiles in America, it ignored the assimilation of Mexicans. At times, the government welcomed Mexicans, and instituted programs that guaranteed their presence, but only as *brazos*. Only as a cyclical supply of cheap labor did they summon attention. "Mexicans," said Briggs, "have been welcomed as workers but not as settlers."[122]

4. The Value of Being a Cuban Political Immigrant

Methods

As we have seen in the portraits drawn, the processes by which Cuban exiles and Mexican laborers became incorporated into American society were vastly different. The overarching argument of this book is that, as political and economic immigrants, the differences in their incorporation are due in part to government policy. In instituting programs for Cuban political immigrants that facilitated their secondary structural assimilation, the state reinforced their initial advantage of social class origin, giving way to a process of cumulative advantage; the lack of policy and supportive programs for Mexican immigrants reinforced their initial disadvantage of social class origin, resulting in a process of cumulative disadvantage.

To support this argument, the data analyzed comes from the 1970 U.S. census, a unique data set in that it was the first census since the 1930 census to ask the question on year of immigration.[1] The 1980 census would provide us with more recent data on the labor force outcomes, in earnings and occupational attainment, of Cuban and Mexican immigrants. But the research design requires the use of the 1970 census. To provide evidence for the impact of government policy in facilitating the secondary structural assimilation of Cuban refugees, I will compare Cubans and Mexicans who came to the United States during the period of political immigration with those who immigrated prior to that period. That is, I will compare Cubans and Mexicans who immigrated as adults (at least 25 years of age) from 1960 to 1970, when Cubans were political immigrants, and those who immigrated from 1945 to 1959, when Cubans were economic immigrants. A person 36 years of age in 1950 would in 1970 be 56 years old—still in the labor force, with an occupation and earnings. But a person 36 years of age in 1950 would in 1980 be 66 years old—out of the labor force. Hence, the research design that seeks to buttress my argument requires that we utilize the data of the 1970 census.

Working with aggregate data sets has limits. The effect of govern-ment policy programs extended to Cuban political immigrants and not extended to Mexican economic immigrants cannot be tested directly. But sociologists have long used comparative statistics to infer the unequal social processes operating for social groups. For example, the classic studies of Otis Dudley Duncan, "Inheritance of Poverty or Inheritance of Race?,"[2] and Paul Siegel, "On the Cost of Being a Negro,"[3] argued that blacks suffered undue discrimina-tion on the basis of the residual difference between the outcomes of blacks and whites when controlling for all their differences in age, education, occupation, and the like, which could lead to unequal incomes. In essence, I will use the same comparative statistical method, arguing that the residual difference between the outcomes of Cubans and Mexicans is due to their differential incorporation in America as political and economic immigrants.[4] Ultimately the in-terpretation relies on the analytic social histories presented in the previous chapters, the mechanisms of incorporation that led me to say that the state lent Cubans a firm hand but ignored Mexicans. Not only is there historical support for my interpretation, but also the research design specifically seeks to buttress the overarching argument.

To translate the larger argument of this research into a question amenable to statistical indicators, I will seek a precise answer to this question: *Are Cubans still more successful than Mexicans when the differences in their individual characteristics are taken into account?* That is, if we control for the differences between Cubans and Mexicans in their social characteristics, such as social class origin and length of experience in the United States, do Cuban political immigrants fare better than Mexicans?

If so, we can argue the positive impact of the Cuban Refugee Pro-gram. But first the research design needs to provide an additional brace. For if, after controlling for all the unequal social characteris-tics, Cubans should always fare better than Mexicans, one could argue a cultural difference. And our argument is that there is some-thing distinct about being a political immigrant beyond the initial social class advantage: the government policy of extensive social support that enabled Cubans to make their Cuban credentials valu-able in America.

To demonstrate this, the analysis will be extended beyond the period of political immigration. Cubans who immigrated prior to the revolution were not political immigrants, but neither did they ever constitute a controlled and restricted migrant labor pool, such as the *bracero* program. That part of the Mexican immigration that entered the United States and worked under the restrictions and impositions of the *bracero* program and that suffered the deportations of Operation Wetback has no counterpart in the Cuban migration. Why Cubans, even as economic immigrants, never constituted an agricultural migrant labor work force in America, as Mexicans consistently did, is a larger question than can be addressed here. But I would like to suggest that an explanation that simply stresses that bordering countries share a frontier is insufficient. Attention ought to be paid to the different manner in which agriculture was organized in Cuba and Mexico: even prior to the revolution Cubans never formed part of a seasonal and intermittent agricultural labor force, as economic immigrants Cubans were also more educated and of a higher social class than Mexicans. This point will be useful for the research design carried out here.

To brace the argument that, beyond the different individual characteristics of Cubans and Mexicans, there is something distinctive about their being political and economic immigrants—the role of government policy—I will ask another question: *Is the advantage of Cubans over Mexicans greater in the political migration period than in the economic migration period?*

To answer this second question, we need to consider two periods of migration: that from 1960 to 1970, when Cubans were political immigrants, and that prior to 1960, when Cubans were economic immigrants. To compare their labor force outcomes we will use two indexes of secondary structural assimilation: occupational prestige and annual earnings. If the difference in the outcomes of Cubans and Mexicans were significant and consistent—if both as economic and political immigrants Cubans fared significantly better in prestige and earnings than Mexicans—one would have to argue that a cultural difference existed, and our larger argument would remain undemonstrated. But if we compare Cubans and Mexicans who immigrated in the period of economic immigration (prior to 1960) and find no significant difference in their outcomes, whereas their outcomes are significantly different in the period of Cuban political immigration (1960 to 1970), with Cubans faring better, then we can say that being a political immigrant is distinctly different. On the basis of the analytic histories I argue that the difference lies in the government's supportive role in facilitating the secondary structural assimilation of Cuban refugees.

To answer the two questions I will carry out a regression analysis on the two indexes of structural assimilation, prestige and earnings. Having Cuban and Mexican immigrants together in the same equation allows us to control for the differences in their individual characteristics, as independent variables determinant of the attainment of desirable occupations and earnings. An additional independent variable, *nationality*, allows us to answer the first question by telling us what the value is of being a Cuban (as opposed to being a Mexican) when all differences in their social characteristics (social class origin, length of U.S. experience, agricultural employment, and the like) are taken into account.

Running separate equations for the time of immigration, prior to 1960 and after 1960, allows us to answer the second question. Approximately 80 percent of the Cuban immigrants in the United States came after the revolution, while about 25 percent of the Mexican immigrants in the United States arrived before 1945.[5] To compare Cubans and Mexicans as economic immigrants, I chose only those who immigrated from 1945 to 1959, since the time of insertion into the American economy (during the Depression or World War II) would affect current outcomes.[6] Furthermore, the end of World War II corresponds to the inception of the *bracero* program, which lasted until 1964.

Moreover, we know that women's experiences in the labor force (occupational segregation, occupational sex typing, part-time work, intermittency, and discrimination) are very different from men's. Hence, I analyze men and women separately. Cuban men are compared to Mexican men, Cuban women to Mexican women.

The Immigrants' Backgrounds

Since overall the social class origin of the Cubans is higher than that of the Mexicans, it was necessary to control for this difference in the analyses. An index was needed that would grossly differentiate the social class composition of Cubans and Mexicans. But neither of the sample questionnaires of the 1970 census collected any information on father's occupation or education, classic indexes of family background,[7] or on the occupation or education of the immigrants in their country of origin. Nor could we use Erik Olin Wright and Luca Perrone's quantification of the concept of social class, since the census contains no information on employing or supervising others, which their definition incorporates.[8] Instead, I used the educational attainment of adult immigrants as an index for their social class origin.[9]

Sociologists often use educational attainment as a dependent variable, one of the outcomes that in America they want to explain. But I chose adult immigrants whose basic education took place in their native country, so that their education was *prior* to everything that ever happened to them in America. In this way, it takes on the qualities of an independent variable, serving as an index for their social class origin.

In fact, the educational attainment of adult immigrants is better than an index for social class. The meaning of educational systems differs across societies. In societies in which the general level of education of the population is high, as in the United States and other developed countries where educational institutions are available to all and compulsory education to a certain age insures access, the educational system links to social classes via the *quality* of schooling. Then several educational systems operate simultaneously (e.g., Ivy League colleges vs. community colleges), both in selection and recruitment as well as in differential outcomes.[10] In this case, the distribution of educational attainment is not an index for social class, since it measures quantity and not quality of schooling.

But in societies in which compulsory education is effectively absent and educational facilities are not accessible to all (as was the case in Cuba in 1960 and is still effectively so in Mexico), the educational system links to social classes via *access* to schooling. Hence the distribution of educational attainment is an index for social class origin. Table 5 shows the distribution of educational attainment in Cuba (1953) and Mexico (1960) in comparison to that in the United States (1959). When 24 to 40 percent of the population had no formal education and slightly more than 1 percent attended college, educational attainment is a good indicator of social class.

Table 6 shows the educational attainment of immigrants who were 25 years of age or older at the time of immigration, according to their period of immigration (1945–1959 or 1960–1970) and by sex. We can see that the overall educational attainment of adult immigrants is higher for Cubans who immigrated after 1960, as political immigrants (when 25.3 percent of the men had attended college), than for those who immigrated prior to 1960, as economic immigrants (when only 14.0 percent of the men had attended college). For Mexicans, the time of immigration does not greatly alter their educational attainment, since at all times they constitute an economic migration—both migrant labor and brain drain.

As Table 7 shows, the educational attainment of Cubans who immigrated during the decade of the 1960s dropped over time.

Table 5. *Comparative Educational Attainment of the Population in the United States, 1959; Mexico, 1960; and Cuba, 1953 (in Percentages)*

Years of School Completed	U.S. 1959[a]	Mexico 1960[b]	Cuba 1953[c]
None	1.9	40.0	24.0
Elementary school			
1–4 years	5.0	36.7	41.2
5–7 years	12.0	16.4	22.9
8 years	16.6	1.5	5.9
High school			
1–3 years	22.4	3.3	2.4
4 years[d]	26.8	0.9	2.2
College			
1–4 years	12.9	0.9	0.9
5 years or more	2.4	0.2	0.6
Total percentage	100.0	99.9	100.1
N	120,834,000	38,714,922	3,690,333

Note: Data are for population 14–15 years of age or older.

[a] U.S. Bureau of the Census, *Current Population Reports*, Series P-20, No. 99, "Literacy and Educational Attainment: March 1959," Table 1.

[b] México, *VIII Censo General de Población, 1960*, Table 20.

[c] Cuba, *Censos de Población, Viviendas y Electoral, 1953*, Tables 36 and 37.

[d] The equivalent of high school in Latin America is *bachillerato*, which takes five years to complete. Those who completed *bachillerato* are included here with those completing four years of high school in the United States.

Among adults, 36.4 percent of Cuban men who immigrated during 1960–1964 had attended college, while among those who immigrated during 1965–1970 only half that many (17.5 percent) were college-educated. Cuban men who either had no schooling or only an elementary education constituted only a third of the 1960–1964 immigrants, but more than half the 1965–1970 immigrants.

For Mexican immigrants, on the other hand, the proportion of immigrants who had attended college tripled—2.2 percent of the men who immigrated during 1960–1964, compared to 7.4 percent of the men who immigrated during 1965–1970. This is probably the result of the 1965 amendment to the Immigration and Nationality Act, which encouraged the immigration of professional workers in fields where there was a domestic shortage. But the vast

Table 6. Educational Attainment of Cuban and Mexican Immigrants, by Period of Immigration (1945–1959, 1960–1970) and by Sex (in Percentages)

Years of school Completed	Immigrated 1960–1970				Immigrated 1945–1959			
	Cubans		Mexicans		Cubans		Mexicans	
	Males	Females	Males	Females	Males	Females	Males	Females
None	2.0	2.6	16.6	14.6	2.6	4.1	18.8	27.6
Elementary school	45.4	51.2	64.2	67.1	42.6	49.3	63.8	56.1
1–4 years	6.2	6.2	27.6	28.6	0.9	10.8	28.8	25.7
5–7 years	23.7	26.7	28.9	30.8	21.7	23.6	28.2	23.2
8 years	15.5	18.3	7.7	7.7	20.0	14.9	6.8	7.2
High school	78.3	30.0	13.8	13.3	40.9	36.5	12.1	13.4
1–3 years	8.9	7.8	5.9	5.9	11.3	8.1	5.9	5.6
4 years	18.4	22.2	7.9	7.4	29.6	28.4	6.2	7.8
College	25.3	16.1	5.4	5.0	14.0	10.2	5.3	2.8
1–3 years	10.0	6.3	3.1	3.3	7.0	6.1	2.9	0.6
4 years	5.7	5.4	0.3	0.8	3.5	3.4	1.5	1.3
5 years or more	9.6	4.4	2.0	0.9	3.5	0.7	0.9	0.9
Total percentage	100.0	99.9	100.0	100.0	100.1	100.1	100.0	99.9
N	902	1,137	609	639	155	148	340	319

Note: Data are for immigrants who were 25 years of age or older at the time of immigration.
Source: U.S. Bureau of the Census, 1970 Public Use State Sample.

Table 7. Educational Attainment of Cubans and Mexicans Who Immigrated during the Sixties, by Sex (in Percentages)

Educational Level	Immigrated 1960–1964				Immigrated 1965–1970			
	Cubans		Mexicans		Cubans		Mexicans	
	Males	Females	Males	Females	Males	Females	Males	Females
None or elementary	34.2	42.4	87.5	87.0	56.7	61.2	76.7	78.8
High school	29.4	35.1	10.3	9.9	25.8	26.8	15.9	15.2
College	36.4	22.4	2.2	3.1	17.5	12.1	7.4	6.0
Total percentage	100.0	99.9	100.0	100.0	100.0	100.1	100.0	100.0
N	371	441	232	223	531	695	377	415

Note: Data are for immigrants who were 25 years of age or older at the time of immigration.
Source: U.S. Bureau of the Census, 1970 Public Use State Sample.

majority of Mexican immigrants continue to be the poor and the un-skilled in search of better opportunities—87.5 percent of the men who immigrated during 1960–1964 and 76.6 percent of the men who immigrated during 1965–1970 had either no schooling or only an elementary education.

Before I turn to a comparison of the mean prestige and earnings of Cuban and Mexican immigrants by level of education attained, I will describe the data and variables.

Data and Variables

The data used in this analysis are all Cuban and Mexican immigrants from the 5 percent questionnaire, 1/100 Public Use State Sample from the 1970 U.S. census.[11] The regression analysis is for those who were in the labor force—who worked full time or part time and who reported data on current occupation and earnings.[12] Cuban and Mexican immigrants in the labor force numbered 6,288. Of these, 2,574 were Mexican men and 1,416 Cuban men; 1,239 were Mexican women and 1,059 Cuban women. To use the educational attainment of adult immigrants as an index for their social class origin, we restricted the analyses to those who were 25 years of age or older at the time of immigration. This yielded a total of 2,802 immigrants: 853 Mexican men and 901 Cuban men; 365 Mexican women and 683 Cuban women. Since the data are from the 1/100 Public Use Sample from the U.S. census, these numbers should be read as hundreds of workers; the sample represented one in one hundred of the labor force.[13] Thus this sample represents over 280,000 Cuban and Mexican immigrants: a labor force of approximately 85,300 Mexican men and 90,100 Cuban men, and 36,500 Mexican women and 68,300 Cuban women who were at least 25 years old when they immigrated.

Dependent Variables

The two dependent variables chosen as indexes of structural assimilation into American society are the individual's annual earnings and occupational prestige. *Annual earnings* is a variable built from the three census variables on earnings in 1969 that represent work-related income.[14] The annual earnings of the respondent are ex-pressed in dollar units rather than the natural logarithm. Although analyses often use the logged form of this variable in the litera-ture,[15] in plotting the relationship of earnings to years of schooling I found that at least for Cuban and Mexican immigrants this relationship is linear, so that their earnings are more closely approximated by a linear than a log function.[16] The second dependent variable is *occupational prestige*, expressed by the National Opinion Research Center's prestige scores.[17] A prestige scaling of occupations is used not truly as an indicator of prestige in its classical sense of patterned relationships of deference, acceptance, or derogation, but as a measure of occupational attainment given the perceived hierarchy of occupational desirability.

Table 8 presents the mean prestige and earnings of Cuban and Mexican workers by whether they immigrated during the political or the economic period, and by sex. Two-tailed T-ratios test whether the difference in scores between Cubans and Mexicans is significant.

When Cubans are economic immigrants, it is less educated Cubans (those who are not high school graduates) who do better than Mexicans—men fare better both in their prestige and annual earnings, women only in their prestige. In other words, when Cubans are economic immigrants, Cuban women and Mexican women earn the same at all levels of education, but less educated Cuban women fare better than Mexican women in desirable occupations. Among less educated men, Cuban men attain distinctly higher prestige and earnings than Mexican men. But among the well educated, the mean prestige and earnings of Cuban and Mexican college graduates are indistinguishable.

When Cubans are political immigrants, it is still less educated Cubans who fare better than Mexicans, both men and women, and both in prestige and earnings. The immigrants of the period of political migration are also distinct in that, contrary to popular images, when we compare the college graduates the mean prestige score for Cubans is significantly *lower* than for Mexicans, both for men and women. The earnings of the college graduates, on the other hand, do not differ significantly. It seems clear that the differences among Cubans and Mexicans in the mean prestige and earnings they attained are not due to their different educational backgrounds.

Let us now turn to a more detailed examination of these differences. The regression analysis employs one equation for both Cubans and Mexicans together, controlling all the differences in social composition among the two groups. Thus we can ask whether there is a significant difference in being a Cuban (as opposed to being a Mexican) among political versus economic immigrants. But first we need to describe the independent variables, the immigrants' social characteristics I deemed important to include.

Table 8. Mean Prestige and Earnings of Cuban and Mexican Immigrants, by Educational Level, by Period of Immigration, and by Sex

	Mean Occupational Prestige						
	Cuban Males			Mexican Males			
Educational Level	Mean	S.D.	N	Mean	S.D.	N	T Ratio
Immigrated, 1960–1970							
Less than high school graduation	31.46	9.84	463	24.81	8.48	515	11.27**
High school graduation or more	40.81	17.72	383	36.76	19.21	77	1.71
College graduation or more	51.67	19.51	135	66.57	18.65	14	-2.83**
Immigrated 1945–1959							
Less than high school graduation	30.29	10.13	62	25.57	9.63	281	3.35**
High school graduation or more	39.24	14.36	49	39.37	16.13	38	-0.04
College graduation or more	55.62	18.24	8	53.12	24.34	8	0.23

	Mean Annual Earnings[a]						
	Cuban Males			Mexican Males			
Educational Level	Mean	S.D.	N	Mean	S.D.	N	T Ratio
Immigrated, 1960–1970							
Less than high school graduation	47.14	31.55	463	42.19	26.83	515	2.67**
High school graduation or more	71.07	58.89	382	64.23	65.02	77	0.86
College graduation or more	91.00	78.10	135	114.64	124.27	14	0.70
Immigrated 1945–1959							
Less than high school graduation	64.08	43.29	62	47.10	35.73	281	2.88**
High school graduation or more	82.85	66.08	48	87.18	97.89	37	-0.23
College graduation or more	162.00	126.48	8	172.87	181.01	8	-0.14

| | Cuban Females | | | Mexican Females | | | |
Educational Level	Mean	S.D.	N	Mean	S.D.	N	T Ratio
Immigrated, 1960–1970							
Less than high school graduation	28.42	8.38	372	23.81	8.17	274	6.98**
High school graduation or more	36.52	13.90	338	34.04	13.08	45	1.19
College graduation or more	42.61	17.51	98	55.67	15.40	6	-2.00*
Immigrated 1945–1959							
Less than high school graduation	27.10	8.38	68	23.53	7.41	140	3.00**
High school graduation or more	31.45	11.23	44	36.11	13.81	19	-1.30
College graduation or more	36.20	16.54	5	37.00	10.72	5	-0.09

Mean Annual Earnings[a]

| | Cuban Females | | | Mexican Females | | | |
Educational Level	Mean	S.D.	N	Mean	S.D.	N	T Ratio
Immigrated, 1960–1970							
Less than high school graduation	25.00	18.78	372	16.70	16.22	274	6.01**
High school graduation or more	34.52	25.69	338	20.90	23.95	45	3.56**
College graduation or more	43.30	30.97	98	32.17	37.95	6	0.70
Immigrated 1945–1959							
Less than high school graduation	24.60	19.53	68	19.29	23.86	140	1.71
High school graduation or more	26.36	22.31	44	35.76	25.30	19	-1.40
College graduation or more	27.90	30.56	5	39.30	15.16	5	-0.75

Note: Data are for immigrants who were 25 years of age or older at the time of immigration.
Source: U.S. Bureau of the Census, 1970 Public Use State Sample.
* Significant at the 0.05 level, two-tailed.
** Significant at the 0.01 level or higher, two-tailed.
[a] In hundreds of dollars.

Independent Variables

Since the educational attainment of adult immigrants serves as an index of social class origin, I specified it in two ways: as the individual's *years of school completed*; and by two dummy variables for being a *high school graduate* and being a *college graduate*.[18] These dummy variables aim to measure the extent to which educational certification, graduation from high school and from college, has an impact on earnings and occupational attainment beyond that of simply years of schooling. Specifying the educational attainment in this dual manner allows for possession of certificates in a society where credentials are so often a requisite to enter occupations. As expected, education was the most important predictor of earnings and occupational attainment.[19]

To incorporate the migrant labor aspect of the Mexican immigration, which has no counterpart in the Cuban migration, not even prior to 1960, I included a dummy variable for *agricultural employment*. While migrant labor is not only agricultural labor and Mexican immigrants increasingly work in industry and service, it is in agriculture where the worker as worker is least protected (by unions, wage contracts and benefits, length of contract) and where the largest and most deliberate worker recruitment efforts (as well as deportations) always took place. Including a dummy variable for agricultural employment also solves the problem posed by the census definition of urban and rural.[20] Thus employment in agriculture was also used as a measure of urbanism versus rurality.

Since it normally makes a difference in the determination of prestige and earnings, *age* was also used as a control variable. Given job mobility or promotion, increasing age should be reflected in increased earnings.

Length of U.S. experience was also included as a determinant, particularly of earnings. Working within a framework of investment in human capital, Barry Chiswick argued that for an immigrant this is an important variable: as time passes the immigrant gains knowledge of the new American circumstances, learns the language, and modifies his or her skills accordingly. That is, the immigrant undergoes a process of "Americanization," or skill adjustment—thus improving earnings.[21] Length of U.S. experience is also included as a control for differences in this respect among Cuban and Mexican immigrants.

Those who work at *skilled jobs* (professionals, managers, clerical, crafts, operatives) versus those who do unskilled jobs (farm, service, household) constituted another dummy variable. It serves to control for the differences in earnings for the two types of work as well as for the differences in occupational distribution among Cuban and Mexican immigrants. Since this is an occupational classification, it is not included as a predictor variable for the regression on occupational prestige, but only for the regression on earnings.

Region of residence was taken into account as a dichotomy between the rest of the country and the *South*.[22] It is a necessary predictor because earnings are lower in the South (as is the cost of living) than in the rest of the country. Thus it controls for regional differences in wages. Moreover, it is also important because the geographical distribution of Cuban and Mexican immigrants across the nation varies markedly. As is well known, Mexican immigrants are most heavily concentrated in the South (Texas) and the West (California), while Cuban immigrants are most heavily concentrated in the Northeast (New York–New Jersey) and the South (Florida), especially since 1960, when the reception and programs extended to Cuban arrivals in Miami helped to set up and reinforce a Cuban ethnic enclave. Thus residence in the South is also a control for the differential geographic dispersion of Cuban and Mexican immigrants. The meaning of living and working in the South, however, is radically different for Cuban and Mexican immigrants. Fully 89 percent of Cuban immigrants currently living in the South live in Florida, while 96 percent of Mexican immigrants currently living in the South live in Texas. Thus the coefficient for the variable South means the impact of living in Florida for Cubans and the impact of living in Texas for Mexicans.

Whether or not the individual worker received any form of *vocational training* was also included as a dummy variable. It aims to equalize any differences that exist between Cuban and Mexican immigrants in their access to language courses or adult education programs that might have opened up job possibilities.

The average *number of weeks worked* is a necessary predictor since earnings included both those who work part time and full time. It is also a control for the larger proportion of Mexican immigrants who work in agriculture, given the seasonality of agricultural work.

Citizenship is introduced as a predictor variable to see whether the impact of citizenship on earnings and educational attainment differs for Cuban and Mexican immigrants.[23]

Last, for this first set of equations, *nationality* is included to answer these two questions:

1. *What is the value of being a Cuban (as opposed to being a*

Table 9. *Means and Standard Deviations for the Social Characteristics of Cuban and Mexican Immigrants, by Period of Immigration and by Sex*

	Cuban Males		Mexican Males	
	Mean	S.D.	Mean	S.D.
Immigrated 1960–1970				
Annual earnings[a]	61.21	46.81	47.69	34.28
Occupational prestige	35.62	14.79	26.43	11.13
Age	45.19	10.07	38.71	10.42
Length of U.S. experience	4.71	2.48	4.45	2.44
Skilled work	0.81	0.39	0.52	0.50
South	0.52	0.50	0.19	0.39
Vocational training	0.28	0.45	0.10	0.30
Agricultural employment	0.01	0.07	0.24	0.42
Citizenship	0.20	0.40	0.25	0.43
Weeks worked	45.54	11.30	44.30	11.20
Years of school completed	10.20	4.37	5.52	4.15
High school graduation	0.45	0.50	0.13	0.34
College graduation	0.16	0.37	0.02	0.15
N	796		555	
Immigrated 1945–1959				
Annual earnings[a]	75.69	53.89	55.09	48.60
Occupational prestige	34.15	12.69	27.41	11.56
Age	51.11	6.29	50.73	6.88
Length of U.S. experience	14.69	3.32	15.17	3.46
Skilled work	0.79	0.41	0.51	0.50
South	0.46	0.50	0.26	0.45
Vocational training	0.23	0.42	0.09	0.28
Agricultural employment	0.01	0.10	0.19	0.39
Citizenship	0.57	0.50	0.28	0.45
Weeks worked	47.76	8.12	44.40	11.10
Years of school completed	9.82	3.67	5.39	4.12
High school graduation	0.44	0.50	0.12	0.33
College graduation	0.08	0.27	0.02	0.15
N	105		298	

Table 9 (*continued*)

| | Cuban Females | | Mexican Females | |
	Mean	S.D.	Mean	S.D.
Immigrated 1960–1970				
Annual earnings[a]	35.03	20.76	22.36	17.04
Occupational prestige	32.04	11.94	24.95	9.21
Age	43.34	9.51	39.62	9.16
Length of U.S. experience	4.74	2.50	4.55	2.46
Skilled work	0.87	0.34	0.56	0.50
South	0.54	0.50	0.20	0.40
Vocational training	0.26	0.44	0.10	0.30
Agricultural employment	0.00	0.00	0.16	0.36
Citizenship	0.17	0.38	0.28	0.45
Weeks worked	40.26	14.70	33.81	17.41
Years of school completed	10.23	4.09	5.66	4.03
High school graduation	0.49	0.50	0.13	0.34
College graduation	0.15	0.35	0.02	0.13
N	595		244	
Immigrated 1945–1959				
Annual earnings[a]	32.06	18.02	27.78	24.77
Occupational prestige	28.58	10.15	25.19	9.41
Age	51.17	6.48	51.07	7.38
Length of U.S. experience	14.43	3.43	15.39	3.70
Skilled work	0.86	0.35	0.59	0.49
South	0.48	0.50	0.23	0.42
Vocational training	0.20	0.41	0.12	0.32
Agricultural employment	0.00	0.00	0.12	0.33
Citizenship	0.48	0.50	0.29	0.46
Weeks worked	42.55	12.70	39.15	14.80
Years of school completed	8.83	3.89	5.46	4.44
High school graduation	0.39	0.49	0.12	0.33
College graduation	0.05	0.21	0.04	0.20
N	88		121	

Note: Data are for immigrants who were 25 years of age or older at the time of immigration.

Source: U.S. Bureau of the Census, 1970 Public Use State Sample.

[a] In hundreds of dollars.

Mexican) when the differences in the individual characteristics just specified are taken into account?

2. *Is the advantage of Cubans over Mexicans greater in the political migration period than in the economic migration period?*

To answer these questions, two regression equations, on prestige and earnings, are estimated for those who immigrated from 1945 to 1959 (when Cubans were economic immigrants) and from 1960 to 1970 (when Cubans were political immigrants).

Before turning to the regression results, the differences in the characteristics of Cuban and Mexican immigrants that were controlled for should be specified. Table 9 shows the mean values and standard deviations of the characteristics of Cuban and Mexican immigrants by whether they immigrated in the political or economic period, and by sex. The zero-order correlations among variables can be found in Appendix A. Some of the characteristics show little difference; I will point out the most salient.

Looking at those who immigrated during 1960–1970, we see that four-fifths of the Cubans are working at skilled jobs compared to only half of the Mexicans. Half of the Cubans live in the South (Florida), while only one-fifth of the Mexicans live there (Texas).

While only one-tenth of the Mexicans had some vocational training, one-fourth of the Cubans had some form of vocational training. But more Mexicans (0.25 of the men, 0.28 of the women) became naturalized citizens than Cubans (0.20 of the men, 0.17 of the women).

There are virtually no Cubans employed in agriculture, where 24 percent of Mexican men and 16 percent of Mexican women work. On the average, Cubans show a slightly higher number of weeks worked (45.54 for men, 40.26 for women) than Mexicans (44.30 for men, 33.81 for women).

As we saw, the largest difference is in their education. The number of years of schooling is almost twice as high for Cubans (10.2 years) as for Mexicans (5.6 years). Furthermore, there are three times more high school graduates among Cubans (0.45 for men, 0.49 for women) than among Mexicans (0.13 for both men and women) and the proportion of college graduates is eight times larger among Cubans (0.16 for men, 0.15 for women) than Mexicans (0.02 for both men and women).

Looking at those who immigrated during 1945–1959, we see that the proportion of those living in the South is slightly lower for Cubans (0.46 men, 0.48 women) than for the more recent immigrants, but for Mexicans it is slightly higher (0.26 men, 0.23 women) than for the more recent migration. The same differences obtain in the proportion of those working at skilled jobs. Cuban women are more likely than Cuban men to be doing skilled work (0.86 vs. 0.79), and Mexican women are also more likely than Mexican men to be doing skilled work (0.59 vs. 0.51), but, as before, four-fifths of the Cubans in contrast to only about one-half of the Mexicans are working at skilled jobs.

Like the more recent immigrants, Cubans are twice as likely to have received some form of vocational training as Mexicans. But among the early immigrants, the pattern of citizenship is reversed. Cubans are twice as likely (0.57 for men, 0.48 for women) to be citizens as Mexicans (0.28 for men, 0.29 for women).

Again, there are virtually no Cubans who work in agriculture. While the proportion of Mexicans of the earlier immigration who work in agriculture is still sizable (19 percent of the men, 12 percent of the women), it is lower than for the more recent immigrants. On the average, Cubans worked four more weeks (48 weeks for men; 43 weeks for women) than Mexicans (44 weeks for men; 39 weeks for women).

The largest difference between the early and the more recent migrations is that when Cubans were economic immigrants, they were less well educated. The average number of years of school completed is still high (9.8 years for men; 8.8 years for women); and the proportion of high school graduates is still three times higher for Cubans (0.44 for men, 0.39 for women) than for Mexicans (0.12 for both men and women). But among the early immigrants the proportion of those who graduated from college is now only half as high for the men (0.08) and only one-third as high for the women (0.05) as in the period of political migration (0.16 for men; 0.15 for women). For Mexicans, on the other hand, the average education of those who immigrated during 1945–1959 is virtually the same as those who immigrated during 1960–1970. Only 0.02 of the men and 0.04 of the women graduated from college.

Although the characteristics of women hardly differ from those of men with whom they share the same nationality, the average annual earnings of working women are only half those of men.

The Value of Being a Cuban

We now turn to the regression results. The first question is: Are Cubans still more successful than Mexicans when the differences in their characteristics are taken into account? To address this question, Table 10 summarizes the results of the regressions on prestige and earnings for men and women by time of immigration

Table 10. *Partial (b) Regression Coefficients and Standard Error (b) of the Nationality Variable for Cuban and Mexican Immigrants, by Period of Immigration and by Sex*

		Nationality Variable				
	Occupational Prestige			Annual Earnings[a]		
	b	S.E.	(b)	b	S.E.	(b)
Immigrated 1960–1970						
Males	2.79		0.81	4.32		2.62
	R^2 = 0.375			R^2 = 0.293		
	N = 1351			N = 1351		
Females	2.76		0.95	6.17		1.37
	R^2 = 0.283			R^2 = 0.583		
	N = 839			N = 839		
Immigrated 1945–1959						
Males	−0.30		1.29	2.24		5.40
	R^2 = 0.386			R^2 = 0.386		
	N = 403			N = 403		
Females	−0.03		1.37	−2.34		3.16
	R^2 = 0.311			R^2 = 0.305		
	N	209		N	= 209	

Note: Data are for immigrants who were 25 years of age or older at the time of immigration.
Source: U.S. Bureau of the Census, 1970 Public Use State Sample.
[a] In hundreds of dollars.

when controlling for all these differences in their social characteristics. The value of the coefficient of *nationality* gives us the value of being a Cuban (as opposed to being a Mexican) when all the differences in their characteristics are taken into account.

This brings us to the second question: Is the advantage of being a Cuban greater in the political migration period than in the economic migration period? To address this question, I employed a Z-test for the difference in the value of being a Cuban in the two periods of immigration.[24] Table 11 shows the results.

In three out of four instances the advantage of being a Cuban over being a Mexican is significantly greater as political immigrants than as economic immigrants.

In more detail, Table 10 shows that, as political immigrants, being a Cuban *raises* the level of prestige by 2.79 points for the men and by 2.76 points for the women, over and beyond the differences in the social characteristics of Cubans and Mexicans who immigrated in the sixties. In sharp contrast, as economic immigrants, being a Cuban *lowered* the level of prestige by -0.30 for the men and by -0.03 points for the women when taking all the differences in the social characteristics of Cubans and Mexicans into account.

In other words, beyond the differences in the social characteristics of Cuban and Mexican immigrants—differences in social class origin, agricultural employment, length of U.S. experience, and the like—being a Cuban has no value whatsoever in prestige over being a Mexican, neither for the men nor the women, when both are economic immigrants. Therefore, a cultural difference cannot be argued. But when Cubans are political immigrants, there is a value to being a Cuban over and beyond the differences in social class origin, agricultural employment, length of U.S. experience, and the like. Both for men and women it means a rise in prestige, or occupational attainment, of nearly 3.0 points. Hence, regarding the occupations Cubans attained, we can infer the role of government policy in helping Cubans to structurally assimilate in America.

The picture is somewhat different for their earnings. As political immigrants, being a Cuban raises the earnings of men by $432. But this is not a significantly larger amount than Cubans attained as economic immigrants, when the value of being a Cuban was $224 over and beyond the differences in the social characteristics of Cubans and Mexicans. In contrast, being a political immigrant raises the earnings of women by as much as $617 a year, while as economic immigrants the value of being a Cuban was a cost: Cuban

Table 11. Z-Test for the Partial Coefficients of the Nationality Variable for the Difference between the Migrations of the Political Period (1960–1970) and the Economic Period (1945–1959), by Sex

	Nationality Variable	
	Occupational Prestige	Annual Earnings
Males	1.94 *	0.35
Females	1.67 *	2.47 * *

* Significant at the 0.05 level, one-tail test.
* * Significant at the 0.01 level, one-tail test.

women earned $234 *less* a year. Thus, regarding the earnings Cubans received, the role of government policy can be clearly inferred in the case of women, but not in the case of men.

As political immigrants, Cuban women benefited from both greater prestige and greater earnings. This can easily be understood. Many of the programs instituted by the government (for example, teacher retraining) targeted the essentially female occupations. Access to these labor markets entailed a rise in both prestige and earnings.

For Cuban men as political immigrants, the role of the state facilitated their acquisition of both prestige and earnings, but the earnings difference was not as large as for women. In addition, as economic immigrants, Cuban men received higher earnings than Mexican men when controlling for the differences in their characteristics.

In sum, over and beyond the differences in their individual social characteristics, the analysis has shown that as political immigrants Cuban men have a distinct advantage over Mexican men in the prestige they attained, and Cuban women have a distinct advantage over Mexican women in both the prestige and earnings they attained. As economic immigrants only Cuban men have an advantage over Mexicans, and solely in earnings. We can, therefore, conclude that being a political immigrant is distinctly different: distinct in that the supportive role the state played facilitated the structural assimilation of Cuban political émigrés.

Returns to the Human Capital of Cubans and Mexicans

If political immigrants are distinctly different from economic immigrants, next we would want to know: Is their *process of attainment* of prestige and earnings different?

To answer this question, at the outset I set it within the human capital framework, an economic model with a sociological counterpart in the status attainment school of stratification research.[25] For the last two decades, the central concern of these economic and sociological perspectives has been to measure the *returns* to workers, in prestige or earnings, to their social characteristics, to their investment in human capital. Investments in human capital, Gary Becker explained, concern the activities "that influence future monetary and psychic income by increasing the resources in people."[26] Those investments differ in their effects or in the size of the returns. They take many forms, including schooling, on-the-job training, medical care, migration, and information search, all of which "improve skills, knowledge, or health, and thereby raise money or psychic incomes."[27] The empirical studies typically focused on education, since it best exemplifies the notion of investment in human capital: the more highly educated and skilled tend to earn more than others.[28] This perspective disregards the social relations of production, which the next chapter on segmented labor markets incorporates. But for now we will concentrate simply on the response to the human capital of the worker. Invariably, this perspective asks this question: What are the returns to the individual characteristics of workers? Given the argument of this study, that question becomes comparative and specifically asks: *Do the returns to the characteristics of Cuban and Mexican immigrant workers really differ?*

Separate equations for Cubans and Mexicans in both periods of migration enable us to answer the question by comparing the returns in prestige and earnings to the characteristics of Cubans and Mexicans who immigrated in the same historical period, 1960–1970 or 1945–1959.[29] We then ask whether the returns to their social characteristics really differ when we compare Cuban political immigrants to Mexican economic immigrants as well as when we compare Cubans to Mexicans both as economic immigrants. Tables 12 and 13 present the results of the regression on prestige and earnings separately for Cubans and Mexicans, by period of immigration (1960–1970 or 1945–1959) and by sex. The characteristics of workers predict their prestige and earnings very well—from about 28 percent to 45 percent of the variance.

To evaluate the return to a particular characteristic, or independent variable, we turn to the *B* values, or partial regression coefficients. For example, the partial regression coefficient for years of school completed indicates the average number of prestige points or the average number of dollars a year produced by an additional year of schooling. In comparing different populations, Cubans and Mexicans, it is particularly appropriate that we look at the partial *B*s rather than the standardized *Beta*s, since the partial *B*s allow the variation within each sample to remain, and this variation among the two populations constitutes one of their differences in the process of attainment.[30]

To determine whether the comparative process of attainment is really different for Cuban and Mexican immigrants, I employed a Z-test for the difference between Cubans and Mexicans in the size of the returns in prestige or earnings to a particular social characteristic.[31] Table 14 presents the results of the Z-test, two-tailed since differences in either direction are important. The discussion of re-

Table 12. Partial (b) Regression Coefficients and Standard Error (b) for the Effect of Specified Variables on Occupational Prestige, for Cuban and Mexican Immigrants, by Period of Immigration and by Sex

	Immigrated 1960–1970		Immigrated 1945–1959		Immigrated 1960–1970		Immigrated 1945–1959	
	Cuban Males	Mexican Males	Cuban Males	Mexican Males	Cuban Females	Mexican Females	Cuban Females	Mexican Females
Age	-0.16 (0.05)	-0.05 (0.04)	0.26 (0.18)	-0.06 (0.09)	-0.06 (0.05)	-0.04 (0.07)	-0.17 (0.16)	0.01 (0.12)
Length of U.S. Experience	0.37 (0.20)	0.18 (0.16)	0.07 (0.36)	0.21 (0.18)	0.01 (0.20)	-0.15 (0.23)	-0.03 (0.31)	0.13 (0.22)
South	0.85 (0.91)	2.36 (0.91)	2.59 (2.16)	3.96 (1.31)	-2.13 (0.88)	-1.25 (1.27)	-2.33 (2.04)	-0.76 (1.80)
Vocational training	2.04 (1.05)	3.73 (1.25)	-0.03 (2.67)	4.36 (2.06)	3.98 (1.05)	1.94 (2.03)	8.72 (2.56)	6.08 (2.43)
Employment in agriculture	-16.01 (6.40)	-8.06 (0.90)	-11.52 (11.26)	-7.52 (1.54)	...	-5.61 (1.57)	...	-5.19 (2.40)

Citizenship	2.49	−0.55	6.34	0.90	3.61	−1.48	5.51	3.04
	(1.18)	(0.82)	(2.36)	(1.29)	(1.20)	(1.15)	(2.09)	(1.65)
Weeks worked	−0.04	0.08	0.13	−0.01	0.02	0.03	−0.01	0.09
	(0.04)	(0.03)	(0.14)	(0.05)	(0.03)	(0.03)	(0.08)	(0.05)
Years of school completed	0.84	0.06	0.64	0.59	0.71	0.52	0.08	0.14
	(0.25)	(0.14)	(0.59)	(0.22)	(0.27)	(0.20)	(0.51)	(0.26)
High school graduation	−2.06	2.25	−1.12	1.34	0.03	−0.55	1.41	8.15
	(1.77)	(1.57)	(3.70)	(2.61)	(1.81)	(2.39)	(3.69)	(3.21)
College graduation	12.98	32.90	21.43	16.84	5.67	17.50	2.64	0.26
	(1.77)	(2.67)	(5.47)	(4.18)	(1.78)	(4.47)	(5.41)	(4.61)
R^2	0.280	0.452	0.396	0.355	0.224	0.284	0.286	0.346
N	796	555	105	298	595	244	88	121

Note: Data are for immigrants who were 25 years of age or older at the time of immigration.
Note: Standard errors are in parentheses.
Source: U.S. Bureau of the Census, 1970 Public Use State Sample.

Table 13. *Partial (b) Regression Coefficients and Standard Error (b) for the Effect of Specified Variables on Annual Earnings,* [a] *for Cuban and Mexican Immigrants, by Period of Immigration and by Sex*

	Immigrated 1960–1970		Immigrated 1945–1959		Immigrated 1960–1970		Immigrated 1945–1959	
	Cuban Males	Mexican Males	Cuban Males	Mexican Males	Cuban Females	Mexican Females	Cuban Females	Mexican Females
Age	-0.54	-0.23	1.19	-1.06	-0.16	-0.04	-0.32	-0.27
	(0.15)	(0.13)	(0.75)	(0.37)	(0.07)	(0.11)	(0.27)	(0.31)
Length of U.S. experience	2.08	2.77	-1.73	1.43	0.73	0.07	-0.32	-0.15
	(0.63)	(0.56)	(1.46)	(0.74)	(0.27)	(0.37)	(0.52)	(0.60)
Skilled work	13.07	4.67	17.79	12.31	5.60	4.90	9.73	-6.76
	(3.74)	(3.03)	(10.94)	(5.33)	(1.75)	(1.96)	(5.02)	(4.68)
South	-5.08	-13.75	-3.74	-21.19	-4.33	-6.53	-1.82	12.23
	(2.87)	(3.16)	(8.98)	(5.32)	(1.19)	(2.06)	(3.49)	(4.87)
Vocational training	5.12	11.66	-25.21	-14.69	2.23	2.83	14.21	-1.54
	(3.30)	(4.33)	(10.98)	(8.39)	(1.42)	(3.26)	(4.32)	(6.47)

Employment in agriculture	10.33	−7.99	−48.28	−11.75	...	−0.16	...	10.86
	(20.40)	(3.67)	(47.03)	(6.80)		(2.76)		(7.01)
Citizenship	16.76	2.25	31.35	−1.41	10.51	1.60	−1.68	7.38
	(3.72)	(2.84)	(9.79)	(5.24)	(1.61)	(1.85)	(3.54)	(4.41)
Weeks worked	1.11	0.84	0.87	0.61	0.77	0.54	0.64	0.52
	(0.13)	(0.11)	(0.56)	(0.22)	(0.04)	(0.05)	(0.14)	(0.14)
Years of school completed	2.08	0.26	5.91	1.85	0.77	0.34	0.75	1.60
	(0.78)	(0.49)	(2.42)	(0.90)	(0.36)	(0.33)	(0.85)	(0.71)
High school graduation	−7.73	2.30	−30.84	−8.23	−2.82	−1.24	0.33	7.04
	(5.56)	(5.42)	(15.17)	(10.58)	(2.45)	(3.86)	(6.17)	(8.57)
College graduation	19.87	68.79	86.49	126.28	8.40	17.94	−15.50	−14.99
	(5.59)	(9.29)	(22.43)	(16.98)	(2.40)	(7.20)	(9.08)	(12.26)
R^2	0.291	0.309	0.446	0.401	0.533	0.463	0.375	0.338
N	796	555	105	298	595	244	88	121

Note: Data are for immigrants who were 25 years of age or older at the time of immigration.
Note: Standard errors are in parentheses.
Source: U.S. Bureau of the Census, 1970 Public Use State Sample.
[a]In hundreds of dollars.

Table 14. Z-Test for the Difference between the Partial Coefficients of the Social Characteristics of Cuban and Mexican Immigrants, by Period of Immigration and by Sex

	Prestige		Earnings	
	Males	Females	Males	Females
Cubans vs. Mexicans Who Immigrated 1960–1970				
Age	−1.72	− .23	−1.57	− .92
Length of U.S. experience	.72	.52	.82	1.44
Skilled work	N.A.	N.A.	1.75	.27
South	−1.17	− .57	2.03*	.92
Vocational training	1.04	.89	−1.20	− .17
Employment in agriculture	−1.23	...	.88	...
Citizenship	2.12*	3.07	3.10**	3.63
Weeks worked	−2.40*	− .24	1.59	3.59
Years of school completed	2.72**	.56	1.98*	.88
High school graduation	−1.82	.19	−1.29	− .35
College graduation	−6.23**	−2.46	−4.51**	−1.26
Cubans vs. Mexicans Who Immigrated 1945–1959				
Age	1.60	.90	2.69**	− .12
Length of U.S. experience	− .35	.42	−1.94	− .21
Skilled work	N.A.	N.A.	.45	2.40
South	− .54	− .58	1.67	1.74
Vocational training	− .86	.75	− .76	2.02
Employment in agriculture	− .35	...	− .77	...
Citizenship	2.02*	.93	2.95**	−1.60
Weeks worked	.93	−1.06	.43	.61
Years of school completed	.08	− .10	1.57	− .77
High school graduation	− .54	−1.38	−1.22	− .64
College graduation	.67	.33	−1.41	− .03

N.A. = not applicable.
* Significant at the 0.05 level, two-tail test.
** Significant at the 0.01 level, two-tail test.

sults focuses on the returns to those characteristics (Tables 12 and 13) that the Z-test tells us are significantly different (Table 14). We should remember, however, that these characteristics are the only ones that are significantly different when controlling for all the other characteristics.

Given the overarching argument of this study, we can expect that when Cubans and Mexicans are both economic immigrants (1945–1959), they will resemble each other greatly and their process of attainment of prestige and earnings will differ only slightly. We can also expect that Cuban political immigrants will differ substantially from Mexican economic immigrants of the sixties in their process of attainment of prestige and earnings.

Cubans and Mexicans Who Immigrated during 1960–1970

The most striking difference between Cuban and Mexican immigrants of this period is in the rates of return to citizenship. Both for men and women, being a naturalized American citizen has a much larger payoff for Cubans than for Mexicans. This is true both for prestige and earnings. For Cubans, being a citizen entails a return of 2.49 prestige points for men and 3.61 prestige points for women, while for Mexicans the returns entail a cost, of −0.55 prestige points for men and −1.48 prestige points for women. In earnings, being a citizen brings Cuban men $1,676 more a year and Cuban women $1,051 more, while in comparison the return is very small for Mexicans—only $225 more for men and only $160 more for women.

In discussing these results, it is useful to contrast the immigrants of the sixties to the early immigrants. For those who immigrated in the period 1945–1959, the same pattern holds true for men, but not for women. That is, citizenship also has a strong impact for Cuban men, raising their prestige by 6.34 points and their income by $3,135 more a year. For Mexican men, on the other hand, citizenship makes a negligible difference in prestige (0.90) and represents a cost in earnings (−$141). For Cuban and Mexican women who immigrated prior to 1960, however, the difference in their returns to being a citizen is not significant, in either prestige or earnings.

Two very different meanings of citizenship seem to be at stake. A citizenship that has so little impact on prestige and earnings, as is invariably the case for Mexican men and women, is likely to be a citizenship acquired through marriage to an American citizen, Chicano or Anglo, or through bearing a child in America. Evidence from the type of visa Mexicans obtain corroborates this. Alejandro Portes stressed the kinship ties upon which Mexicans base their claims for U.S. residence. Of the 48,076 immigrant visas issued to Mexicans in 1971, over 16,000 were in the categories IR-1, IR-2, IR-5—spouses, children, and parents of U.S. citizens.[32] This type of citizenship enables the worker to legally remain or return and continue to work in the United States, but it in no way changes the nature of the worker's place in the American work force. For example, if a Mexican man first came to the United States under the *bracero* program and thereafter married a U.S. citizen, he could thus become a legal resident and be eligible for citizenship in a few years. In addition, at the end of his contract he could not be repatriated or obligated to return to Mexico, but rather he would be able to stay and continue working. He would continue working, however, at *bracero*-type work. Likewise, during the sixties, marriage to a U.S. citizen would enable an illegal alien to become legal, to remain or reenter the United States to work. He would continue working, however, at work of the illegal-alien type.

On the other hand, a citizenship that does have a salient impact on prestige and earnings, as is the case for Cuban men in both the political and economic migrations and for Cuban women who are political immigrants, must be a citzenship that implies access to those more lucrative and prestigious occupations that require it. The next chapter will provide the evidence. For Cuban women who immigrated prior to 1960 as economic immigrants, the returns to being a naturalized U.S. citizen are not significantly different from the returns Mexican women received. Perhaps it means that their citizenship was, like that of Mexicans, acquired through marriage or child-bearing; perhaps it means that they were also inserted in those labor markets for which it is irrelevant. As economic immigrants, Cuban men were already inserted in those labor markets where being a citizen paid off in prestige and earnings. We could argue that the government policy programs for Cuban political immigrants facilitated the entry of Cuban women into those labor markets—for example, via the teacher retraining and professional retraining programs. This is a sensible interpretation since as political immigrants Cuban women have a higher return to being a citizen in prestige (3.61 points) than Cuban men (2.49), although their return in earnings is less, as one might expect.

Other differences in returns exist among Cubans and Mexicans who immigrated during the sixties. In prestige, the number of weeks worked shows a significant difference for men, but in fact the coefficients are too small (0.08 for Mexicans; −0.04 for Cubans) to warrant attention.

Looking at education, long the focus of human capital research, we see that completing an additional year of school, when controlling for high school and college graduation, provides Cuban men with 0.84 points more prestige and $208 a year more in earnings, while it provides Mexican men with only an additional 0.06 points of prestige and $26.00.

The real difference, however, lies in the impact of being a college graduate. Hand in hand with our distinction between political and

economic immigrants, college graduation means more in determining the occupational attainment of Mexican "brain drain" than of
Cuban political immigrants. College graduation has a very large
impact for Mexican men: 32.90 more prestige points and $6,879
more a year while for Cuban men it represents only 12.98 points
more in prestige and only $1,987 more in earnings. Likewise, col-
lege graduation raises the prestige of Mexican women by 17.50
points, but that of Cuban women by only 5.67 points. There is no
significant difference, however, in the earnings return to Cuban and
Mexican women who are college graduates. As women, they are not
very well rewarded with income even when they hold credentials.

The marked disparity in the returns to college graduation for
Cubans and Mexicans hinges on their different motivations for
emigration. Cuban political immigrants came to the United States
due to their political disaffection, without the promise of a good
job beckoning. Mexican "brain drain" immigrants, on the other
hand, could only be motivated to leave their excellent social positions at home for very rewarding ones in America. All the more so
since the 1965 amendments to the Immigration and Nationality
Act encouraged the immigration of professionals in fields with a
domestic shortage. As we saw earlier, the proportion of college-
educated Mexican immigrants increased in the decade of the sixties. Since as a whole the proportion of Cubans who are college
graduates is much higher than for Mexicans (see Table 6), aggregate
figures for all Cuban and Mexican immigrants obscure the higher
achievement of Mexican college graduates. Demographers call this
a composition effect. But as the regression analysis shows, the returns in prestige and earnings are much higher for Mexican college
graduates than for Cubans.

For Cuban and Mexican women, in addition to the different payoff in earnings that being a citizen entails, the only other difference
was that an additional week of work means $77 more for Cuban
women and $54 more for Mexican women.

The earnings of Cuban and Mexican men who immigrated after
1960 evidence another difference. While living and working in the
South always depresses income, in comparison to living anywhere
else in the country, working in Florida lowers the income of Cuban men less (−$508) than living in Texas does for Mexican men
(−$1,375). For those who immigrated prior to 1960, the difference
in earnings is not significant. The reason would seem to be that in
the decade of the sixties, a large internal migration took place.
Mexican-Americans and Mexican immigrants moved in large numbers from Texas to California and to other urban centers in the

Midwest where better educational and job opportunities exist.[33] Therefore, those who remained in Texas remained at a disadvantage with respect to those working elsewhere, beyond the effect of being in the South. For Cuban men, on the other hand, the effect of living in the South is only half as large since one of the side effects of the Cuban Refugee Program was to create and reinforce a strong Cuban ethnic enclave there.

Cubans and Mexicans Who Immigrated during 1945–1959

Most striking about the difference in returns to the characteristics of Cubans and Mexicans when they are both economic immigrants is that, as we expected, there are very few real differences.

For men, besides the difference already discussed—that citizenship entails very different returns—no other characteristic shows a significant difference in its impact on their prestige. For the women, not even that difference exists. Even the impact of being a college graduate is the same for Cuban and Mexican men when both are economic immigrants. In earnings, besides the difference in the value of citizenship already discussed, only the return to age is really different for men. For Cuban men increasing age represents $119 more a year, for Mexican men $106 less a year. This reflects the lack of lifetime job mobility of Mexican men, a situation typical of *bracero* workers.

For women, only two characteristics make a significant difference in their earnings: doing skilled work and having had vocational training. Working at a skilled job represents a gain of $973 a year for Cuban women, while it means a loss of $676 a year for Mexican women, who fare better financially as farm workers, service workers, and domestics. While these are less desirable labor markets, Mexican women must have more access to them. The difference in the returns to having had some form of vocational training is similar—Cuban women increase their income by $1,421 a year while Mexican women lose $154. Both in prestige and earnings, being a college graduate returns substantially the same to Cuban and Mexican women when both are economic immigrants.

In sum, looking at the process of attainment of prestige and earnings—the returns to the individual characteristics of Cubans and Mexicans—shows the following. When Cubans and Mexicans are economic immigrants, the differences in the returns to their characteristics are few. In particular, they do not involve different returns to levels of education and especially not to college graduation—as they do for the political versus economic immigrants of the sixties. *Do the returns to the characteristics of Cuban and Mexican immigrant workers really differ?* We can now answer: hardly, when both are economic immigrants, but substantially when Cubans are political immigrants and Mexicans are economic immigrants.

5. Workers in Labor Markets: Cubans and Mexicans

Segmented Labor Markets

The problem with the status-attainment or human-capital approach to stratification research, as Patrick Horan contends, is not that it is atheoretical but that, "quite the contrary, it is heavily theory-laden."[1] This theoretical perspective typically asks the question: What are the returns to the characteristics of workers? That question issues from the theoretical assumptions of Kingsley Davis and Wilbert Moore's functionalist theory of stratification that sees the social position achieved as the reward to the importance of occupational roles performed; hence, the reward to the societal value of the characteristics (or human capital) of workers.[2] While Davis and Moore's stark theory of stratification received much criticism,[3] its theoretical assumptions became embedded, though covert, in the status-attainment approach to stratification that later became a dominant trend in stratification research.

In the last few years, sociologists and economists have contested the limitations embedded in these assumptions. While all criticized the focus on individual characteristics, the alternatives proposed varied. Ross Stolzenberg, for example, argued that it was time "to bring employers back into the sociological study of employment," as it is employers who provide jobs.[4] To merge thinking about employers with the occupational attainment and earnings of individuals, Stolzenberg introduced the size of the organization into the analysis. He showed that there were real differences between the processes of socioeconomic achievement in large organizations and those in small or medium-sized organizations. The empirical evidence provided, he stressed, "a compelling argument for systematically drawing organizational research into the study of social stratification."[5]

A more developed and widespread critique took the form of the dual labor market approach to stratification in its various forms of dual economy, dual labor markets, and labor force segmentation.[6] This competing perspective also arose out of the effort to correct the individualistic orientation embodied in the returns to the characteristics of workers and to recapture the fundamental notion of social relations of production as that which affects the interplay of worker characteristics and stratification outcomes.[7] This literature strives to show that industrial capitalism, in its advanced stage,[8] entails a differentiation of the industrial structure into *core* and *periphery* sectors "within which employers and workers face fundamentally different conditions and operate according to fundamentally different rules."[9] Hence, the returns to the characteristics of workers depend not only on their human capital (such as education) but on whether they are placed in the fundamentally different opportunity structures of the core and the periphery.

This is precisely what E. M. Beck, Patrick Horan, and Charles Tolbert showed in their quantitative analysis of earnings determination. Indeed, a different labor force composition partly defined the industrial sectors of core and periphery—core workers had more human capital in education, credentials, social background, and were more likely to be male and white than periphery workers. But they also showed that sectoral location had an effect beyond that due to the characteristics of their workers. Doing separate regressions on earnings in the core and periphery sectors enabled them to estimate the costs and benefits of sectoral location for workers. By applying the regression slopes of those in the core to the means of those in the periphery, and vice versa, they obtained that the "cost" of being in the periphery for the average periphery worker was $1,037 a year and the "benefit" of being in the core for the average core worker was $979—beyond the returns due to the characteristics of individuals.

Nonetheless, the problem with this new structural perspective is that the distinction between core and periphery industrial sectors is too simple and not theoretically grounded enough. For in effect what distinguishes the core from the periphery is the capital-intensive, monopolistic basis of the former versus the labor-intensive, competitive basis of the latter. As an effort to capture what Horan called "structural entities which derive from the nature of modern industrial capitalism,"[10] it supposes that the process of development from the early stage of capitalism to its advanced stage entailed an increasing *simplification* of the labor force that can be captured by distinctions based only on the degree of monopolization and capital investment. In fact, while we have no theory that adequately incorporates the process of transformation of the labor force that is one of the hallmarks of the development of industrial capitalism, it is quite clear that this process resulted in an increasingly *variegated* labor force—who not only produce and invest but who also command, catalogue, manage, mediate, and service.[11] That variegation cannot be wrapped in only two labor markets simply distinguished by capital layout and degree of monopolization.

This "new structuralism" in stratification research, James Baron and William Bielby pointed out, failed to provide an explicit conceptualization of the structure underlying the process of attainment and failed to incorporate the organization of work. The organization of work is what mediates the relationship between structure and individual attainment; it is "the interplay between technical and administrative imperatives on the one hand, and relations among people, positions, and objects within the workplace on the other."[12] Moving the focus to the organization of work implies the possibility that very different factors may shape attainment in different work settings, or that the same factor, say education, "may *mean* something very different in each sector."[13] To incorporate the organization of work, Baron and Bielby argued, it is necessary not only to bring the boss back in, but also to bring the firms back in. Arthur Stinchcombe's theory of social mobility in industrial labor markets recaptures both bosses and firms.

Stinchcombe's theory of social mobility retains the very important concept of labor market segments but incorporates the differentiation of the labor force as well as of the nature of production in advanced capitalist societies.[14] As Stinchcombe defines them, labor market segments are bounded areas within the labor market such that people within them hardly compete with people outside them. Noncompetitive labor market segments are the result of the organization of the product and commodity markets (degree of monopolization and licensing), the characteristics of workers within them (such as skill differences), the binding of job and property ownership, and the organization of labor, as well as the way in which labor is recruited and selected (or not selected) from within, and the criteria for promotion. Hence, segmented labor markets not only look different but function differently. And this has consequences for the patterns of social mobility of workers.

Using these criteria, Stinchcombe distinguished seven industrial labor markets: primary, classical capitalist, small-skilled, engineering, petty bourgeois, professional, and bureaucratic. I will briefly summarize Stinchcombe's description of each. In the analyses that follow, these seven labor markets were coded using the industrial classification of the 1970 census. The coding scheme is included in Appendix B.

Traditional primary industries (for example, farming and fishing) tend to be organized with family property in small enterprises, and labor is recruited from the family (i.e., farmers are sons of farmers). Since this labor market has generally declined in demand and in proportion of the total labor force, wages are driven down low enough to force a large part of its labor out of the industry and into urban jobs. Hence, immigrant "guest workers" or contract labor, such as the *braceros*, fill in.

Classical capitalist industries (for example, textile, clothing, and shoe manufacture; sand and gravel mining; quarrying; food and drink industries) are those vividly depicted by Marx and Ricardo. Since higher productivity comes from the "stretch out" of getting more labor out of cheaper laborers and not from technical improvements, they are characterized by relatively small firms in a competitive commodity market that uses unskilled labor with "an authoritarian 'people-driving' administrative apparatus."[15] Hence they typically recruit labor from whoever the underprivileged may be—blacks, women, and immigrant or guest workers—"the reserve army of the unemployed" who accept low wages and insecure jobs. Virtually no positions of privilege to be defended by trade unions exist, and seniority systems are not highly developed.

Small-scale industries with skilled workers (for example, metal goods, electrical repair, technical and scientific instrument production, construction) are characterized by a small-firm structure, competitive commodity or service markets, and a skilled, generally well-organized, manual work force that cannot be replaced by workers from the reserve army of the unemployed. Hence labor is organized as "craft."

Large-scale engineering-based industries (for example, coal, oil, and metal ore mining; chemical, petroleum, and rubber products; transportation equipment; post and telecommunications) are characterized by a large middle-class labor force that is organized bureaucratically by "careers." Usually two separate career lines exist, one for the middle class (which is recruited from higher education) and another for the working class (where good jobs are allocated strictly by the criterion of seniority). Level of education plays a large role, determining the speed of promotion and the ultimate level of achievement since these industries "do depend on abstract knowledge, and because education is one of the criteria of merit which is easiest to defend normatively when authority has to be unequally distributed."[16]

The *petty bourgeois trade and services* (for example, wholesale and retail trades, hotels and restaurants, taxis, real estate, personal services) are characterized by a labor force that is largely self-employed, or are small employers of very few employees. Since the enterprises are small and competitive only locally, they are organized with few career structures and weak seniority provisions. They also recruit workers from the reserve army of the unemployed (women, guest workers, racial minorities, youth), for whom the situation is much like that of the classical capitalist industries. The middle classes here engage mostly in borrowing and paying back (as well as inheriting), so that education amounts to little in shaping careers.

Professional services (for example, education and health, religion, engineering, publishing, the military) have as their central feature that "the professionals have a status obtained by education which is valuable in many different organizations, which is often protected by formal monopolies (e.g., lawyers), by the service being provided by the state itself (e.g., in most countries, education), or by both (e.g., in many countries, medicine)."[17] Other workers in professional services are either aspiring professionals (e.g., young researchers), subordinate professionals (e.g., nurses), or service communications personnel (e.g., secretaries or janitors). They are disproportionately recruited from the underprivileged, especially women, but also guest workers, racial minorities, and youth, who are vastly underpaid. Given the internal status system, apprentices to the professions are often rewarded with scholastic credits or certificates of professional competence rather than wages.

Bureaucratic services (for example, the government, banks, insurance organizations, nonprofit interest organizations) process claims of one sort or another and exhibit a general tendency toward monopoly. Hence, they developed extensive bureaucratic career structures. Unlike professional services, however, there is little transferability of competence from one organization to another and, unlike engineering-based industries, they lack the subordinate skilled manual workers.

Stinchcombe argued further that, since these seven labor markets not only look different but also function differently, they have consequences for social mobility. For example, those industries characterized by a bureaucratic organization of labor promote from within. By contrast, in the professional industries there are few promotions from within, but a great deal of hiring "at the top" from without. Given the emphasis of the status-attainment or human-capital approach on the individual characteristics of workers, this alternative perspective means that not only will the labor markets be distinguished by a different composition of workers (they do clearly recruit differently) but that in fact the same characteristics may well be variously rewarded in the different labor markets. Hence this chapter is devoted to resetting the questions asked earlier within this theoretical perspective of industrial labor markets that incorporates the organization of work.

Cubans and Mexicans in Labor Markets

Of course, the first question that we want to ask is this: *In what labor markets are Cubans and Mexicans inserted?* Table 15 shows

Table 15. *Cuban and Mexican Immigrants Working in Labor Markets, by Period of Immigration and by Sex*

	Males				Females			
	Cubans		Mexicans		Cubans		Mexicans	
Type of Industry	N	%	N	%	N	%	N	%
Immigrated 1960–1970								
Primary	11	1.3	156	26.4	1	0.1	55	17.3
Classical capitalist	115	13.6	72	12.2	269	37.9	89	27.9
Small skilled	166	19.6	128	21.6	60	8.4	18	5.7
Engineering-based	131	15.5	76	12.8	58	8.2	17	5.3
Petty bourgeois services	267	31.6	116	19.6	172	24.2	109	34.2
Professional	105	12.4	34	5.7	119	16.8	30	9.4
Bureaucratic	51	6.0	10	1.7	31	4.4	1	0.0
Total	846	100.0	592	100.0	710	100.0	319	99.8
Immigrated 1945–1959								
Primary	1	0.9	68	21.3	0	0.0	23	14.5
Classical capitalist	11	9.9	28	8.8	66	58.9	51	32.1
Small skilled	28	25.2	84	26.3	4	3.6	8	5.0
Engineering-based	17	15.3	44	13.8	3	2.7	6	3.8
Petty bourgeois services	37	33.3	74	23.2	28	25.0	54	34.0
Professional	11	9.9	18	5.6	9	8.0	16	10.1
Bureaucratic	6	5.4	3	0.9	2	1.8	1	0.6
Total	111	99.9	319	99.9	112	100.0	159	100.1

Note: Data are for immigrants who were 25 years of age or older at the time of immigration.
Source: U.S. Bureau of the Census, 1970 Public Use State Sample.

their differential insertion into the seven labor markets by period of immigration and by sex.

Clearly, Cubans and Mexicans differ in their insertion into labor markets, and the differences are large. About one-quarter of all Mexican men work in the primary labor market, where there are no Cubans; nearly one-third of Cubans but only one-fifth of Mexicans work in petty bourgeois services; and there are three times more Cubans working in professional and bureaucratic industries than Mexicans.

But there are also differences in the insertion of Cubans into labor markets as political versus economic immigrants. As political immigrants a larger proportion of Cuban men but fewer women work in the classical capitalist industries (13.6 percent of the political immigrants vs. 9.9 percent of the economic immigrants for the men; 37.9 percent vs. 58.9 percent for the women). Fewer men but more women work in the small-skilled sector (19.6 percent of the political immigrants vs. 25.2 percent of the economic immigrants for the men; 8.4 percent vs. 3.6 percent for the women). And a much larger proportion works in the professional industries (12.4 percent of the political immigrants vs. 9.9 percent of the economic immigrants for the men; for women the proportion of professionals doubled, 16.8 percent vs. 8.0 percent).

Given the differential labor market insertion of Cubans and Mexicans, next we would want to know: *Do the mean prestige and earnings of Cubans and Mexicans in the same labor market differ?* Tables 16 and 17 compare the mean occupational prestige and earnings of Cuban and Mexican men and women in each labor market by period of immigration. T-ratios, sensitive to small numbers of cases, test whether the difference in the means is significant.

Comparing those who immigrated prior to 1960, when Cubans were economic immigrants, we see that Cuban men attain distinctly better occupations in only two of the labor markets for which the number of cases allows comparison: the small-skilled industries and the petty bourgeois services. They attain distinctly higher earnings only when they work in the engineering-based industries.

The lack of cases in some labor markets does not allow comparisons between Cubans and Mexicans. This lack is due not only to a case base that, divided by sex, period of immigration, and seven labor markets yielded too few cases but also to the historical difference in labor market insertion of Cubans and Mexicans in America. We cannot compare Cubans and Mexicans in the primary and bureaucratic industries because Cubans never have been, either as economic or as political immigrants, part of the migrant labor work force in agriculture. We cannot compare Cubans and Mexicans in the bureaucratic industries because there are virtually no Mexicans in bureaucratic industries in America.

Comparing those who immigrated after 1960, when Cubans were political immigrants, we see that Cuban men fare significantly better than Mexican men in occupations attained in all seven labor markets. But Cubans never translate this advantage of being in better social slots within the same labor market—which may be *partly* due to the facilitating role of government policy—into earnings that are distinctly higher than the earnings of Mexicans.

For women who immigrated before 1960, the small number of cases allows comparison in only three labor markets: classical capitalist, petty bourgeois, and professional. Only in the petty bourgeois industries do Cuban women fare occupationally better than Mexican women. As economic immigrants, in none of the three do they fare better in income.

As political immigrants, Cuban women attain better occupational slots in three out of five labor markets we can compare—not only in the petty bourgeois services but also in the classical capitalist and professional industries. As we saw in the last chapter, for Cuban women, government policy facilitated their attainment of both better occupations and distinctly higher incomes. While as economic immigrants the earnings of Cuban and Mexican women are essentially the same, as political immigrants Cuban women earn significantly more than Mexican women in four out of five labor markets—classical capitalist, small-skilled, petty bourgeois, and professional.

The Value of Being a Cuban

To reset the questions asked earlier within this perspective of segmented labor markets, the seven labor markets were added as six dummy variables to the same initial regression equation of Chapter 4 for both Cubans and Mexicans together, with nationality included as an independent variable.[18] Prestige and earnings were regressed separately for political and economic immigrants. This enables us to compare the results of two equations. The equation that corresponded to the question *What is the value of being a Cuban political immigrant?* can be compared with this one, which corresponds to the question *What is the value of being a Cuban political immigrant when we take the labor markets into account?*

Table 18 summarizes the results of the regressions on prestige

Table 16. Mean Prestige and Earnings of Cuban and Mexican Male Immigrant Workers, by Labor Market Type and by Period of Immigration

| | Mean Occupational Prestige | | | | | | |
| | Cuban Males | | | Mexican Males | | | |
Type of Industry	Mean	S.D.	N	Mean	S.D.	N	T Ratio
Immigrated 1960–1970							
Primary	26.55	10.32	11	19.34	4.15	156	2.30*
Classical capitalist	31.97	7.72	115	26.53	8.00	72	4.59**
Small skilled	34.04	9.44	166	28.78	9.81	128	4.63**
Engineering-based	35.72	11.33	131	29.84	10.03	76	3.87**
Petty bourgeois	30.71	12.07	267	26.06	8.54	116	4.29**
Professional	51.30	22.47	105	41.06	23.50	34	2.23*
Bureaucratic	45.29	15.89	51	31.20	21.10	10	2.00*
Immigrated 1945–1959							
Primary	...	...	1	19.71	5.40	68	...
Classical capitalist	30.64	7.57	11	28.71	6.15	28	0.75
Small skilled	34.14	9.87	28	29.65	11.13	84	2.02*
Engineering-based	33.53	10.23	17	29.48	11.77	44	1.33
Petty bourgeois	33.03	12.56	37	27.53	10.46	74	2.29*
Professional	41.36	22.77	11	32.11	21.91	18	1.08
Bureaucratic	...	...	3	...	...	...	...

Mean Annual Earnings[a]

Type of Industry	Cuban Males			Mexican Males			
	Mean	S.D.	N	Mean	S.D.	N	T Ratio
Immigrated 1960–1970							
Primary	23.68	33.69	11	33.22	22.70	156	−0.92
Classical capitalist	51.32	31.19	115	44.64	26.09	72	1.58
Small skilled	53.98	36.22	166	50.67	32.49	128	0.82
Engineering-based	57.25	30.44	131	52.01	26.30	76	1.30
Petty bourgeois	52.12	39.66	267	45.53	28.29	116	1.84
Professional	89.86	86.90	105	63.79	89.49	34	1.49
Bureaucratic	59.97	45.29	51	38.90	35.57	10	1.63
Immigrated 1945–1959							
Primary	...	...	1	28.79	19.55	68	...
Classical capitalist	55.32	29.85	11	49.18	34.51	28	0.55
Small skilled	72.11	35.43	28	64.19	51.60	84	0.90
Engineering-based	74.03	20.67	17	58.98	31.06	44	2.19*
Petty bourgeois	63.11	48.90	37	47.68	30.63	74	1.74
Professional	103.05	117.55	11	78.61	132.81	18	0.52
Bureaucratic	...	...	3	...	...	6	...

Note: Data are for immigrants who were 25 years of age or older at the time of immigration.
Source: U.S. Bureau of the Census, 1970 Public Use State Sample.
[a] In hundreds of dollars.
 * Significant at the 0.05 level, two-tailed.
 ** Significant at the 0.01 level or higher, two-tailed.

Table 17. Mean Prestige and Earnings of Cuban and Mexican Female Immigrant Workers, by Labor Market Type and by Period of Immigration

	Mean Occupational Prestige						
	Cuban Females			Mexican Females			
Type of Industry	Mean	S.D.	N	Mean	S.D.	N	T Ratio
Immigrated 1960–1970							
Primary	...	...	1	18.18	1.39	55	...
Classical capitalist	27.52	6.57	269	25.75	4.56	89	2.82**
Small skilled	30.33	8.78	60	31.00	9.76	18	0.26
Engineering-based	33.93	7.92	58	31.35	9.47	17	1.02
Petty bourgeois	28.90	9.45	172	23.31	7.75	109	5.40**
Professional	45.16	16.78	119	36.53	18.53	30	2.32*
Bureaucratic	43.97	8.11	31	...	...	1	...
Immigrated 1945–1959							
Primary	...	...	...	18.83	3.06	23	...
Classical capitalist	27.15	5.50	66	25.82	4.63	51	1.42
Small skilled	...	...	4	...	...	8	...
Engineering-based	...	...	3	...	...	6	...
Petty bourgeois	29.14	11.02	28	23.02	8.42	54	2.58**
Professional	38.56	20.05	9	34.19	18.16	16	0.54
Bureaucratic	...	...	2	...	...	2	...

Mean Annual Earnings[a]

Type of Industry	Cuban Females			Mexican Females			
	Mean	S.D.	N	Mean	S.D.	N	T Ratio
Immigrated 1960–1970							
Primary	...	...	1	8.23	9.68	55	...
Classical capitalist	27.28	18.35	269	20.46	16.83	89	3.24**
Small skilled	33.05	19.96	60	19.22	14.91	18	3.17**
Engineering-based	36.00	23.43	58	34.91	22.67	17	0.17
Petty bourgeois	23.15	20.11	172	14.26	16.14	109	4.08**
Professional	34.97	30.26	119	24.30	22.27	30	2.17*
Bureaucratic	45.63	27.74	31	...	...	1	...
Immigrated 1945–1959							
Primary	...	...	...	10.59	15.19	23	...
Classical capitalist	24.42	18.08	66	22.40	16.59	51	0.53
Small skilled	...	...	4	...	...	8	...
Engineering-based	...	...	3	...	...	6	...
Petty bourgeois	23.11	22.81	28	20.06	30.05	54	0.51
Professional	37.39	32.15	9	25.94	30.47	16	0.87
Bureaucratic	...	...	2	...	...	1	...

Note: Data are for immigrants who were 25 years of age or older at the time of immigration.
Source: U.S. Bureau of the Census, 1970 Public Use State Sample.
[a]In hundreds of dollars.
* Significant at the 0.05 level, two-tailed.
** Significant at the 0.01 level or higher, two-tailed.

Table 18. *Partial (b) Regression Coefficients and Standard Error (b) of the Nationality Variable for Cuban and Mexican Immigrants, with Labor Markets Included, by Period of Immigration and by Sex*

	Nationality Variable			
	Occupational Prestige		Annual Earnings[a]	
	b	S.E. (b)	b	S.E. (b)
Immigrated 1960–1970				
Males	3.26	0.78	5.55	2.62
	R² = 0.428		R² = 0.307	
	N = 1351		N = 1351	
Females	2.31	0.89	6.17	1.37
	R² = 0.413		R² = 0.554	
	N = 839		N = 839	
Immigrated 1945–1959				
Males	−0.57	1.32	1.34	5.42
	R² = 0.385		R² = 0.402	
	N = 403		N = 403	
Females	0.11	1.38	−2.35	3.21
	R² = 0.364		R² = 0.328	
	N = 209		N = 209	

Note: Data are for immigrants who were 25 years of age or older at the time of immigration.
Source: U.S. Bureau of the Census, 1970 Public Use Sample.
[a] In hundreds of dollars.

and earnings for both men and women who immigrated during 1960–1970 and during 1945–1959. As before, a Z-test for the difference between the nationality coefficients in the political and economic migrations tells us the value of being a Cuban political immigrant when we take into account the differential labor market insertion of Cubans and Mexicans.

Table 19 shows that, taking the differential labor market insertion of Cubans and Mexicans into account, being a Cuban political immigrant is still significantly different (and positive) for men in their occupational prestige and for women in their earnings—but no longer for women's occupational attainment. In other words, the prestige advantage of Cuban women as political immigrants that we found earlier is possibly due entirely to the differential labor market insertion of Cuban and Mexican women, and particularly of

Cuban women as political versus economic migrants. I argued that many of the specific programs instituted by the state to facilitate the structural assimilation of Cuban political immigrants targeted the essentially female occupations and opened access to those professions that otherwise would have remained largely inaccessible. Comparing political to economic immigrants, Table 15 indeed shows the large decrease of Cuban women working in the classical capitalist industries and the large increase of Cuban women working in the professional and bureaucratic labor markets. Thus when the difference in their labor market insertion is taken into account, the advantage in occupational prestige that Cuban women have as political immigrants "washes out." But that differential labor market insertion is at least partly an effect of the helping hand the state extended. The advantage that they have in earnings, on the other hand, is over and beyond that produced by differential labor market insertion. As we saw, as political immigrants Cuban women earn significantly more than Mexican women in nearly all the labor markets.

Likewise, for men, the advantage in occupational prestige Cuban men as political immigrants have is over and beyond that produced by their differential labor market insertion. As we saw, as political immigrants Cuban men are placed in distinctly better occupational slots than Mexicans in every labor market. I argue that this is at least partly due to the helping hand of the state.

Labor markets, as described, are partly characterized by the composition of their workers—by differences in skill and education—and their recruitment of the underprivileged or fortunate. For men and women who immigrated in the sixties, Tables 20 and 21 present the mean values of the social characteristics of Cubans and Mexicans in each labor market. They confirm the unequal com-

Table 19. *Z-Test for the Partial Coefficients of the Nationality Variable for the Difference between the Migrations of the Political Period (1960–1970) and the Economic Period (1945–1959), with Labor Markets Included, by Sex*

	Nationality Variable	
	Occupational Prestige	Annual Earnings
Males	2.50 *	0.70
Females	1.34	2.44 *

* Significant at the 0.01 level, one-tail test.

Table 20. *Means and Standard Deviations for the Social Characteristics of Cuban and Mexican Males Working in Labor Markets Who Immigrated during 1960–1970*

	Cuban Males		Mexican Males	
Type of Industry	*Mean*	*S.D.*	*Mean*	*S.D.*
Primary				
Age	⋯	⋯	42.15	11.05
Length of U.S. experience	⋯	⋯	4.84	2.50
Skilled work	⋯	⋯	0.04	0.20
South	⋯	⋯	0.18	0.38
Vocational training	⋯	⋯	0.03	0.18
Citizenship	⋯	⋯	0.19	0.40
Weeks worked	⋯	⋯	42.40	12.04
Years of school completed	⋯	⋯	3.19	2.86
High school graduation	⋯	⋯	0.02	0.14
College graduation	⋯	⋯	0.00	0.00
N	7		145	
Classical capitalist				
Age	44.44	9.57	35.52	8.93
Length of U.S. experience	4.43	2.44	3.79	2.20
Skilled work	0.95	0.21	0.86	0.35
South	0.48	0.50	0.24	0.43
Vocational training	0.19	0.40	0.09	0.29
Citizenship	0.20	0.40	0.30	0.46
Weeks worked	44.09	3.80	44.74	10.40
Years of school completed	8.73	3.80	6.52	4.04
High school graduation	0.31	0.47	0.17	0.38
College graduation	0.06	0.25	0.02	0.12
N	109		66	
Small skilled				
Age	43.09	8.99	38.24	9.57
Length of U.S. experience	4.17	2.36	4.39	2.43
Skilled work	0.90	0.30	0.67	0.47
South	0.59	0.49	0.21	0.41
Vocational training	0.21	0.41	0.11	0.31
Citizenship	0.16	0.37	0.24	0.42
Weeks worked	43.34	13.77	44.80	9.97
Years of school completed	8.35	4.05	5.06	3.44
High school graduation	0.28	0.45	0.07	0.25
College graduation	0.07	0.25	0.01	0.09
N	162		122	
Engineering-based				
Age	43.26	8.76	37.30	9.23
Length of U.S. experience	4.61	2.48	4.80	2.51
Skilled work	0.91	0.29	0.78	0.41
South	0.44	0.50	0.09	0.30
Vocational training	0.31	0.46	0.09	0.29
Citizenship	0.23	0.42	0.24	0.43

Table 20 (*continued*)

Type of Industry	Cuban Males		Mexican Males	
	Mean	S.D.	Mean	S.D.
Weeks worked	46.12	10.71	45.88	11.05
Years of school completed	10.42	4.12	5.88	3.43
High school graduation	0.49	0.50	0.11	0.31
College graduation	0.17	0.37	0.01	0.12
N	121		74	
Petty bourgeois				
Age	46.86	10.88	38.09	8.90
Length of U.S. experience	4.88	2.50	4.43	2.44
Skilled work	0.63	0.48	0.50	0.50
South	0.59	0.49	0.18	0.39
Vocational training	0.27	0.45	0.13	0.34
Citizenship	0.16	0.37	0.30	0.46
Weeks worked	46.86	9.49	44.73	1.80
Years of school completed	9.81	3.65	6.35	4.06
High school graduation	0.43	0.50	0.19	0.40
College graduation	0.07	0.25	0.00	0.00
N	256		109	
Professional				
Age	48.35	9.58	38.03	16.24
Length of U.S. experience	5.48	2.47	3.59	2.10
Skilled work	0.87	0.34	0.81	0.40
South	0.47	0.50	0.34	0.48
Vocational training	0.39	0.49	0.28	0.46
Citizenship	0.29	0.46	0.31	0.47
Weeks worked	46.63	10.48	43.98	12.26
Years of school completed	14.03	4.45	11.37	5.54
High school graduation	0.74	0.44	0.56	0.40
College graduation	0.54	0.50	0.31	0.47
N	99		32	
Bureaucratic				
Age	42.62	9.82	...	...
Length of U.S. experience	4.88	2.53	...	...
Skilled work	0.88	0.33	...	...
South	0.26	0.44	...	...
Vocational training	0.48	0.51	...	...
Citizenship	0.36	0.48	...	...
Weeks worked	48.05	9.39	...	...
Years of school completed	14.29	3.17	...	...
High school graduation	0.90	0.30	...	...
College graduation	0.43	0.50	...	...
N	42		7	

Note: Data are for immigrants who were 25 years of age or older at the time of immigration.
Source: U.S. Bureau of the Census, 1970 Public Use State Sample.

Table 21. *Means and Standard Deviations for the Social Characteristics of Cuban and Mexican Females Working in Labor Markets Who Immigrated during 1960–1970*

	Cuban Females		Mexican Females	
Type of Industry	Mean	S.D.	Mean	S.D.
Primary				
Age	⋯	⋯	41.50	8.89
Length of U.S. experience	⋯	⋯	4.52	2.48
Skilled work	⋯	⋯	0.02	0.15
South	⋯	⋯	0.19	0.40
Vocational training	⋯	⋯	0.00	0.00
Citizenship	⋯	⋯	0.26	0.44
Weeks worked	⋯	⋯	18.60	16.80
Years of school completed	⋯	⋯	3.64	2.67
High school graduation	⋯	⋯	0.02	0.15
College graduation	⋯	⋯	0.00	0.00
N	1		42	
Classical capitalist				
Age	43.88	9.50	40.29	8.74
Length of U.S. experience	4.50	2.45	4.75	2.51
Skilled work	0.98	0.14	0.96	0.21
South	0.57	0.50	0.20	0.40
Vocational training	0.17	0.37	0.12	0.32
Citizenship	0.12	0.33	0.30	0.46
Weeks worked	39.71	14.73	36.48	17.51
Years of school completed	8.82	3.66	5.77	3.57
High school graduation	0.30	0.46	0.07	0.26
College graduation	0.09	0.28	0.01	0.12
N	238		69	
Small skilled				
Age	39.49	8.23	⋯	⋯
Length of U.S. experience	4.48	2.47	⋯	⋯
Skilled work	0.91	0.30	⋯	⋯
South	0.40	0.49	⋯	⋯
Vocational training	0.26	0.45	⋯	⋯
Citizenship	0.21	0.41	⋯	⋯
Weeks worked	41.98	14.26	⋯	⋯
Years of school completed	9.68	4.46	⋯	⋯
High school graduation	0.45	0.50	⋯	⋯
College graduation	0.13	0.34	⋯	⋯
N	53		18	
Engineering-based				
Age	41.24	10.90	⋯	⋯
Length of U.S. experience	4.17	2.38	⋯	⋯
Skilled work	0.98	0.14	⋯	⋯
South	0.39	0.50	⋯	⋯
Vocational training	0.49	0.37	⋯	⋯
Citizenship	0.16	12.50	⋯	⋯

Table 21 (*continued*)

Type of Industry	Cuban Females		Mexican Females	
	Mean	*S.D.*	*Mean*	*S.D.*
Weeks worked	43.47	3.31	...	...
Years of school completed	11.16	0.49	...	...
High school graduation	0.61	0.30	...	...
College graduation	0.10	7.52	...	...
N		51		17
Petty bourgeois				
Age	45.23	9.66	40.56	9.65
Length of U.S. experience	5.02	2.51	4.58	2.48
Skilled work	0.65	0.48	0.42	0.50
South	0.73	0.45	0.30	0.46
Vocational training	0.25	0.43	0.10	0.31
Citizenship	0.17	0.38	0.30	0.46
Weeks worked	37.75	16.01	35.39	16.39
Years of school completed	9.95	3.43	5.47	4.07
High school graduation	0.51	0.50	0.16	0.36
College graduation	0.05	0.22	0.00	0.00
N		133		77
Professional				
Age	43.54	8.70	35.62	9.13
Length of U.S. experience	5.13	2.51	4.42	2.48
Skilled work	0.76	0.43	0.42	0.50
South	0.41	0.49	0.19	0.40
Vocational training	0.37	0.48	0.19	0.40
Citizenship	0.24	0.43	0.35	0.49
Weeks worked	40.84	14.24	37.67	15.92
Years of school completed	13.00	4.36	8.12	5.04
High school graduation	0.77	0.42	0.35	0.49
College graduation	0.40	0.49	0.12	0.33
N		93		2(
Bureaucratic				
Age	40.22	8.09	...	...
Length of U.S. experience	5.83	2.40	...	...
Skilled work	0.96	0.19	...	...
South	0.44	0.51	...	...
Vocational training	0.37	0.49	...	...
Citizenship	0.37	0.49	...	...
Weeks worked	46.02	11.80	...	...
Years of school completed	13.81	3.23	...	...
High school graduation	0.85	0.36	...	...
College graduation	0.37	0.49	...	...
N		27		1

Note: Data are for immigrants who were 25 years of age or older at the time of immigration.

Source: U.S. Bureau of the Census, 1970 Public Use State Sample.

Table 22. Z-Test for the Partial Coefficients of the Nationality Variable for the Difference between the Two Equations with and without Labor Markets Included, by Period of Immigration and by Sex

	Nationality Variable	
	Occupational Prestige	Annual Earnings
Immigrated 1960–1970		
Males	−0.42	−0.33
Females	0.35	0.00
Immigrated 1945–1959		
Males	0.15	0.12
Females	−0.07	0.00

position of the labor forces the seven labor markets hold. So much so, that if we compare the former equation, which did not include the labor market dummies (see Chapter 4), with this equation, which does, as Table 22 shows, there is no significant difference in the nationality coefficient between the two. That is, adding the labor market dummies does not appreciably reduce the size of the nationality coefficient because the compositional differences (in age, proportion who do skilled work, or were college graduates, and the like) that partly characterize the labor markets were already present. Hence, the impact of differential insertion into the various labor markets has yet to be accounted for.

Labor Market Consequences

Reset within the labor markets perspective, the argument of this study—that what is distinct about Cuban political immigrants is not only their higher social class origin but also the facilitating role the state played—takes two forms. First, as political immigrants Cubans fare distinctly better than Mexicans in some labor markets (either in occupations or earnings attained within them), while as economic immigrants Cubans differ from Mexicans in few respects. Furthermore, Cuban political immigrants fare better than Cuban economic immigrants in some labor markets. Second, as I stressed, part of the difference between Cubans and Mexicans lies in their differential insertion into labor markets. This is especially true of Cuban political immigrants, whose access to the professional and bureaucratic labor markets opened up with the helping hand of the state. This is particularly important because, as Stinch-combe argued, not only do labor markets look different in their labor force composition, but they function differently, which holds consequences for social mobility and outcomes. Hence a new question arises: *How much of a difference does differential insertion into the labor markets make?*

As Tables 16 and 17 show, the mean prestige and earnings of workers in the seven labor markets differ substantially,[19] irrespective of who works in them (Cubans, Mexicans, women, or men). Thus being inserted in a certain labor market is tantamount to being inserted in a certain *opportunity structure* with ceilings and floors on what men and women can achieve there. In Chapter 4, we compared Cuban and Mexican adult immigrants with the same educational level, as an index of their social class origin, and we consistently found that, whether they immigrated before or after 1960, it was Cubans without high school diplomas who achieved distinctly higher occupations and income. To examine the reason, Table 23 presents the differential labor market insertion of Cuban and Mexican men who immigrated during the sixties without high school diplomas. Mexicans are overwhelmingly inserted in the primary labor market (29.7 percent), where there are no Cubans (1.51 percent). The primary labor market obviously presents the least opportunity to attain desirable occupations and wages. This accounts

Table 23. *Labor Market Insertion of Cuban and Mexican Males Who Immigrated during 1960–1970 with Less than High School Graduation (in Percentages)*

Type of Industry	Cuban Males	Mexican Males
Primary	1.51	29.71
Classical capitalist	17.06	11.65
Small skilled	26.13	23.31
Engineering	14.47	13.20
Petty bourgeois	33.05	18.05
Professional	5.62	3.11
Bureaucratic	2.16	0.97
Total percentage	100.00	100.00
N	463	515

Note: Data are for immigrants who were 25 years of age or older at the time of immigration.
Source: U.S. Bureau of the Census, 1970 Public Use State Sample.

for the difference in achievement found earlier. As throughout the long history of their immigration, Mexicans continue to serve as a source of cheap labor for agriculture.

Returns to the Human Capital of Cubans and Mexicans

Labor markets are partly characterized by the composition of their workers. Tables 20 and 21 clearly show that, for example, there are virtually no college graduates in the classical capitalist or petty bourgeois industries, while a large proportion of those engaged in the professional services are college graduates. To witness the effect of segmented labor markets, we return to the classic question of status-attainment research addressed in the last chapter: *What are the returns to the characteristics of workers—in the same labor market?*

Tables 24 and 25 present the results of the regressions on prestige and earnings for Cuban and Mexican men who immigrated during 1960–1970 in the four labor markets that we can compare: classical capitalist, small-skilled, engineering, and petty bourgeois. Within each labor market, a Z-test was employed for the difference between the returns to the social characteristics of Cuban and Mexican men in the same labor market. Table 26 shows the results of the Z-test.

The answer is quite clear: there are no real differences in the returns to the characteristics of Cuban and Mexican workers who work in the same industrial labor market. Only a few individual characteristics show a significant difference: age in the classical capitalist and small-skilled industries; length of U.S. experience in the small-skilled sector; and number of weeks worked in the small-skilled and petty bourgeois sectors. But the partial coefficients are terribly small: they hardly produce a return in either prestige or earnings. The differences in the return to college graduation show up as significantly different in two instances: in the small-skilled and engineering-based industries, Mexican college graduates do better than Cuban college graduates. But there are no Mexican college graduates to speak of in either of these industries (1 percent, see Table 20). Hence, no major differences exist in the returns to the individual characteristics of workers in the same industrial labor market.

Impact of Labor Markets

It is most important that there are no real differences in the returns to the characteristics of Cubans and Mexicans in the same labor

Table 24. Partial (b) Regression Coefficients and Standard Error (b) for the Effects of Specified Variables on Occupational Prestige, for Cuban and Mexican Males Who Immigrated during 1960–1970, by Labor Market Type

	Classical Capitalist		Small Skilled		Engineering		Petty Bourgeois		Professional	
	Cuban Males	Mexican Males	Cuban Males	Mexican Males	Cuban Males	Mexican Males	Cuban Males	Mexican Males	Cuban Males	Mexican Males
Age	0.13 (0.08)	−0.24 (0.13)	−0.25 (0.08)	0.06 (0.10)	−0.43 (0.12)	−0.11 (0.15)	−0.12 (0.07)	−0.22 (0.11)	−0.14 (0.17)	...
Length of U.S. experience	0.22 (0.32)	0.60 (0.52)	0.30 (0.33)	−0.79 (0.37)	0.41 (0.44)	0.50 (0.54)	0.40 (0.32)	0.61 (0.38)	−0.74 (0.76)	...
South	2.69 (1.36)	3.66 (2.37)	−1.30 (1.47)	−2.71 (2.07)	4.59 (1.99)	9.61 (4.45)	0.16 (1.54)	4.81 (2.08)	1.61 (3.24)	...
Vocational training	6.11 (1.83)	9.26 (3.57)	1.31 (1.82)	2.77 (2.80)	1.47 (2.31)	0.69 (4.19)	2.38 (1.72)	1.71 (2.46)	−0.43 (3.33)	...
Citizenship	0.01 (1.69)	−0.64 (2.21)	−1.00 (2.02)	−2.44 (1.91)	−1.84 (2.36)	3.06 (2.82)	−0.21 (2.10)	0.67 (1.75)	10.02 (4.00)	...
Weeks worked	−0.02 (0.06)	−0.05 (0.10)	0.04 (0.05)	0.27 (0.09)	−0.12 (0.09)	−0.05 (0.11)	0.10 (0.08)	0.12 (0.07)	−0.26 (0.16)	...
Years of school completed	0.51 (0.36)	0.02 (0.38)	−0.25 (0.34)	−0.12 (0.31)	0.41 (0.59)	0.53 (0.49)	0.79 (0.42)	0.23 (0.30)	3.23 (1.10)	...
High school graduation	−2.81 (2.54)	1.74 (3.83)	2.90 (2.79)	1.09 (4.09)	0.61 (4.01)	−1.90 (5.52)	−2.88 (2.75)	2.22 (2.97)	−4.77 (7.96)	...
College graduation	2.35 (3.62)	−1.63 (8.70)	9.73 (3.51)	43.37 (10.64)	2.46 (3.55)	17.39 (11.10)	0.70 (3.85)	...	5.79 (6.21)	...
R^2	0.254	0.205	0.158	0.264	0.201	0.231	0.079	0.167	0.566	...
N	109	66	162	122	121	74	256	109	99	...

Note: Data are for immigrants who were 25 years of age or older at the time of immigration. Standard errors are in parentheses.
Source: U.S. Bureau of the Census, 1970 Public Use State Sample.

Table 25. *Partial (b) Regression Coefficients and Standard Error (b) for the Effects of Specified Variables on Annual Earnings[a], for Cuban and Mexican Males Who Immigrated during 1960–1970, by Labor Market Type*

	Classical Capitalist		Small Skilled		Engineering		Petty Bourgeois		Professional	
	Cuban Males	Mexican Males	Cuban Males	Mexican Males	Cuban Males	Mexican Males	Cuban Males	Mexican Males	Cuban Males	Mexican Males
Age	−0.78	−0.54	−0.43	−0.02	−0.47	0.30	−0.49	−0.54	−1.43	...
	(0.25)	(0.37)	(0.27)	(0.30)	(0.28)	(0.34)	(0.22)	(0.34)	(0.81)	...
Length of U.S. experience	4.19	2.73	1.79	1.40	3.10	1.03	1.41	3.76	−1.49	...
	(1.01)	(1.48)	(1.07)	(1.15)	(1.05)	(1.24)	(0.95)	(1.21)	(3.52)	...
Skilled work	12.67	−4.66	−5.66	−2.71	8.36	7.14	12.31	10.00	21.99	...
	(10.39)	(8.24)	(8.02)	(5.47)	(7.95)	(6.40)	(4.79)	(5.31)	(23.87)	...
South	−3.50	−1.44	−14.79	−23.58	−8.71	−18.86	−5.59	−5.53	−0.03	...
	(4.33)	(6.76)	(4.85)	(6.61)	(4.76)	(10.41)	(4.60)	(6.78)	(15.09)	...
Vocational training	16.51	2.64	1.27	13.12	11.94	16.97	0.61	−14.10	9.89	...
	(5.86)	(10.11)	(5.91)	(8.63)	(5.51)	(9.60)	(5.15)	(7.97)	(15.34)	...

Citizenship	0.11	−5.72	7.53	0.39	−3.93	10.04	8.15	−3.98	64.83	⋮
	(5.39)	(6.24)	(6.60)	(5.88)	(5.61)	(6.47)	(6.28)	(5.53)	(18.51)	⋮
Weeks worked	1.19	0.64	1.25	1.19	0.92	0.84	1.09	0.40	1.95	⋮
	(0.19)	(0.27)	(0.17)	(0.28)	(0.22)	(0.25)	(0.24)	(0.21)	(0.75)	⋮
Years of school completed	1.47	2.26	−0.82	0.89	−0.07	−0.28	2.21	−0.23	8.01	⋮
	(1.15)	(1.08)	(1.09)	(0.95)	(1.40)	(1.12)	(1.25)	(0.96)	(5.10)	⋮
High school graduation	−9.53	−4.23	10.08	4.79	−2.92	3.45	−1.70	13.71	−40.19	⋮
	(8.21)	(10.86)	(9.07)	(12.61)	(9.56)	(12.68)	(8.21)	(9.44)	(36.74)	⋮
College graduation	6.31	−33.21	15.81	6.59	2.01	63.79	−15.06	⋯	15.25	⋮
	(11.52)	(24.47)	(11.44)	(33.17)	(8.46)	(25.47)	(10.71)	⋯	(28.79)	⋮
R^2	0.509	0.281	0.385	0.322	0.305	0.373	0.218	0.206	0.394	⋮
N	109	66	162	122	121	74	256	109	99	⋮

Note: Data are for immigrants who were 25 years of age or older at the time of immigration.

Source: U.S. Bureau of the Census, 1970 Public Use State Sample.

Note: Standard errors are in parentheses.

[a] In hundreds of dollars.

Table 26. Z-Test for the Difference between the Partial Coefficients of the Social Characteristics of Cuban and Mexican Male Workers Who Immigrated during 1960–1970, by Labor Market Type

| | Cubans vs. Mexicans in Each Labor Market | | | | | | | |
| | Classical Capitalist | | Small Skilled | | Engineering | | Petty Bourgeois | |
	Prestige	Earnings	Prestige	Earnings	Prestige	Earnings	Prestige	Earnings
Age	2.42*	-0.54	-2.42*	1.02	1.67	-1.75	0.76	0.12
Length of U.S. experience	-0.62	0.82	2.20*	0.25	0.13	1.28	-0.42	-1.53
Skilled work	N.A.	1.31	N.A.	0.30	N.A.	0.12	N.A.	0.32
South	0.36	-0.26	0.48	1.07	-1.03	0.89	-1.80	-0.01
Vocational training	-0.79	1.18	-0.44	1.13	0.16	-0.45	0.22	1.55
Citizenship	0.23	0.71	0.52	0.81	-1.33	-1.63	-0.32	1.45
Weeks worked	0.26	1.67	-2.23*	0.18	-0.49	0.24	0.19	2.16*
Years of school completed	0.94	-0.50	0.28	-1.18	-0.16	0.12	1.08	1.55
High school graduation	-0.99	-0.39	0.37	0.34	-0.19	-0.40	-1.26	1.23
College graduation	0.42	1.46	-3.00**	0.26	-1.28	-2.30*	...	...

N.A. = not applicable.

* Significant at the 0.05 level, two-tail test.
** Significant at the 0.01 level, two-tail test.

Table 27. *Partial (b) Regression Coefficients and Standard Error (b) of the Citizenship Variable for Cuban Males Who Immigrated during 1960–1970, by Labor Market Type*

	Citizenship Variable			
	Occupational Prestige		Annual Earnings[a]	
Type of Industry	b	S.E. (b)	b	S.E. (b)
Primary	...	...	...	...
Classical capitalist	0.01	1.69	0.11	5.39
Small skilled	−1.00	2.02	7.53	6.60
Engineering-based	−1.84	2.36	−3.93	5.61
Petty bourgeois	−0.21	2.10	8.15	6.28
Professional	10.02	4.00	64.83	18.51
Bureaucratic	...	...	...	...

Note: Data are for immigrants who were 25 years of age or older at the time of immigration.
Source: U.S. Bureau of the Census, 1970 Public Use State Sample.
[a] In hundreds of dollars.

market. It means that virtually all the differences between them that we found in the last chapter—in the impact of citizenship, weeks worked, or college graduation on prestige and earnings— were due to their differential labor market insertion, not only because the labor markets look different but moreover because they function differently.

How differently, then, do they function? Stinchcombe's argument that the labor markets function differently and hold consequences for social mobility can be demonstrated empirically by focusing on the returns to the same characteristic in the different industries.

Take, for example, citizenship, which in the last chapter we found to be a large and consistent difference between Cubans and Mexicans. Table 27 presents the coefficients of the variable citizenship in five labor markets for Cuban men who immigrated during the sixties. We have already seen that there is no significant difference in the returns to citizenship between Cuban and Mexican males in the four labor markets we could compare. Now focusing on Cubans alone allows us to see how different the labor markets function and to watch the payoff citizenship has in the professional industry.

We do not need a Z-test to see the enormous difference that labor market insertion makes. Workers who are citizens working in the classical capitalist industry receive a meager increase of 0.01 prestige points and $11.00 more a year. But workers who are citizens in the professional labor market receive an astounding increase of 10.02 prestige points and $6,483 more a year. Hence the difference in the returns to being a citizen that we observed in the last chapter is explained, for while the proportion who are citizens does not differ greatly for Cuban and Mexican men who immigrated in the decade of the sixties, their labor market insertion does. About 20 percent of Cuban men and 25 percent of Mexican men are citizens (see Table 9). But Mexicans are overwhelmingly concentrated in the primary sector, where citizenship has absolutely no payoff. For Mexicans working in the primary labor market, being a citizen entails a cost of 1.06 prestige points and $99 in earnings.[20] This is a citizenship that lacks any other value than to enable the worker to remain in this country and continue to work. In contrast, Cubans are inserted in those labor markets—the professional and bureaucratic—where citizenship makes a dramatic difference. This explains the differences in the returns to the individual characteristics of Cubans and Mexicans that we observed in the last chapter.

More important, we have seen how different the segmented labor markets function and their various consequences for the processes of social mobility. Thus the theoretical assumptions of the status-attainment or human-capital approach to stratification are critically contested. Their focus on the individual characteristics of workers missed the organization of industry and work.

It was Marx's insight that the manner in which human beings produce is critically determinant of their social relations. In the early stages of capitalism that fundamental relation could be encompassed, conceptually and empirically, by stark categories of capitalists versus workers. That corresponded to the reality of that initial period of industrialization when the middle classes had not yet emerged and the state played a far less arbitrating and administering role. With the process of development of capitalism and the accompanying transformation of the labor force that it entailed, all sorts of people indeed emerged who by no stretch of the conceptual or empirical imagination can be fitted into these initial categories.[21] That cannot be denied. But neither should it be ignored that human beings still stand in relations of production before one another. More variegated and less stark as these have become, they still hold consequences for the lives of individuals.

6. The Functions of Political and Economic Migration

The Type of Migration and the Role of the State

Political refugees and economic immigrants. Their markings come from two separate sources: their attitudes and their states. Their attitudes mark them. Without doubt, all societies are simultaneously political and economic. Thus political and economic conditions often entangle in the attitudes of individuals, particularly in the consequential decision to emigrate from the land of birth. But the snarl was not the same for Cubans and Mexicans. Cubans emigrated feeling politically disaffected with the Cuban revolution, even when economic reasons lay at the source of their disaffection. In the beginning years of the revolution, political disaffection easily resulted when government policies that changed the basic economic allocation dislocated people, causing them to lose their economic, social, and ideological "place." Thereafter, Cuba rebuilt itself on the Eastern European model of communism as a new system of political *and* economic organization. Then either the lack of civil liberties or the frustrated economic aspirations or the weight of both led Cubans to political disaffection. Mexicans, on the other hand, always emigrated in search of better job opportunities. Their search never entailed political disaffection.

Their states also marked them. Once on American shores, the U.S. government classified them as political and economic immigrants. The reception of the new Haitian immigrants in the 1980s makes this role of the government clear. In the countries they left, the state also branded them as political and economic émigrés. For nearly two decades after the Cuban revolution, until the Dialogue between the Cuban community in the United States and the Cuban government, Cuba barred the exiles from returning to Cuba, even to visit relatives. Mexican immigrants, on the other hand, have always freely returned to Mexico, with the sole proof of a birth certificate. In addition, as we have seen, in the United States the state lent Cubans a firm helping hand while it ignored Mexicans. We have seen the effects of this varying treatment. We ought now to explain this marked contrast in attention.

To understand the varying roles of these states, we must consider the functions of the two types of migration. By a functional explanation, as Arthur Stinchcombe defined it, "we mean one in which the *consequences* of some behavior or social arrangement are essential elements of the *causes* of that behavior."[1] The Mexican migration provided Mexico with a fortuitous safety valve, the United States with a dependable source of cheap labor. Thus a system of economic migration developed and America largely ignored the assimilation of Mexicans. The Cuban political migration provided Cuba with a chance to externalize dissent, the United States with symbols around which to build legitimacy during the Cold War. Hence a system of political migration ensued, and in America Cubans encountered a generous reception.

Theories of the State

The states played critical roles in defining the immigrants and arranging their exit and reception. Yet, as Anthony Giddens pointed out, despite the expanding role of the state in social life over the course of this century, until fairly recently "the state has been largely ignored in sociology—by those of a Marxist persuasion as well as by others."[2] Likewise, over a decade ago, J. P. Nettl complained of "the relative 'statelessness' of American social science."[3]

Over the last decade, interest in the role of the state as a social actor has emerged, particularly in Marxist debates. These Marxist debates can be summarized as two contrasting positions: the instrumentalist versus the expressive views of the state.[4] In brief, the instrumentalist view of the state, typified by the analysis of Ralph Milliband, saw the state as an instrument of the ruling, capitalist class.[5] This ruling class was, first, unified by common interests, purposes, backgrounds, and life-styles, and, second, able to manipulate the state at will. The expressive view of the state, typified by the structural Marxism of Nicos Poulantzas, saw the state as possessing a "relative autonomy" from the capitalist class.[6] To preserve the functioning of the whole capitalist society, the state sometimes needed to favor other groups at the expense of the capitalist class—hence, it expressed all social classes. Poulantzas's emphasis on the relative autonomy of the state and its shifting role regarding social classes bore closer resemblance to social reality than the instrumentalist notion of a state that is but a horse to a rider. But Poulantzas's analysis suffered from the shortcoming of structuralism: its failure to incorporate living, breathing, thinking human beings who struggle to affect their social environment.[7] Moreover, both views failed to recognize what Giddens stressed: that the state is an independent source of power, sometimes horse, sometimes rider, always a national actor.[8]

Among theories of the state Charles Tilly distinguished three families: developmental, functional, and historical theories.[9] While not necessarily incompatible, and encompassing much variation, the focus of these theories differed. Essentially, developmental theories of the state are evolutionary, often focusing on the origins of the state or on the expectation that underdeveloped countries would follow the path of political development and modernization.[10] As Tilly observed, their "extreme concentration on the individual nation, political system, society, *or* state has drawn attention away from the international structures of power within which 'development' takes place."[11] And that interdependence of international political structures often shapes development.

Functional theories of the state focus on the functions the state must try to fulfill. In James O'Connor's analysis, for example, the capitalist state must serve to promote accumulation and legitimization, "two basic and often mutually contradictory functions."[12] The advantage of functional theories of the state, Tilly noted, is that they highlight what the developmental theories obscure: the relationship between state policy and the system of stratification as well as their use of coercion. Their disadvantage, however, lies in that the problems to be solved, accumulation and legitimization, are of such breadth that they do no serve to define the capitalist state. For example, communist societies must also try to fulfill these two basic and often contradictory functions. Hence, it is not what functions the state serves that distinguishes among nations, but how they go about serving them.

Last, historical theories of the state are those that see the characteristics of any particular government as deriving from "its individual relationship to some historical transformation affecting the world as a whole."[13] For example, dependency theory, such as André Gunder Frank's analysis of the development of underdevelopment or Immanuel Wallerstein's theory of the birth of one modern world-system, saw nation states as shaped by the large-scale international, economic processes that enveloped them.[14] While dependency theory had the virtue of placing the problem of underdevelopment onto the stage of the international arena of political and economic power that conditions the possibilities for development, its prognosis that underdeveloped countries would remain in stagnation flew in the face of the sustained development of some nations in the periphery, such as Brazil.[15] Moreover, the grand sweep of dependency theory ignored the contribution of modernization theory with its stress on the internal actors involved in the process of development, such as the state and social classes in underdeveloped nations.[16] These theories, then, were not only historical, as Tilly called them, but global in scope; hence, they failed to distinguish the enormous variation that now exists among nations faced with a common situation of inequality.

To understand the state as a significant political and social actor, a different type of historical theory of the state is necessary: one that is less global and enmeshed in worldwide transformations but that still focuses on the legacy of particular histories. As Tilly later argued, the value of historical sociology lies in its "systematic appreciation of the significance of time and place for social processes."[17] J. P. Nettl aimed to bring the analysis of the state back into the comparative analysis of societies, where the state itself would be regarded as a conceptual variable. In assessing the substance of their political life, different societies could be compared according to what Nettl called their "degree of stateness." As such, the notion of the state was to be "not merely a ragbag synonym of government" but a center of "the *institutionalization* of power."[18] Nettl considered the functions and structures that corresponded to the state to be among its variable components.

For Nettl, the degree of stateness depended on the degree of state autonomy vis-à-vis other institutions; the cultural disposition to identify the nation with the state and to recognize it as a significant actor in political and social life; the impact of federalism; the structuring of dissent; the effective institutionalization of public opinion through elections and political parties; the extent of development of state bureaucracy; and its very notion as cognitively expressed. All these varied among Western societies, yet all concerned the internal role of the state. The state, as Nettl observed, has another role, invariant among societies: in the international arena the state is an "international diplomatic persona."[19] Whatever the state may be regarding civil society—the degree of stateness that varies across societies—its sovereignty and autonomy as an international actor are indivisible and uncontested.

Migration policy lies at the crossroads of the internal and international roles of the state. When migration policy hinges on the interests of foreign policy, as it did when the United States supported Cuban exiles during the period of the Cold War, the state acts in its international role of national actor. When migration policy reacts to domestic exigencies, as it did when the United States deported illegal aliens during times of recession and unemployment, the state acts in its internal role. Regarding immigration the role of the state lies at the crossroads of its two roles, internal and international; hence, it is impossible to predict what actions the state will pursue regarding immigrants. But neither should the analysis of immigration fail to incorporate it—nor should the analysis of modern societies. The varying functions of the Cuban and Mexican migration show the need to bring the state back in; not, however, with set predictions as to its role but with an eye to assess the courses taken at different times and places. In concert, the policies of the two states in the sending and receiving societies set in motion systems of political and economic migration.

The Functions of Economic Migration

Source of Cheap Labor: The United States

In the wake of the urgency and alarm that surrounds discussions of Mexican immigration in the United States, together with the growing recognition of the prevalence of "guest worker" programs in developed capitalist societies across Western Europe and South Africa,[20] attention turned from compiling its legal and social history to theoretical attempts to explain the functions of economic migration. The question became: *Why should developed capitalist countries wittingly and unwittingly allow so many poor, unskilled immigrants in their midst?* Because immigrants from underdeveloped nations are a source of cheap labor.

Recent theoretical analyses have stressed the increased significance of immigrant workers in developed capitalist societies as a way of counteracting the traditional perspective of studies of labor migration that focused on the migrants themselves, their reasons for migration, and its consequences for them. With different emphases, Michael Burawoy's comparative analysis of the United States and South Africa, Manuel Castells's comparative analysis of Western European nations, and Alejandro Portes's analysis of Mexican immigration to the United States reformulated the problem by examining the structural sources and social and economic implications of labor migration.[21] In a nutshell, all three agreed that migrant labor—as immigrant and as labor—has structural causes. Hence, it performs important functions for the society that receives them. They disagree, however, on the precise formulation of why labor migration exists.[22]

In his analysis of labor migration, Burawoy began with the Marxist concept of reproduction. The reproduction of the labor force involves both its renewal and maintenance. He defined migrant labor institutionally as a system that separates the functions of renewal and maintenance, physically and institutionally. The function of renewal takes place in the less developed society (such as Mexico), while only the function of maintenance takes place in the developed capitalist society (such as the United States), thus externalizing the costs of labor force renewal to the less developed country. The less developed society is dependent on the developed capitalist country because of its own inability to support the reproduction of all its labor force. Hence, a mutually beneficial system of labor migration ensues.

Castells, on the other hand, defined labor migration not institutionally but economically. Migrant labor is cheap labor that "causes a relative lowering of wages thus contributing to the structural countertendency which helps delay the fall in the rate of profit."[23] Burawoy criticized Castells's definition of migrant labor because it left unanswered the questions of cheap for whom, cheap with respect to what, and cheap under what conditions.

Like Castells, Portes defined migrant labor as cheap labor, whose historical function under capitalism is to maintain the rate of profit. Not a Marxist, Portes attempted to answer the questions of cheap for whom and with respect to what. The answer lies in what he termed the paradox of illegal immigration: "while denounced on the one hand as a national calamity, it is permitted to continue."[24] Clearly, the flow could be averted. The migrants could be physically prevented from crossing the border by increasing the Border Patrol—understaffed and porous as it now is. In addition, during times of unemployment and recession, concerted deportation drives could be repeated, such as those effected during the Depression, "Operation Wetback," or the recent "Operation Jobs." Alternatively, as Portes argued, fining employers who hire illegal workers could undermine the incentives for their coming. The flux of immigration continues because it serves economic functions, providing cheap labor for certain enterprises with respect to domestic labor.

Flows of immigrant labor are flows of cheap labor. But for Portes, unlike Castells, the function of this cheap labor is not to counteract the overall tendency of capitalism toward a falling rate of profit.

Nor is it to serve those enterprises having alternatives for generating profit despite the inelasticity of domestic labor caused by the floor on wages established by the organized working class and welfare. Rather, immigrant labor provides cheap labor—not for the larger capital-intensive enterprises that can solve the profit problem by either undertaking capital-intensive technological innovations or by locating in areas where cheap labor resides, but for the small and medium-sized enterprises for which such alternatives hardly exist.

In several Western European nations, the construction industry is an example. "It has remained largely small-scale and based on labor-intensive methods," Portes said, "because the presence of immigrant workers has contributed, directly and indirectly, to maintain conditions of low wages and intensive exploitation."[25] In the United States, as we saw earlier, agriculture has relied most on immigrant labor, but more recently so have other small and medium-sized urban enterprises, such as factories, restaurants, and repair shops, which "have come to progressively rely on illegal migration as their defense against high labor costs."[26] Thus, Portes further argued, the role of immigrant labor is central to a developed capitalist economy.

While Mexican immigrants cannot be said to be structurally assimilated into American society, from this point of view they can be said to be structurally *integrated*. In addition, as Portes underlined, illegality does not change the functions of legal labor migration, but only serves "to reinforce the very conditions which make immigrant labor economically useful."[27] Those conditions are the vulnerability and powerlessness of the immigrants. Their vulnerability and powerlessness stem from the restrictions on the length of their stay as well as the type of work that they may pursue; from the lack of collective organization typical of most industries where they work; and from their legal status, which hardly empowers them to make demands or to bargain. In all, these conditions constitute a denial of citizenship, both in its concrete sense and in the larger sense that while these individuals are accountable to the state, they have no claim on it. Part of the differential treatment Cuban and Mexican immigrants received consisted of making citizenship (both in its concrete and larger senses) easily available to Cubans, who do not constitute a system of labor migration, but unavailable to Mexicans, who do in part.

Despite the varying emphases in the analyses of Burawoy, Castells, and Portes, they fundamentally agreed that immigrant labor has structural causes and that, as immigrant labor and as labor, it

has a central role in the functioning of developed capitalist societies. They also agreed on its consequences for the internal class
structure and the organization of labor. One consequence lies in
the conflict that develops between immigrant labor and the organized working class in America over wages, efforts at unionization, and the like. César Chávez, for example, complained that one
of his difficulties in organizing Chicano farm workers in California
comes from growers who use illegal aliens as strikebreakers to forestall the spread of the United Farm Workers.[28] As Portes emphasized, "To this day, many local unions and ethnic organizations are
not certain whether they should oppose and denounce illegal immigrants, embrace them as part of the same community, or adopt
some intermediate attitude."[29]

   Another consequence lies in the limited possibilities for social
mobility that the immigrants encounter as the result of the restrictions on the length of their stay and the type of work they may perform: *bracero* work in the past or that deemed licit by labor certification today. Last, their participation in society as immigrants
and as laborers becomes perceived and interpreted as problems of
ethnic relations. Thus Barry Chiswick interpreted the low earnings
of Mexican Americans and Mexican immigrants as an ethnic-group
effect;[30] Paul Bullock argued that the problem stemmed from the
cultural traits of Mexicans: familism, male dominance, and an orientation toward immediate gratification, all of which led to the low
participation of women in the work force, the preference for manual
jobs over intellectual work, the emphasis on early work for males
in preference to continuing school, and the low interest in maxi-
mizing job opportunities.[31]

   These social consequences of labor migration stem from the restrictions placed on the immigrants as temporary sources of labor
along with their powerlessness and vulnerability. Given the functions of cheap labor migration, it is scarcely surprising that the
state should have made so few attempts to assist the structural assimilation of Mexican immigrants in America. As Castells said,
"immigrant workers do not exist because there are 'arduous and
badly paid' jobs to be done, but, rather, arduous and badly paid jobs
exist because immigrant workers are present or can be sent for to
do them."[32]

   Contrary to the cry of public officials that if illegal immigration
ceased more jobs would become available for American workers,
Portes also underscored that "many such jobs *could not exist*, at
least at their present wage levels, were not immigrant workers
available to perform them."[33]

The Safety Valve: Mexico

Less attention has been paid to the functions of labor migration from the perspective of the underdeveloped country that the migrants leave. The question remains: *Why should Mexico allow so many of its young and clearly energetic citizens to leave?* Because while the immigration of Mexican laborers serves the function of cheap labor in the United States, for Mexico, analysts have consistently argued, this migration functions as a safety valve. The safety valve function is as old as the history of Mexican emigration to the United States. Tracing the history of Mexican policy toward labor emigration to the United States, Arthur Corwin demonstrated its ambivalence.[34] At the beginning of this century, Mexican nationalism protested the exodus of workers to the north—some cried out against the ungrateful workers themselves, others against government liability. The Mexican Revolution deepened this nationalism. For some intellectuals it became intertwined with the need for pro-natalist policies, what Corwin called a "demographic nationalism."[35]

When World War I spurred the dramatic increase of Mexican emigration, regarded in the United States as the first silent invasion, in Mexico the newly formed labor unions took up the nationalistic cry for strict control of emigration. But, Corwin argued, "the early revolutionary regimes of Carranza, De la Huerta, Obregón and Calles, covering the period 1915–1934, regarded an open border as an 'escape valve' for revolutionary unrest and political enemies." In addition, they were aware that Mexico had little to offer them "except unfulfilled revolutionary promises."[36] Hence, they permitted American labor contractors to recruit workers. Yet, while not preventing the emigration, at the same time successive governments applied nationalistic policies. As Corwin showed, these centered on two efforts: dissuasion and protectionism. During the massive migration of the World War I period, the Mexican state insisted on the emigrants' registering; tried to dissuade them from following a mere illusion, especially from leaving without contracts; sought to protect them from army conscription in the north as well as from abuses of their labor; and tried to eliminate the exploitative *coyotes*, the smugglers who profited from the flow. Yet, despite the protectionism, in the 1920s Mexico resisted U.S. efforts to place quotas on the Western Hemisphere, which would have limited the Mexican immigration. And to date, in what is a very long history, the Mexican government has never restricted or halted the flow. "The question of border control," said Corwin, "has always been enmeshed in a complex of ambivalent policies and feelings."[37]

When, after the repatriation drives of the Depression, World War II spurred the second major wave of Mexican migration, the Mexican government continued its efforts to dissuade and protect. "The difference," noted Corwin, "is that the government tried to use the bracero program to channel surplus labor to the United States."[38] For the first time Mexico attained real control over the emigration but used it only to regulate the flow.

On occasion, as Corwin showed, the Mexican government considered terminating the *bracero* program in its distress over the wetback problem. But ultimately it was unable to resolve the swelling wetbackism other than by enlarging the protectionism of *bracero* contracting and by relying on the U.S. Border Patrol. Corwin underscored that Mexico never abandoned its policy of discouragement; it always encouraged *Mexicanidad*, the continuing identification with Mexico and its culture, and it always left the door open for repatriation. Yet, with the problem created by the rapid population explosion, "more and more, the United States was regarded as an outlet for surplus people—no matter how much political critics and social reformers shouted down the concept of surplus population."[39] In the end, as we saw, it was the United States, not Mexico, that terminated the *bracero* program.

Mexico resisted the termination of the *bracero* program in part because of the economic benefits of the program. Richard Craig stressed that, in all likelihood, this was the paramount reason for Mexico's desire to prolong it: "What the ambassador did not say, but what was understood by all students of the bracero program, was that each bracero supported an average of four persons."[40] Even after the termination of the *bracero* program, other analysts stressed the positive effect of income remittances workers sent back home. Wayne Cornelius, as well as David North and Marion Houstoun, sought to estimate the actual magnitude of these remittances sent back to Mexico.[41] Yet Sidney Weintraub and Stanley Ross rightly found fault with their methods.[42]

More central than the actual amount of money remitted, however, is whether it can be said to contribute to the Mexican economy. In their analysis of the migration in another area of the world, from poor Arab countries to oil-rich ones, J. S. Birks and C. A. Sinclair pointed to the limited role remittances play.[43] While conventional wisdom sees the income remitted as having an impact on the overall economy by providing foreign exchange and hard currency, "mobilizing remittances for productive investment has proved difficult because of the individual nature of remittances."[44] In the absence of a national strategy to channel the remittances into savings and productive investments, they typically get spent on consumption items that enhance the daily life of the family back home.[45] Hence, while remittances are real, whatever their actual magnitude, they function not to promote Mexican development but to extend the safety valve—to provide the workers and their families what Mexico cannot give.

Amidst the rising tide of illegal aliens that typified the mid-sixties and seventies, in 1974, under President Echeverría's government, Mexico passed a population law providing for national population planning as well as for control of labor recruiting and smuggling.[46] But, as Portes argued, the population explosion was not the sole cause of the massive emigration. The development model that Mexico pursued also played a part: "the sources of this illegal immigration are not to be found in a backward and traditional rural economy but in the very contradictions accompanying Mexican *development.*"[47]

Four major contradictions, said Portes, characterized the process of capitalist industrialization in Mexico. First, it broke the peasants' ties to the land without offering industrial employment or forms of social security. Hence, it resulted in massive unemployment and underemployment. Second, economic growth went side by side with a growing inequality in income distribution. Third, standards of modern consumerism permeated Mexico while the majority of the population, particularly the working classes in cities, remained without access to the new patterns of consumption. Last, Mexico's development took place amid a contradiction between "a formally nationalistic government policy and an international reality of increasing dependence involving control of the Mexican economy by foreign sources" in the shape of multinational corporations.[48] While this development model was enormously successful, that success was not shared by most of the people.

Echeverría's government undertook some internal reforms: it substantially raised minimum wages, promoted family planning, and expanded the infrastructure, such as rural electrification and roads.[49] But given a development strategy that slighted the rural *campesinos* as well as the urban lower-middle classes, Mexico's migration continued to function as a safety valve. Those whom the development strategy failed to incorporate, faced with no alternatives, continued choosing to leave. Thus, Mexico opposed the possibility of the United States fining employers of illegal aliens. As Corwin underscored, "Since land distribution had run its course and industrialization could not fully absorb population growth, the

Echeverría government came to regard emigration not only as income compensation for the closing of the bracero programs, but as an outlet for unemployed millions otherwise open to demagoguery." Building a "Berlin Wall" would have amounted to a confession of national failure on the government's part, and would have "shut off an economic and psychological safety valve." [50]

With the apprehensions of illegals soaring by the end of the 1970s, President López Portillo inherited an already bad situation that was aggravated by the new American limit of 20,000 Mexican immigrants a year, relatives excepted. López Portillo's strategy, the Production Alliance, devolved on internal economic development, with particular emphasis on labor-intensive industries and border development programs as well as efforts to reduce population growth.[51] In addition, the Mexican government advocated that the United States take certain cooperative steps regarding both illegal immigration in the United States and patterns of American investment in Mexico. But despite acknowledging the problem of migration, Mexico refused to engage in efforts to control the border. Hence, as Corwin concluded, "López Portillo's policy was essentially that of his predecessors since World War II: to maintain the status quo of a half-open border—the safety valve. . . ." [52]

From its beginnings in the nineteenth century, the Mexican migration provided the United States with a source of cheap services and labor, Mexico with an outlet for its dearth of employment. Hence Jorge Bustamante and Gerónimo Martínez correctly dubbed it "beyond borders but within systems." [53]

Yet as the 1980s opened, the United States faced a deepening unemployment and the increasing visibility of the many homeless while Mexico endured the distress of devaluation and the austerity measures demanded by the renegotiation of its international debt. At the border, in 1982 and 1983, apprehensions soared.[54] For the first time, Mexican needs and American needs contradict one another. The system of economic migration may well have come to an end.

The Functions of Political Migration

Externalizing Dissent: Cuba

Political migration can also constitute a system when its functions mutually benefit the two countries involved. Unlike the majority of exile movements, the Cuban exodus to the United States was an organized one, based on mutual arrangements of the Cuban and

American governments.[55] The "push" and "pull" that repelled and attracted the exodus rested not only on the hardships of life under the revolution and the magnet of the land of opportunity, but also on the policies of Cuba and the United States. Their governments, acting in concert, set in motion a system of political migration.

The Cuban migration constituted a system of political migration both at the level of institutions and functions. The instances of institutional collaboration multiply: both countries collaborated in the arrangements that facilitated and channeled the migration. Over the course of many years, the freedom flights brought hundreds of exiles daily from Havana to Miami, transporting over a quarter of a million Cubans.[56] Furthermore, the United States and Cuban governments drafted agreements, such as the Memorandum of Understanding, to approve and regulate an orderly departure. In addition, the United States set up the Cuban Refugee Emergency Center and the many-faceted Cuban Refugee Program, previously unknown in its breadth and scope. Even the failure of the Bay of Pigs invasion by American-trained Cuban exiles sparked collaboration. The U.S. and Cuban governments traded the imprisoned fighters for food and medical supplies. Despite the chaos of the Mariel exodus, President Carter's ambivalent response, and President Castro's spiteful dumping of his social undesirables, ultimately the two governments collaborated, allowing the émigrés exit and entry.

This institutional collaboration requires us to examine the functions of political migration. The question becomes: *Why should Cuba allow so many of its able and enterprising citizens to leave?* Because Cuba benefited from the flight of dissenters. In externalizing dissent, the Cuban government effectively controlled it.

The revolution effected radical social and economic change that went hand in hand with increasing social control over people's lives. On both fronts Cuba generated a great deal of dissension. At the same time, the government suppressed dissent. The institutions that could incorporate interest groups founded on divergent opinions and criticism of goals ceased to exist. Initially, the Cuban government justified this as a necessity mandated by the swift and abrupt transition from capitalism to communism. In later years, during the period of institutionalization, the party retained irrevocable power.[57]

In authoritarian societies, both of the left and right, only two alternatives exist for effectively dealing with the dissent they inevitably generate: emigration and imprisonment. Over the course of more than twenty years, Cuba exercised both.

Although the Cuban government never released public statistics on the number of its political prisoners, neither did it deny their existence. Throughout the sixties, estimates ranged between 15,000 and 30,000.[58] In 1975, Amnesty International reported that Cuba held from 4,000 to 5,000 political prisoners, a rough approximation that applied only to "those prisoners whom the Cuban authorities (and in particular the courts who pass sentence) recognize as being detained on political charges."[59] A year later, the Inter-American Human Rights Commission appealed to the Cuban government to end the "cruel, inhuman, and degrading" treatment of political prisoners.[60] As a result of the Dialogue, Cuba gradually released 3,600 political prisoners. Others remained behind.[61] Clearly, imprisonment was a solution to the dissent that the revolution generated.

Of the two means available to suppress dissent, emigration is the most effective because externalizing dissent saps its force: it insures that from without exiles will be less able to undermine the revolution than from within. The defeat of the Bay of Pigs and the failure of political groups of exiles, such as Alpha 66, to overturn the Castro regime testify to the policy's success. Externalizing dissent also serves to break the ties between dissenters at home and abroad, hindering their capacity for joint actions. Even more, externalizing dissent removes the likelihood of developing an internal dynamic for change. Solidarity, the Polish workers' movement, could hardly have evolved among people who had carried away their grievances and discontent.

Fidel Castro was well aware that emigration served the function of externalizing dissent. As on many other occasions, during the exodus from Camarioca Harbor in 1965, he explained, "In this country, when we say to someone, 'If you want to leave, we aren't going to stop you; you are free to leave,' this country doesn't lose a citizen. Why? Because that citizen could never be considered— from our revolutionary point of view, from our Marxist point of view—a citizen of this country."[62] Thus rhetoric as well as policy aimed to externalize dissent.

Yet hand in hand with the benefits went the costs: the emigration also eroded the social and economic base of the revolution. In the beginning years of the revolution, the departure of the professional, managerial, and administrative classes drained Cuba of needed skills and resources. For example, of the 158 senior professors who taught at the University of Havana Medical School, all but 17 fled the country. A third of all doctors, more than 2,000, left.[63] From 1965 on, increasingly the exodus drew from the working classes and the small entrepreneurs. The exodus of exiles helped to consolidate the revolution politically by externalizing dissent and rendering it impotent. But at the same time it eroded Cuba's human resources and skills. A content analysis of the speeches of the main spokesmen of the revolution reveals this contradiction, one that is reflected in the changing attitudes toward the émigrés.

At the outset of the revolution, prior to the Bay of Pigs victory that consolidated it, dissent peaked as the transition to communism progressed. The Cuban government suppressed the existing independent press; broke up protest demonstrations; equated the anticommunism of revolutionaries such as Huber Matos with counterrevolution; fought rebel forces in the Escambray Mountains; seized the independent television and radio stations; executed counterrevolutionaries; jailed thousands of dissenters for treason; assailed those who left as traitors; and, faced with sabotage, emigration, and counterrevolution, created the Committees for the Defense of the Revolution for surveillance.[64] The slogan "With the revolution or against the revolution" expressed the only possibilities.

In this first stage of the revolution, Fidel Castro repeatedly stated that those who wished to leave could. Yet, faced with the costs— the loss of thousands of professionals and technicians to manage the newly nationalized enterprises—he also tightened up exit regulations and assailed emigrants for treason: "Those who escape their duty, taking the road to the north, have lost the right to be worthy sons of the fatherland."[65]

Cuba banned from exit many professionals and technicians—engineers, petroleum specialists, government employees, executives of industry—all of whom needed to obtain special permits to allow them to leave.[66] In addition, the government undertook a campaign designed to halt the exodus of professionals. For example, a mass meeting of professionals was held at the University of Havana in November 1960 to repudiate the thousands who had left. President Dorticós underscored the need for professionals to stand "together with the nation and against treason," and urged those present to take an oath to stay and place their knowledge and efforts at the service of the government.[67] Six months later, on the eve of the Bay of Pigs invasion, when addressing a meeting of engineers, architects, and technicians at the Confederation of Cuban Workers, Premier Castro also urged the professionals not to leave Cuba. The exodus, he explained, was motivated by "the enemies of the revolution," who wished to "deprive a country on the road to development, in a period of construction and growth, of those it so much needs, the professionals and technicians." The Americans, he added, had done everything in their power "to economically strangle the revolution" and to snatch "our doctors, our engineers, our architects, and technicians that the nation so much needs at present." Then, he reminded them of their duty to serve their country and urged them to identify themselves "100 percent with the revolution."[68]

After Cuba defeated the Bay of Pigs invaders, Castro applauded the exit of the émigrés, derisively called *gusanos*. His brother Raúl, minister of the armed forces, underscored the benefits of externalizing dissent: "It is the normal exodus that takes place when the people take the power in their own hands and liquidate exploitation and the privileged classes. Their departure does not damage the revolution, but fortifies it, as it is a spontaneous purification."[69]

Warning that the Bay of Pigs incident was imperialism's first but not last battle, Raúl Castro called for strengthening Cuba's military defense and increasing surveillance. Members of the Committees for the Defense of the Revolution were told to keep their eyes and hands on the "internal reaction."[70]

With the revolution consolidated, the exodus of Cubans turned into a veritable flood. The shortage of doctors, engineers, technicians, and teachers seriously hindered Cuba's efforts to industrialize as well as expand its educational and health services. At a conference of delegates to the national literacy program, Fidel Castro announced that doctors, engineers, and other technicians who had fled to the United States would be deprived of their citizenship and barred from returning to Cuba. Imperialism, Castro stated, was to blame for taking from the revolution the doctors, professors, engineers, and technicians: a deliberate effort "to deprive it of competent men, to deprive it of intelligence, the resources the revolution could rely on." As soon as possible, the revolution aimed to prepare many new professionals and technicians, "whom imperialism would never be able to conquer." The spread of education throughout the country, the thousands of scholarships provided to study in Havana, and the continuation of the literacy campaign in the countryside were all needed to replace the "miserable traitors" who had left the revolution wanting.[71] Yet just a few weeks later it was not the costs but the benefits that became paramount. At a speech in the Plaza of the Revolution, Castro stressed that the *gusanos'* exit would remove thoughtless consumers whose property would go to the working people of Cuba. "If some more want to go to Miami," Castro said, "let them go to Miami! Each time that a boatload of parasites leaves . . . the Republic comes out ahead."[72]

After the Cuban Missile Crisis the flights ceased and only Cubans who managed to cross the sea on rafts and rowboats left. Due to both economic and political pressures, discontent and dissent again accumulated. Repeated party purges accompanied the leanest years of the revolution until, as Hans Magnus Enzensberger showed, Castro wrested control of the party from the old Communists.[73] In September 1965 Castro offered to allow Cubans to migrate to the "Yankee paradise." In a speech commemorating the fifth anniversary of the Committees for the Defense of the Revolution, Castro blamed the United States for impeding the migration. Speaking of those who nevertheless had risked the exit, he said, "Now they are leaving in small boats, many of them drowning, and they (the Americans) use this as propaganda . . . Now those who want to leave can leave, because there are many here remaining who struggle for the people." Challenging the United States to reopen the exodus, Castro added, "Now we shall see what the imperialists will do or say."[74]

To back up his offer, Castro offered two free flights daily from Havana to the United States.[75] President Johnson replied with the open door policy, resulting in the freedom flights that lasted eight years. The Cuban government barred men of military age from departing—as well as political prisoners and persons with professional and technical skills, such as doctors, "whose departure might produce grave disturbance to production or to a social service because of the lack of a replacement."[76] The United States paid for the refugee flights, and Cuba benefited from externalizing dissent— so much so that Fidel Castro repeatedly requested that the United States open its doors wider to allow more Cubans to enter: "Now we ask them: Why don't you take everyone out of here who wants to go, once and for all? For each one who goes, we will have that much more in resources for giving a scholarship to the son of a farm worker, or a canecutter."[77]

Still, the costs of the exodus went hand in hand. Castro announced his willingness to allow some doctors to leave. "But," he underscored, "we have only contempt—which they merit—for all those who desert the honorable ranks of our doctors."[78] Upon leaving, the exiles had always lost their property; now the Cuban government ordered those who applied for exit fired from their jobs and their belongings itemized.[79] For many, this turned into years of waiting with neither honor nor income.

The exodus took such force that, only a year after challenging the United States to open its doors wider, Castro complained that the lack of technical and professional people posed serious problems for Cuba's economy. "The mission of the Universities," Castro stressed, "is not to train just technicians, but revolutionary technicians."[80]

But it was really in 1968 that, as Fagen et al. pointed out, Castro's attitude toward those who intended to leave grew harsh. The revolutionary offensive involved the takeover and "eradication" of private "parasite" activities, such as street vendors, the self-employed, artisans, small bars, small groceries, small family restaurants, laundries. When these "loafers" vanished, Castro announced, Cuba would be farther down the road to the "pure communism" under construction.[81] "*El pueblo*," a recent Cuban exile told me, "began to turn." When those in whose name the revolution was made wanted to leave, Castro enforced agricultural work upon them. "The *gusanos*," he declared, "are no longer on holiday, waiting three years, living at the expense of others, yearning for the day when they will enter the Yankee 'paradise.' Not any more. The way to Miami now runs through the countryside, through the canefields, through work."[82]

The party and the intellectuals suffered as well. The trial of "the microfaction," as it came to be called, yielded a party that, for all its organization, committees, and members, ultimately lay under the unlimited sovereignty of Fidel Castro. "Such an unlimited sovereignty," underlined Enzensberger, "can turn into arbitrariness."[83] The artist also suffered a serious blow. After Heberto Padilla's poem, "Fuera del juego" ("Out of the Game"), sparked the Padilla affair, writers and intellectuals could choose to write only on approved revolutionary themes. The slogan that conveyed the message read, "With the revolution, everything. Outside the revolution, nothing."[84] Writers then needed to fulfill their revolutionary mission. Purges of intellectuals ensued.[85]

Dissent peaked again among the working classes, the political elites, and the intellectuals. But Cuba proceeded to tighten its grip on emigration. By May 1966 over 350,000 persons had applied for the airlift, but after that date the Cuban government refused to accept new applications. In 1970 Cuba closed the door to emigration through other countries, mainly Spain and Mexico.[86] When the airlift ended in April 1973, it had transported over a quarter of a million Cubans from Cuba. Thereafter, the solution to dissent once again devolved on imprisonment. Labor absenteeism was summarily dealt with. The government declared vagrancy unlawful and made work an obligation for women and men. Under this law, by 1974 the government had jailed 50,000.[87] In 1975 Cuba began a new foreign policy period, the "proletarian internationalism" that prompted Cubans to fight in Angola.[88] Amnesty International estimated that Cuba held at least 4,000 to 5,000 political prisoners. A year later the Inter-American Human Rights Commission reported that Cuba treated its political prisoners with complete disdain.

Yet in 1978 the Dialogue gave birth to a new period of liberalization. Cuba welcomed the return visits of the exiles, gradually released over 3,600 political prisoners, and signaled the new era by exchanging *gusanos* for the respectful and inclusive members of the Cuban community abroad. The Dialogue, in the broadest sense of the word, died with the 1980 Mariel exodus. As is well known, the latest exiles earned the new label of *escoria* (scum), the "antisocial elements."

Capitalizing on the spontaneous exodus, the Cuban government again seized the opportunity to externalize dissent. *Granma*, the official newspaper of the Cuban Communist Party, printed an editorial on Cuba's position:

> Our working people are of the opinion: "Let them go, the loafers, the antisocial and lumpen elements, the criminals and the scum!"
>
> As always, Cuba gladly opened the doors for them, as it had done before with all the rabble that opposed socialism and the revolution . . .[89]

Again Castro explained the benefit of externalizing dissent: "I think that those of them remaining here are people with whom we can work better, much better! . . . So we need not worry if we lose some flab. We are left with the muscle and bone of the people. We are left with the strong parts."[90] Again the costs were evident. Cuba barred youths of military age and those holding university degrees from exit. University graduates, explained Castro, could not leave because a minimum number of years of working is "indispensable" to repay society for what it has spent on them.[91] Both the good-riddance attitude and the restrictions imposed on the exit expressed, as always, the benefits and costs of the exodus. But for the first time the Cuban government did more than that.

To discredit the many decent working people whose exit belied the promises of the revolution, Castro emptied the jails and asylums onto the boats. He assailed the Americans: "In the past they used to take away our doctors, engineers, teachers, all highly qualified personnel. Now it was their turn to take away our lumpen."[92] The American press, almost obligingly, focused on the criminal element and the insane, and photographed the blatantly homosexual. Thus they left the majority blurred: the decent working people, the former Communist Party members, the onetime members of the Committees for the Defense of the Revolution, the prominent Cuban writers and intellectuals—all who left after years of quiet dissimulation.[93] Focusing on them would have touched at the heart of totalitarianism: the false promises, the spread of social control over people's lives, the lack of alternatives to participation, and the dissimulation of a life whose truth is shared only with a few and at great risk while another face beams in public.

More than twenty years ago, C. Wright Mills spoke of the need to connect, in our understanding, private troubles and public issues. For two decades, Cuba's public policy toward the exodus stemmed from the contradiction between its costs—the erosion of skill—and its benefits—the externalization of dissent. The troubles this produced left a Mariel refugee bewildered: "I was very surprised when they told me I was leaving," said Gilberto Rodríguez when he arrived in Key West. "Ten years ago they put me in prison for trying to escape Cuba in a boat. Yesterday they put me in a boat and let me have what I had been trying for, for ten years."[94]

Symbols as Weapons: The United States

While the Cuban state utilized the exodus to externalize dissent, on our shores the question remains: *Why should the United States so eagerly receive the exiles?* Because in America during the Cold War years, all the political migrations—the Hungarians, Koreans, Berliners, and Cubans—served a symbolic function. When West and East contested the superiority of their political and economic systems, political exiles who succeeded in the flight to freedom became touching symbols around which to weave the legitimacy needed for foreign policy.

After World War II, the foreign policy of the United States and the Soviet Union went through several distinct phases. The Cold War dawned, peaked, and waned. The Cold War issued the period of real war in Vietnam. Détente followed for some years until the eighties opened with a resurgence of the Cold War. A content analysis of the statements of American public officials reveals that, during the peak years of the Cold War, the multitude of political refugees from communist societies served as touching symbols around which to build legitimacy.

Based on its humanitarian concern, since World War II, America consistently welcomed the refugees from communism. In 1961 President Eisenhower pleaded with Americans to open their homes and hearts to the Cuban refugees as Americans had opened them to the Hungarians. "To grant such asylum," stressed Eisenhower, "is in accordance with the long-standing traditions of the United States."[95] Tracy Vorhees, the president's representative on the Cuban refugee problem, reported their plight and stressed the need for a Cuban relief program, underlining the "opportunity it gives to prove in action the true humanitarian spirit of America."[96] President Kennedy underscored "the tradition of the United States as a humanitarian sanctuary, and the many times it has extended its hand and material help to those who are 'exiles for conscience's sake.'"[97] Fourteen years later, when the United States set up a similar resettlement program for the Vietnamese refugees, L. Dean Brown, director of the task force on Indochinese refugee relief and resettlement, drew upon the Cuban refugee experience: "America has a tradition of extending a warm hand of welcome to those who are forced to flee to our shores."[98] "To do otherwise," urged President Ford, "would be a repudiation of the finest principles and traditions of America."[99]

But the refugees of the peak years of the Cold War served a further function. Beyond the traditional humanitarian concern, public officials repeatedly underscored that it was in our national interest to help them. Richard Brown, director of the Office of Refugee and Migration Affairs, made it clear that, beyond our humanitarian regard, "our assistance demonstrates in concrete form to the enslaved millions in Communist-dominated lands the inherent humanity of free society." In addition, he drew attention to President Kennedy's statement that "the successful re-establishment of refugees . . . is importantly related to free-world political objectives."[100] The political objectives were intimately tied to the Cold War. During the U.S.–Soviet showdown in Berlin, when over a thousand refugees a day streamed from East Berlin to West Berlin, President Kennedy explained the objectives: to continue providing asylum to the oppressed and persecuted, to offer hope to the victims of communism, and to provide "the exemplification by free citizens of free countries, through actions and sacrifices, of the fundamental humanitarianism which constitutes the basic difference between free and captive societies."[101]

At the height of the Cold War, when, as Arthur Schlesinger, Jr., drew it, "two nations bestrode the narrow world and glared at each other across an abyss,"[102] communism's refugees lent themselves as symbols. For example, early in 1962 at the United Nations Cuba charged the United States with intervention and aggression. Adlai Stevenson countered these charges by pointing to the self-imposed isolation of Cuba from the resolutions adopted by the other Western Hemisphere nations, such as their unanimous endorsement of the Alliance for Progress. Stevenson pointed to those who fled communism: ". . . millions of voices will answer them—the voices not only of 150,000 Cubans but of 200,000 Hungarians, of 55,000 Tibetans, of 1,100,000 Chinese, of 2,500,000 East Germans, and many more who have risked their lives to escape from that ideology and that form of government to the free world. And the final confession of ideological bankruptcy is that it takes a wall through the heart of Berlin not to keep the enemies out but to keep their own people in."[103] Such symbols helped build the legitimacy the American government needed to frame its foreign policy. In their comparative analysis of political power in the United States and the Soviet Union, Zbigniew Brzezinski and Samuel P. Huntington outlined the four phases of the policy-making process: initiation, persuasion, decision, and execution.[104] Only the order of these phases varied in the two nations. For example, in their analysis the persuasion phase precedes decision in America whereas it follows decision in the Soviet Union. Whatever the order, in all nations the state must engage in a process of persuasion because persuasion develops consent, one of the sources of legitimacy.

The symbols that political refugees from communist societies represented can be understood only as part of the historical drama of the Cold War. Arthur Schlesinger, Jr., unraveled "the tangled skein" of those years.[105] Beginning after World War II, the bipolar confrontation between the United States and the Soviet Union attained a nearly religious fervor in the 1950s and early 1960s. During its peak, the Hungarians arose, East Berlin built its wall, Korea divided, and the Cuban revolution moved into the Soviet orbit. President Kennedy defined that "basic clash of ideas and wills" as "one of the forces reshaping our globe."[106] As Schlesinger expressed it, "Each superpower believed that its own safety as well as world peace depended on the success of its own peculiar conception of world order. Each superpower, in pursuing its own clearly expressed and ardently cherished principles, only confirmed the fear of the other that it was bent on aggression."[107]

At the outset, the doctrine of collective security guided U.S. strategy; the belief in its role as the guardian of freedom gave it moral sustenance. In time, as both Schlesinger and Robert Burr underscored, the doctrine of collective security degenerated into the principle of unilateral intervention and, particularly in Latin America, America's anticommunism failed to remain prodemocratic.[108] Then, over the course of the ravages of the Vietnam War, at home and overseas America lost its moral sustenance. But in the years immediately following World War II, the containment of Stalinism, with all its brutality, was a moral crusade.[109] The multipolar world resulting from the struggles between the Soviet Union and China, as well as nationalism in the Third World, had not yet appeared, and the Soviet conquest of Europe remained a real fear.[110] In the early 1950s the Cold War moved from sensible defense worries to a nearly religious war.

When the Korean War transformed the European conflict into a global conflict, the domino theory took root.[111] During the Eisenhower presidency, the Cold War peaked, fanning the zealousness of McCarthyism. On this stage appeared the Hungarian uprising and the Cuban revolution. Both the Hungarian and Cuban refugees came to bear proof of the fitness of our struggle. When Vice-president Richard Nixon submitted the report on Hungarian relief problems to President Eisenhower, he recommended that the United States take its full share of these refugees. Nixon stressed the significance of the Hungarian uprising: "The Communist leaders thought they were building a new order in Hungary. Instead they erected a monument which will stand forever in history as proof of the ultimate failure of International Communism. Those people, both inside and outside of Hungary, who had the courage to expose by their actions this evil ideology for what it is deserve all the gratitude and support which we in the Free World are so willingly giving today."[112]

In the United States this conflict between nations, each of which saw humankind as divided between good and evil, resulted in an interventionist foreign policy that helped to overthrow governments under the mere suspicion of communism, as in Guatemala in 1954.[113] As Burr underscored, the U.S. role in Guatemala convinced many Latin Americans that the United States preferred to maintain stable anticommunist regimes than to support democratic governments that sought to radically reform their countries.[114] In the 1950s, the doctrine of collective security, said Schlesinger, "began to narrow into one of unilateral intervention."[115]

Kennedy and Krushchev inherited the Cold War. Together, they fanned it to a new intensity. Krushchev transformed the Cold War by extending its battleground to the Third World. Twice, Kennedy and Krushchev collided head on: over Berlin in 1961 and over the Cuban Missile Crisis in 1962.

Although the Germans did not seek refuge on American soil, the symbolism of this Cold War migration rang the loudest. To be sure, it offered the most striking symbols: 3 million refugees, a city divided by a wall, an exodus that lasted two decades. Since the end of

World War II, Berlin had stood as a symbol of the Cold War. For example, soon after the Hungarian uprising, Eleanor Dulles of the Office of German Affairs had underlined that "never has the meaning of Berlin for the free world been more apparent than since the Hungarian revolution."[116] But it was really the Berlin crisis, the head-on collision between the United States and the Soviet Union over American presence in West Berlin, that gave Berlin its power as a symbol. Walter Dowling, ambassador to Germany in 1961, explained: "The division of Germany is more than a geographic partition or even a political separation. It is really the division between two modes of political thinking, two concepts of morality, two ways of life—one imposed and one freely chosen. It is, in sum, the expression in one country of the division of the world into two opposing camps, and represents the attempt of Communism to overwhelm democracy."[117] When the Soviet Union opposed the presence of the Allied forces in West Berlin, Secretary of State Dean Rusk also invoked the meaning of Berlin as a symbol: "I think first of West Berlin as a symbol—a symbol which has caught the imagination of the world and deeply moved the minds and feelings of men. As a symbol of free men's will to be free, of their capacity to rise to the challenge which history has imposed upon them, West Berlin has played a vibrant role."[118]

Krushchev defended the wall. The exodus continued, and many lost their lives in surmounting the wall. American public officials used the wall to assail the Soviets: "Successful societies do not have to build walls and string barbed wire against their own people," said Rusk. "The Berlin Wall . . . is a monument to failure—the failure of a 'competitive coexistence' that dared not compete."[119]

Why the need for symbols? Because they contributed to the legitimacy needed during the peak Cold War years. In any society governmental power rests on the two foundations of legitimacy and force. In the long run, the stability of power depends more on legitimacy than on naked force. As Dolf Sternberger stressed, popular consent is one of the most important sources of legitimate government.[120]

Historically, governments have rested their claim to legitimacy on different principles, whether traditional ones, such as the divine right of kings, or popular elections, or revolutionary mandates. Whatever the principle, the capacity to govern, the power to act in definite ways on precise issues, depends on the extent to which a government enjoys widespread authentic legitimacy or tries to win such recognition. To create and recreate that recognition, that consent, the state engages in a process of persuasion.

Because the wellsprings of legitimacy vary across societies and history, Max Weber sought to distinguish the ideal types of legitimate domination: traditional, charismatic, and rational.[121] Despite the differences, Weber based his three types on the notion that legitimacy resides in the obedience of the subjects. Without doubt, in democracies, where the people vote, the consent of the public is a crucial source of legitimacy. Hence, the state's efforts at persuasion aim to elicit the consent of the public, who will express it in elections. But, as Arthur Stinchcombe underscored, the public is only one of the centers of power. "The person *over whom power is exercised,*" added Stinchcombe, "is not usually as important as *other power-holders.*"[122] Legitimacy comes from the backing of a power-holder (such as the executive) by other centers of power (such as Congress, public opinion, or the armed forces) that constitute reserve sources of power. The state's efforts to persuade, therefore, aim not only at persuading the public that the state's actions are fit, but also at convincing the other centers of power that the state's decisions deserve backing. Communism's refugees served a symbolic function that aimed to win the consent not only of the American public but also of other centers of power, such as Congress. For example, Kennedy's use of the German refugees as symbols supports this notion of legitimacy. When the United States and the Soviet Union collided in Berlin, in his address to the nation Kennedy's symbolism reached its height:

> If anyone doubts the extent to which our presence is desired by the people of West Berlin compared to East German feelings about their regime, we are ready to have that question submitted to a free vote in Berlin, and, if possible, among all the German people.
>
> And let us hear at the same time from 2,500,000 refugees who have fled the Communist regime in East Germany—voting for Western-type freedom with their feet.[123]

At the same time, Kennedy appealed to the nation for increases in defense. From Congress he requested larger appropriations, more soldiers, draft calls and reserves, as well as more ships and planes, weapons, ammunitions, and equipment. In addition, he called for an increase in civil defense, particularly fallout shelters stocked with the essentials for survival. In all, the new defense budget request came to approximately $3.5 billion, which entailed the possibility of increased taxes. In his appeal he emphasized the sacrifice these measures would demand from the American people and welcomed the cooperation of the Congress. For West Berlin, he underscored, had many roles:

> It is more than a showcase of liberty, a symbol, an island of freedom in a Communist sea. It is even more than a link with the free world, a beacon of hope behind the Iron Curtain, an escape hatch for refugees.
> West Berlin is all of that. But above all it has now become—as never before—the great testing place of Western courage and will . . .[124]

As the result of his appeal, Kennedy won the complete support of the Republican congressional leaders.[125]

That confrontation resolved, two years later Kennedy visited Berlin. Its symbolism redounded upon the showcase of liberty, the defended island of freedom:

> Two thousand years ago the proudest boast was *"Civitas Romanus sum."* Today, in the world of freedom, the proudest boast is *"Ich bin ein Berliner"* . . .
> There are many people in the world who really don't understand, or say they don't, what is the great issue between the free world and the Communist world. Let them come to Berlin. There are some who say that communism is the wave of the future. Let them come to Berlin. And there are some who say in Europe and elsewhere we can work with the Communists. Let them come to Berlin. And there are even a few who say that it is true that communism is an evil system but it permits us to make economic progress. *Lasst Sie nach Berlin kommen.*[126]

Berlin was but the first stage where the U.S.-Soviet confrontation was played out. When the Cuban revolution moved into the Soviet camp, the drama moved to our own hemisphere. The Cuban refugees became the new symbols of the struggle between the two ways of life. On the heels of the Bay of Pigs invasion, U.N. delegates from communist nations charged the United States with intervention and aggression. Adlai Stevenson defended the United States by defending the exiles' effort to restore freedom: "The longing will not cease. Of this we can be sure. A hundred thousand Cubans have escaped already. Thousands more will follow. To them we say that the door is open and that the United States respects and upholds their right of asylum as one of the most fundamental of the rights of man."[127] The symbols of the past accumulated with those of the present. In the areas of tyranny, Stevenson reminded the assembly:

. . . people cannot protest their position publicly or make clear their profound desire for liberty. But it remains a fact that thousands upon thousands have registered their protest in the only way open to them. They have escaped.

Castro's refugees are but a page in this unhappy history. In Korea a great majority, not only of north Korean prisoners but of Chinese prisoners as well, opted not to return to Communist tyranny. Tibetans have streamed across India's frontiers to escape Chinese oppression. Tens of thousands fled from Hungary and now live in many lands here represented. Most revealing of all, over 3 million Germans have escaped from East Germany—"voting with their feet" against the regime. Gentlemen, there is no stream in the opposite sense. People fly to freedom, not away from it.[128]

Cuba and the prevention of other fallen dominoes were at the heart of Kennedy's policies. From Eisenhower, Kennedy inherited the planned Bay of Pigs invasion. After its fiasco, Kennedy's strategy to prevent the spread of communism turned to promoting social and economic reform in the underdeveloped world. In Latin America that effort took the shape of the Alliance for Progress. Kennedy explained his goal: "Those who make peaceful revolution impossible will make violent revolution inevitable."[129] Dean Rusk was even more explicit: "Communism now benefits from the harsh conditions of life in the hemisphere, conditions which the Alliance for Progress was designed to improve as a free alternative to the Castro brand of revolution."[130]

But the alliance, as Eduardo Frei Montalva explained, lost its way.[131] President Johnson's belligerent anticommunism sought the cooperation of the other Latin American nations to act against Cuba because, as the Department of State insisted, "the maintenance of communism in the Americas is not negotiable. Furthermore, the problem of Cuba is not a simple problem of United States–Cuban relations. It is a collective problem for all the states of this hemisphere."[132] Initially, the United States achieved only the exclusion of Cuba from the Organization of American States. In time other Latin American nations cooperated. Other centers of power backed the U.S. claim to power: the OAS imposed the 1964 hemispheric trade embargo.

From the Cold War issued a period of real war: the swift escalation and Americanization of the Vietnam War under presidents Johnson and Nixon. The bleakness that massive destruction wrought, during what Schlesinger called "the messianic phase" of foreign policy, generated the disbelief and dissent of the antiwar movement at home.[133] In Latin America the interventionist image of the United States expanded when President Johnson's vigorous anticommunism led to the invasion of the Dominican Republic. In addition, as Burr emphasized, support intensified for anticommunist regimes in Latin America, irrespective of whether they were democratic or authoritarian and dictatorial.[134]

The Cold War produced the real war, and the real war produced Détente. Under the accords of Détente, both superpowers sought to restore the balance of power, reducing the frenzy of the Cold War.[135] Vietnam had rent the social fabric of American life; Détente demanded a vastly attenuated ideological confrontation. Hence, the South Vietnamese hardly served as symbols. Appeals on behalf of the Vietnamese refugees rested primarily on humanitarian grounds. For example, in his statement before the Senate committee on appropriations to assist South Vietnam, Henry Kissinger pleaded for our compassion: "The human tragedy of Viet-Nam has never been more acute than it now is. Hundreds of thousands of South Vietnamese have sought to flee Communist control and are homeless refugees. They have our compassion, and they must also have our help."[136]

Likewise, L. Dean Brown reminded Congress that "the tragic outcome of events in Indochina has thrust upon the United States a gigantic humanitarian responsibility." In concluding, he added that "America has a tradition of extending a warm hand of welcome to those who are forced to flee to our shores. We are asking for no more today."[137] When Kissinger visited Berlin in 1975, twelve years after Kennedy, he also pointed to Berlin as a symbol of freedom: "To us you symbolize man's unquenchable yearning for freedom; you represent the capacity of democracy to summon the strength to defend its values." Like Kennedy, he called for a visit to Berlin: "I think that all of those who doubt what America has stood for should visit Berlin." But the symbol was quickly reset within the meaning of the period of Détente: "As Berlin was the greatest symbol of the heroism of the immediate postwar period, it is also the acid test of the period we now hope to enter."[138] The political refugees remained symbols of the fitness of our struggle, but outside the peak years of the Cold War those symbols could hardly be invoked to build legitimacy.

In this setting President Carter sought to reweave U.S. foreign policy with antiauthoritarianism and the prodemocratic moral thread of human rights. But as the decade of the 1980s opened, the Cold War, never totally extinguished, returned. With the invasion of Afghanistan, the Soviets returned to territorial expansion; their support for Poland's military repression of the Solidarity movement showed the limits of their own moral progress. President Reagan arrived clearly willing to engage in a renewed contest. The Nicaraguan revolution and the Salvadorean massacre refocused concern on the Latin American dominoes. A massive Cuban exodus rushed to Mariel. President Carter announced that America welcomed the new Cuban refugees "with open heart and open arms." Yet the symbolic value of the Mariel refugees paled when Cuba deliberately dumped criminals onto the boats and our press inordinately focused on them.

In the early sixties, when Cuba, scarcely ninety miles away, entered the spotlight of the Cold War, U.S. foreign policy aimed to undermine Cuba's capacity to endure. Like the Hungarians, Koreans, and Berliners before them, Cuba's refugees then served as symbols the state used to persuade other centers of power to back up its decisions and actions. Hence, in the United States Cubans encountered a generous reception. In the tug of war that ensued between Cuba and the United States, the United States cut diplomatic ties, imposed the trade embargo, supported the Bay of Pigs invasion, and won Latin American condemnation. Those actions aimed to isolate and undermine the Cuban revolution.

Ironically, for twenty years those very actions provided the Cuban state with its own set of symbols around which to weave the legitimacy it also needed. In particular, American actions served to justify the Cuban government's incapacity to satisfy economic aspirations as well as its utter militarization of Cuban society. For example, shortly after the Bay of Pigs incident, Raúl Castro underscored that "in Bay of Pigs imperialism lost its first battle in America . . . it was not its last; rather, many battles remain. That means that we have to insist, over and over again, on strengthening our defense."[139] The embargo likewise served to justify the militarization of Cuba: "U.S. economic aggression constitutes 'the prelude' to a new military aggression." "Bay of Pigs," Raúl Castro warned, "will not be the end. We have to think, rather, that they will return."[140] Seven years later, when Cuba announced the nationalization of the new revolutionary offensive, Fidel Castro promised that in the future compulsory military service would disappear. But, he explained, "The real fact of being so near such a powerful and criminal neighbor has obliged us all to become soldiers."[141]

Exhorting Cubans to work harder to overcome Cuba's economic failures, Raúl Castro plainly acknowledged a decade later that in the past the Cuban government had blamed the embargo for everything, relying on it as "a convenient crutch." "The truly negative consequences of the economic blockade imposed on us, by Yankee imperialism," he revealed, "have been used as pretexts to hide our deficiencies and inefficiencies."[142]

For twenty years, Cuba externalized its dissenters; America welcomed its symbols. Between them, the two governments set in motion a system of political migration. Mariel may well have brought it to an end.

7. Closing Observations

Every schoolchild learns that American history is inextricably tied to immigration. Yet, for all that immigrants fashioned America, immigration has never ceased to be a controversial and divisive issue. At a time when a prolonged recession has shrunken our humanitarian sensibilities, the concern of many has focused on immigration restriction. Arguing that America needs fewer immigrants, Colorado Governor Richard Lamm asked us to "disenthrall ourselves" from our past, an immigrant past that belonged to a frontier society, and to come to grips with the changed reality of our present. In that present, argued Lamm, immigration is at the highest level in our history, serving to aggravate our social epidemic of unemployment and scarcity. "It is usually not recognized," said Lamm, "but the nation's largest number of immigrants came not in 1911 or 1893 but in 1980"—808,000 legal immigrants and over one million apprehensions of illegals, ten times the number in the early 1960s.[1] Yet to understand the meaning of these figures, we must not disenthrall ourselves from our past but rather use it to illuminate our present.

If we compare the number of legal immigrants in 1980 to the years immediately preceding, we immediately see that the 1980 figure is abnormally high. In 1976, for example, total U.S. legal immigration numbered 467,000; in 1977, only 399,000; and in 1978 and 1979, just over 500,000. We must realize that the 808,000 immigrants for 1980 were due in part to the unexpected arrival of 125,000 Cuban and 10,000 Haitian "entrants" and due in part to the 232,000 Cuban and Indochinese refugees who already lived in the United States under "parolee" status, and in 1980 adjusted this status to that of immigrant.[2] Because of that lag time between the year of arrival and the year in which the Immigration and Naturalization Service counts an immigrant—years later, when the immigrants adjust their status—it is more sensible to consider the annual admissions averaged over a decade. In addition, since the United States has grown considerably since the turn of the century, we need to consider the proportion of the total population constituted by the immigrants. Then Governor Lamm's figures lose their capacity to terrify.

Contrary to Lamm's assertions, the decades of highest immigration remain those around the turn of the century. In the decade 1890–1900, immigration constituted 0.6 percent of the population; in the decade 1900–1910, that of the highest admissions, 1.2 percent. By contrast, in the decade 1970–1979, immigration comprised only 0.2 percent of the total population. A further comparison is in order, however. Over the last twenty years, the birth rate has steadily declined as a proportion of population growth. Even so, in the decade 1900–1910, with the population growing at more than 2 percent, immigration accounted for more than 40 percent of the population growth. In the decade 1970–1979, with the population growing at less than 1 percent, immigration accounted for less than 25 percent of that growth.[3] Moreover, as I stressed, the number of apprehensions is not equal to the number of illegals, many of whom are repeatedly arrested. This statistical common sense reduces the problem to its true magnitude: a fraction of a percent of the population cannot be made to bear the brunt of all our social ills. But neither should the issue of immigration reform be ignored.

Over the last few years, beginning with President Carter's administration and continuing under President Reagan's, concern over the adequacy of immigration law and the illegal alien problem mounted. President Carter established the Select Commission on Immigration and Refugee Policy to study the problem. Many of its recommendations were incorporated in the Simpson-Mazzoli bill, a comprehensive immigration reform bill that represented a bipartisan effort designed to curtail unlawful immigration. By a very comfortable majority, the Senate approved it in the spring of 1983; by a narrow margin, the House approved it in June 1984. The bill went to conference, but, as Congress adjourned in the fall, the conference committee failed to reach an agreement.[4] The measure would have been the largest overhaul of immigration law in thirty-two years. Its main provisions consisted of granting amnesty to those who had been in the country illegally for several years; more than doubling the current ceiling on Mexican immigration; and outlawing the hiring of illegal aliens by establishing employer sanctions for those who knowingly hired illegal aliens.

The bill's major strengths rested, first, in its recognition that illegals who have lived here for quite some years are not sojourners, but part of our work force and people who have put down roots in America. Second, while recognizing the need to establish a limit on immigration, the bill also recognized the need to more than double the Mexican ceiling. A new ceiling would turn that many potential illegals into legals, a measure that would protect them as well as provide a sense of bounds to America. Third, establishing for the first time in history employer sanctions to penalize those who now benefit from the illegals should protect both the illegal aliens themselves and American workers. American workers *are* displaced by illegal labor, a situation particularly serious during a severe recession. Yet the blame should hardly be cast on the illegals. If employers were fined, jobs for illegals should cease to be plentiful. In time the message would filter back to Mexico and the tide of aspiring illegals might recede. In the long run, that might control the flow of immigration more than any other direct form of control.

From the start the immigration bills were surrounded by the typical controversy that has always encircled immigration reform. Writing of the controversy that developed around immigration restriction in the 1920s, Thomas Gossett emphasized the "strange alliances" that developed on both sides of the immigration issue.[5] As Gossett showed, favoring the continuation of the large-scale European immigration of the time were both "high-minded" people who defended the immigrants as "real or potential" good Americans and employers who wanted an assured supply of cheap labor. Favoring immigration restriction were both conservatives who thought immigrants would contribute to cementing radicalism and liberals who feared the adverse effect of a continuous supply of cheap labor for American workers and their unions. Now that immigration reform and restriction once again came under debate, those strange alliances visited us again. Conservatives and liberals alike opposed the immigration reform outlined in this bill. Conservatives feared that it would impose additional government burdens on business; liberals, among them civil libertarians and Hispanic leaders, decried the infringement of privacy and the possible discrimination against all Hispanics, legals as well as illegals.[6]

Ultimately the challenge lies in how to frame a humane and realistic immigration policy. In its provisions such a policy needs to recognize not only that historically the United States has benefited from the flows of Mexican immigration but also that poor Americans need to be protected from the adverse effects of excessive immigration. Moreover, as Michael Teitelbaum underscored, one of the basic requirements that a humane and realistic immigration policy must meet is that the de jure policy (such as employer sanctions] "must be enforceable in practice in the real world."[7] If it is not, de facto it will be a different policy (evolving, perhaps, into the employment discrimination Hispanic leaders feared).

Yet immigration, as I hoped to demonstrate in this book, is not only an issue for our borders that, for whatever reasons, close or open to allow fewer or more immigrants in our midst. It is also an issue in the structural assimilation of immigrants—in facilitating the personal path to attainment that ultimately represents a social investment. Governor Lamm asked us to disenthrall ourselves from our past. Once again we will use the immigrants of yesterday and today to draw a different historical comparison.

Expecting the assimilation of minority groups to be an evolutionary process, some analysts have drawn the comparison between the Hispanics of today and the European immigrants of the turn of the century. As Ricardo Otheguy pointed out in his analysis of bilingual education, the comparison is made not out of ill will, but out of a conviction that the problems of Hispanics today are essentially the same ones Europeans had then. Hence, they will be solved in essentially the same way: by a process of natural, evolutionary assimilation that, with the passage of time, will result in their integration into the mainstream.[8] Such a comparison requires that we compare, as Otheguy did, each group—Hispanics of today, Europeans of yesterday—to the mainstream of its time. For it is their access to the mainstream patterns of language, employment, and education, their secondary structural assimilation, that is at stake.

Through various comparisons, Otheguy showed the following. Consider language. The vast majority of households today use English, and the majority of those who do not, use Spanish. By contrast, during the years of European migration, a high proportion of households must have used languages other than English, and no other language was dominant. Consider employment. Hispanics and other minorities today suffer unemployment rates many times higher than white Americans do. At the time of the European migrations, however, the unemployment rates of immigrants and native Americans hardly differed. Consider education. Today a wide gap exists in the achievement of Hispanics and the rest of the population. In the early years of the century, the cleft was not there. While the quality of education was a serious problem, Otheguy underlined that "the situation was as bad for the native as it was for the immigrant."[9] In addition, it was rare for anyone, immigrant or native-born, to attend high school. In 1920, only 16 percent of those 25 to 29 years old had finished high school. In 1977, 65 per-

cent shared that same education. With these and other data comparisons, Otheguy demonstrated that yesterday's Europeans and
today's Hispanics stand in very different relations to the mainstream of their time. The European immigrant experience more
closely resembled that of white natives than the Hispanic experience resembles our mainstream today. To put it simply, Europeans
then were much less *outsiders* than Hispanics are today. Hence,
Otheguy concluded, whatever the merits or demerits of bilingual
education programs and their implementation, the comparison of
Hispanics now and Europeans then renders the opposition to bilingual education untenable. We must not disenthrall ourselves
from our past because our present is radically changed. Historical
evidence and comparative studies can shed light on that very
difference.

Several years ago in his analysis of Mexican migration and the
U.S. labor market, Briggs outlined a number of policy measures he
felt were urgently needed. Some, such as legislation that would
make it a criminal act to employ illegal aliens, were incorporated
in the latest attempt at reform. But beyond the specific issues involving immigration law, his call for special programs that would
assist the Mexican immigrants in settlement went unheeded. The
need remains for government impact funds to school districts and
community organizations that provide services to the immigrant;
for information regarding legal protection; for special English
classes, and for training programs joined to efforts at job placement.[10] In short, the need remains for a Mexican analogue to the
Cuban Refugee Program. As we strive to stem the illegal tide, we
might also consider welcoming Mexicans not only as workers but
also as settlers.

In this comparison of Cuban and Mexican immigrants, I argued
and sought to demonstrate, using both historical and statistical
evidence, the source of the contrast in their secondary structural
assimilation. Throughout, the argument focused on the considerable variation in their process of incorporation into American society. The varying labor force outcomes of Cubans and Mexicans, I
argued, were partly due to the helping hand the state lent. Since
Cubans were political immigrants, the state lent them a firm hand;
since Mexicans were economic immigrants, the state largely ignored them. This reinforced the contrast in their social class origins, giving way to processes of cumulative advantage and disadvantage. The Cuban Refugee Program, in all its facets, staked the
success story of many Cubans in America. If the Cuban experience

can serve to show the benefits of a welcoming hand, that hand should be extended to others: to Mexican immigrants, to the Cuban émigrés of the Mariel exodus, to black Americans, to all who suffer from the lack of access outsiders endure. It is my hope that this analysis will contribute to a better future for both political and economic migrants in America. Ultimately, they will help bear America's future. As they upheld her past.

Appendix A.
Zero-Order Correlations among Variables

		(1)	(2)	(3)	(4)	(5)
Cuban Males Who Immigrated during 1960–1970						
Annual earnings	(1)	···	.462	−.110	.229	.183
Occupational prestige	(2)		···	−.070	.153	.528
Age	(3)			···	.226	−.164
Length of U.S. experience	(4)				···	.044
Skilled work	(5)					···
South	(6)					
Vocational training	(7)					
Agricultural employment	(8)					
Citizenship	(9)					
Weeks worked	(10)					
Years of school completed	(11)					
High school graduation.	(12)					
College graduation	(13)					
Cuban Males Who Immigrated during 1945–1959						
Annual earnings	(1)	···	.599	.125	−.057	.235
Occupational prestige	(2)		···	.168	.079	.480
Age	(3)			···	.299	.002
Length of U.S. experience	(4)				···	−.048
Skilled work	(5)					···
South	(6)					
Vocational training	(7)					
Agricultural employment	(8)					
Citizenship	(9)					
Weeks worked	(10)					
Years of school completed	(11)					
High school graduation	(12)					
College graduation	(13)					

(6)	(7)	(8)	(9)	(10)	(11)	(12)	(13)
084	.126	−.037	.246	.334	.353	.262	.325
001	.153	−.064	.157	.055	.443	.327	.475
134	−.022	−.017	.002	−.008	.005	.015	.067
066	.055	.008	.295	.170	.235	.233	.172
020	.079	−.147	.060	.003	.142	.114	.123
...	−.006	.032	−.070	−.004	−.050	−.021	−.003
	...	−.005	.001	.039	.276	.287	.119
		...	−.036	−.134	.009	.006	.018
			...	.078	.138	.124	.148
				...	.162	.132	.084
					...	.847	.688
						...	.477
							...
057	.048	.012	.246	.216	.391	.177	.462
158	.212	.053	.247	.156	.441	.302	.488
188	−.082	−.017	−.092	−.066	−.067	−.068	.115
028	.017	−.065	.283	−.190	−.026	−.004	−.082
191	.113	−.190	.167	.037	.090	.030	.060
...	−.044	−.090	.061	.128	.140	.153	−.047
	...	.180	.105	.061	.343	.251	.357
		...	−.113	.039	.166	.111	.341
			...	.226	.152	.183	−.114
				...	.130	.087	−.009
					...	.815	.564
						...	.325
							...

		(1)	(2)	(3)	(4)	(5)
Cuban Females Who Immigrated during 1960–1970						
Annual earnings	(1)	⋯	.424	−.077	.238	.16:
Occupational prestige	(2)		⋯	−.074	.115	.28(
Age	(3)			⋯	.300	−.13:
Length of U.S. experience	(4)				⋯	−.02）
Skilled work	(5)					⋯
South	(6)					
Vocational training	(7)					
Agricultural employment	(8)					
Citizenship	(9)					
Weeks worked	(10)					
Years of school completed	(11)					
High school graduation	(12)					
College graduation	(13)					
Cuban Females Who Immigrated during 1945–1959						
Annual earnings	(1)	⋯	.258	−.158	.021	.09（
Occupational prestige	(2)		⋯	−.214	.047	.32！
Age	(3)			⋯	.174	.00！
Length of U.S. experience	(4)				⋯	.08（
Skilled work	(5)					
South	(6)					
Vocational training	(7)					
Agricultural employment	(8)					
Citizenship	(9)					
Weeks worked	(10)					
Years of school completed	(11)					
High school graduation	(12)					
College graduation	(13)					

(6)	(7)	(8)	(9)	(10)	(11)	(12)	(13)
.150	.135	...	.300	.621	.324	.241	.273
.094	.223	...	.163	.101	.409	.339	.344
.110	−.106	...	.057	−.025	−.043	−.052	.036
.061	.084	...	.239	.157	.251	.256	.172
.065	−.023	...	.011	.074	.072	.059	.052
...	.010	...	−.079	−.049	.022	.038	.026
	...	...	−.020	.099	.255	.306	.056
		...	...	...	...	...	...
				.111	.119	.114	.087
				...	.129	.098	.044
					...	.853	.663
						...	.424
							...
.134	.365	...	−.042	.434	.152	.084	.033
.086	.403	...	.308	−.015	.235	.204	.150
.049	−.140	...	−.064	.036	−.261	−.180	−.217
.141	.002	...	.259	.160	−.014	−.039	−.124
.217	−.127	...	.181	−.098	.042	.043	.087
...	.079	...	−.002	−.226	.077	.083	−.099
	...	...	.079	.094	.277	.176	.160
		...	...	...	...	...	...
			...	−.154	.030	.083	−.099
				...	−.136	−.195	.068
					...	.831	.432
						...	.275
							...

		(1)	(2)	(3)	(4)	(5)
Mexican Males Who Immigrated during 1960–1970						
Annual earnings	(1)	⋯	.433	−.055	.158	.216
Occupational prestige	(2)		⋯	−.112	−.040	.650
Age	(3)			⋯	.411	−.150
Length of U.S. experience	(4)				⋯	−.084
Skilled work	(5)					⋯
South	(6)					
Vocational training	(7)					
Agricultural employment	(8)					
Citizenship	(9)					
Weeks worked	(10)					
Years of school completed	(11)					
High school graduation	(12)					
College graduation	(13)					
Mexican Males Who Immigrated during 1945–1959						
Annual earnings	(1)	⋯	.457	−.244	.066	.273
Occupational prestige	(2)		⋯	−.072	.106	.734
Age	(3)			⋯	.370	−.126
Length of U.S. experience	(4)				⋯	.033
Skilled work	(5)					⋯
South	(6)					
Vocational training	(7)					
Agricultural employment	(8)					
Citizenship	(9)					
Weeks worked	(10)					
Years of school completed	(11)					
High school graduation	(12)					
College graduation	(13)					

(6)	(7)	(8)	(9)	(10)	(11)	(12)	(13)
100	.191	−.211	.019	.308	.285	.208	.342
.155	.265	−.394	−.017	.127	.424	.358	.543
.069	−.009	.210	.003	−.048	−.233	−.124	.000
034	−.034	.113	−.001	.072	−.135	−.114	−.026
035	.181	−.573	.028	.090	.276	.196	.150
...	.064	−.003	.023	.064	.010	.053	.136
	...	−.158	−.028	.020	.313	.277	.185
		...	−.076	−.078	−.333	−.191	−.086
			...	.001	−.040	−.028	−.035
				...	.108	.011	.019
					...	.733	.448
						...	.398
							...

(6)	(7)	(8)	(9)	(10)	(11)	(12)	(13)
137	−.017	−.256	.015	.304	.408	.264	.455
213	.200	−.375	.087	.127	.450	.391	.382
119	.014	.143	.171	−.264	−.187	−.078	−.036
104	−.015	.001	.253	.017	.020	.161	.105
099	.162	−.488	.007	.160	.373	.242	.109
...	.005	−.091	.043	−.080	−.023	.107	.160
	...	−.088	−.031	.046	.262	.287	.031
		...	−.085	−.246	−.321	−.178	−.075
			...	−.086	.060	.071	.004
				...	.230	.078	.092
					...	.722	.432
						...	.418
							...

		(1)	(2)	(3)	(4)	(5)
Mexican Females Who Immigrated during 1960–1970						
Annual earnings	(1)	···	.292	−.076	.005	.349
Occupational prestige	(2)		···	−.139	−.094	.481
Age	(3)			···	.435	−.139
Length of U.S. experience	(4)				···	−.012
Skilled work	(5)					···
South	(6)					
Vocational training	(7)					
Agricultural employment	(8)					
Citizenship	(9)					
Weeks worked	(10)					
Years of school completed	(11)					
High school graduation	(12)					
College graduation	(13)					
Mexican Females Who Immigrated during 1945–1959						
Annual earnings	(1)	···	.371	−.185	−.142	.135
Occupational prestige	(2)		···	−.032	.003	.422
Age	(3)			···	.455	−.106
Length of U.S. experience	(4)				···	−.047
Skilled work	(5)					···
South	(6)					
Vocational training	(7)					
Agricultural employment	(8)					
Citizenship	(9)					
Weeks worked	(10)					
Years of school completed	(11)					
High school graduation	(12)					
College graduation	(13)					

(6)	(7)	(8)	(9)	(10)	(11)	(12)	(13)
156	.129	−.319	.093	.604	.251	.156	.195
059	.231	−.325	−.070	.175	.413	.307	.338
012	−.117	.112	.004	−.036	−.289	−.172	.072
010	−.023	.010	−.042	.047	−.125	−.077	−.042
120	.128	−.482	.010	.256	.293	.151	.115
...	.037	−.022	.019	.029	−.069	−.047	.014
	...	−.142	−.085	.044	.408	.524	.174
		...	.006	−.395	−.243	−.133	−.055
			...	.095	−.058	−.055	.062
				...	.111	.038	.027
					...	.731	.372
						...	.332
							...
151	.123	−.226	.205	.401	.390	.265	.097
014	.304	−.289	.222	.287	.429	.445	.262
043	−.053	.109	.113	−.129	−.237	−.052	.054
005	−.039	.147	−.031	−.133	−.077	.045	.062
057	.146	−.448	.017	.243	.369	.265	.174
...	−.076	−.206	−.091	.095	.000	.091	.083
	...	−.058	−.003	.093	.330	.178	.055
		...	−.074	−.286	−.249	−.142	−.078
			...	.070	.111	.147	.142
				...	.279	.186	.116
					...	.681	.514
						...	.552
							...

Appendix B.
Classification of Industrial Labor Markets

1970 Census Industrial Classification	1970 Census Codes
Primary	
Agriculture, fishing, forestry	017–029
Classical Capitalist	
Nonmetallic mining and quarrying	057–058
Lumber and wood products	107–109
Food and drink	268–298
Tobacco products	299
Textiles	307–327
Plastic goods	348–387
Leather products, shoes	388–397
Manufacturing, nondurable	398–399
Small-Skilled	
Nonprimary metals production	157–169
Construction	067–078
Furniture	118
Stone, clay, and glass products	119–138
Machinery, other than electrical	177–198
Professional and photographic equipment, watches	239–257
Ordnance	258
Manufacturing, durable	259–267
Automobile and electrical repair	757–759
Business and repair services	767

1970 Census Industrial Classification	*1970 Census Codes*

Engineering-Based

Coal, metal, and petroleum mining	047–049
Primary metals production	139–149
Electrical machinery, transportation equipment	199–238
Paper products	328–337
Chemical, petroleum, and rubber products except plastic goods	349–379, 347
Transportation, other than taxis	407–408
Trucking	418–429
Radio and telecommunications	447–449
Utilities and sanitary services	467–499
Postal service	907

Petty Bourgeois

Taxicab service	409
Wholesale trade	507–599
Retail trade	607–699
Real estate	718–719
Detective and protective services	747
Personal services	769–799
Sports, entertainment, and recreation	807–817

Professional

Printing, publishing	338–339
Business services	727–739, 748–749
Health, education	828–868
Museums, art, religion	869–877
Engineering, architectural, accounting	888–899
Military	

Bureaucratic

Banking, credit, insurance, investment	707–717
Welfare, nonprofit organizations	878–887
Government: federal, state, local	917–947

Notes

1. Immigrant Assimilation

1. "How the Immigrants Made It in Miami," *Business Week*, 1 May 1971, p. 88.
2. Ibid.
3. Edward J. Linehan, "Cuba's Exiles Bring New Life to Miami," *National Geographic* 144 (July 1973): 95.
4. "A Cuban Success Story—in the United States," *U.S. News & World Report*, 20 March 1967, pp. 104–106.
5. "How the Immigrants Made It in Miami," p. 88.
6. "A Cuban Success Story," p. 104.
7. "Flight from Cuba—Castro's Loss Is U.S. Gain," *U.S. News & World Report*, 31 May 1971, p. 74.
8. Ibid., pp. 74–77; see also "Doctors in Exile," *Time*, 13 April 1962, p. 79; and "It's Your Turn in the Sun," *Time*, 16 October 1978, pp. 51–52.
9. "Migrant Workers' Plight," *Fortune*, November 1959, pp. 274–276.
10. Violence in the Oasis," *Time*, 17 February 1961, p. 18; and "Migrants and Machines," *New Republic*, 24 July 1961, pp. 7–8.
11. "Tossed Salad," *Newsweek*, 20 February 1961, p. 26; "Migrants and Machines," p. 8.
12. "Deathtrap for Wetbacks," *Time*, 11 October 1968, pp. 24–25.
13. "Where Braceros Once Worked," *Business Week*, 16 January 1965, p. 32.
14. "Growers Face Loss of Braceros," *Business Week*, 22 August 1964, p. 120; see also "California: What Help for the Harvest?" *Newsweek*, 2 November 1964, p. 77.
15. "Deathtrap for Wetbacks," p. 25; "Where Braceros Once Worked," p. 33.
16. "Deathtrap for Wetbacks," p. 25.
17. "The Little Strike that Grew to La Causa," *Time*, 4 July 1969, pp. 16–21. See also Richard Severo, "The Flight of the Wetbacks," *New York Times Magazine*, 10 March 1974, pp. 17, 77–84.
18. "California Tries to Dam the Alien Tide," *Business Week*, 12 February 1972, pp. 34–36.
19. Leonard F. Chapman, Jr., " 'Silent Invasion' That Takes Millions of

American Jobs," *U.S. News & World Report*, 9 December 1974, pp. 77–78. See also "'Invasion' by Illegal Aliens, and the Problems They Create," *U.S. News & World Report*, 23 July 1973, pp. 32–35.

20. Robert E. Park, "Racial Assimilation in Secondary Groups," Chapter 16 in *Race and Culture*, p. 204.

21. Robert E. Park, "Our Racial Frontier on the Pacific," Chapter 9 in *Race and Culture*, pp. 138–158.

22. This discussion of assimilation draws on Joe R. Feagin, *Racial and Ethnic Relations*.

23. Milton M. Gordon, *Assimilation in American Life*, pp. 3–18, 233.

24. Milton M. Gordon, "Assimilation in America: Theory and Reality," in *Majority and Minority*, edited by Norman R. Yetman and C. Hoy Steele, p. 233.

25. By limiting the number of immigrants of any nationality to 2 percent of the United States residents of that nationality residing in the country in 1890. The Western Hemisphere aliens were exempt from the quotas. See U.S. Commission on Civil Rights, *The Tarnished Golden Door: Civil Rights Issues in Immigration*, pp. 9–10. See also Oscar Handlin, *The Uprooted*, p. 260.

26. Gordon, "Assimilation in America," pp. 229–230.

27. Ibid., p. 231.

28. Ibid., p. 233.

29. Joe Feagin distinguishes prescriptive from descriptive theories of assimilation. See Feagin, *Racial and Ethnic Relations*, pp. 29, 35.

30. Gordon, *Assimilation in American Life*, p. 67.

31. Ibid., pp. 80–81.

32. Ibid., p. 78.

33. Andrew M. Greeley, *Ethnicity in the United States: A Preliminary Reconnaissance*.

34. Gordon, *Assimilation in American Life*, p. 80. For analyses of intermarriage among Mexican Americans over different generations, see Frank G. Mittelbach and Joan W. Moore, "Ethnic Endogamy—the Case of Mexican Americans," *American Journal of Sociology* 74 (July 1968): 50–62; Robert Schoen and Verne E. Nelson, "Intermarriage among Spanish Surnamed Californians, 1962–1974," *International Migration Review* 12 (Fall 1978): 359–369; and Robert Schoen and Lawrence E. Cohen, "Ethnic Endogamy among Mexican American Grooms: A Reanalysis of Generational and Occupational Effects," *American Journal of Sociology* 86 (September 1980): 359–366. At present, similar studies do not exist for Cubans.

35. See Ruby Jo Reeves Kennedy, "Single or Triple Melting-Pot? Intermarriage Trends in New Haven, 1870–1940," *American Journal of Sociology* 49 (January 1944): 331–339, and its update, "Single or Triple Melting-Pot? Intermarriage in New Haven, 1870–1950," *American Journal of Sociology* 58 (July 1952): 56–59; see also Will Herberg, *Protestant-Catholic-Jew*.

36. Gordon, "Assimilation in America," p. 235. The phrase "a nation

within a nation" was Booker T. Washington's. See Park, "Racial Assimilation," p. 218.

37. Therefore, Gordon thought that a more accurate description was structural pluralism rather than cultural pluralism.

38. Gordon, "Assimilation in America," p. 235.

39. Ibid., p. 243.

40. Feagin, *Racial and Ethnic Relations*, p. 30.

41. They arrived after the 1980 census, but even if they had arrived prior to it, it is unlikely that they could have been sampled by the census while in the refugee camps.

42. The U.S. Bureau of the Census conducted the 1976 Survey of Income and Education from April through July 1976, as a supplement to the yearly Current Population Survey with additional questions to it. Of the 440,815 persons for whom data were obtained, 1,669 persons were Hispanics. In these comparisons, all data for Cubans and Mexicans are for *immigrants* rather than for Mexican and Cuban *origin*, which includes both the immigrants and the native-born. Hence these comparisons differ from others that do not incorporate this distinction. See, for example, Morris J. Newman, "A Profile of Hispanics in the U.S. Work Force," *Monthly Labor Review* 101 (December 1978): 3–14; and U.S. Bureau of the Census, "Persons of Spanish Origin in the United States: March 1979," *Current Population Reports*, Series p-20, no. 354. The fact that data publications of the U.S. government fail to distinguish between immigrants and the native-born renders their excellent published data of little use for studying immigrants. The data presented here also differ from those of Marta Tienda, "A Socioeconomic Profile of Hispanic-American Male Workers: Perspectives on Labor Utilization and Earnings" in *National Symposium on Hispanics and CETA 1980*, edited by Antonio Furino. Although Tienda considers immigrants separately from the native-born and her data are also from the 1976 Survey of Income and Education, she did not distinguish between those Cuban immigrants who immigrated prior to 1960 and those who came to the United States during the period of political immigration.

43. U.S. Commission on Civil Rights, *Social Indicators of Equality for Minorities and Women*, Table 4.3. Aggregate data for whites in the United States are "pulled down" below what they should be because they include Hispanics, 96 percent of whom are classified as white. The U.S. Commission on Civil Rights has rectified this error by publishing data for the "majority," meaning "white, not of Hispanic origin."

44. U.S. Bureau of the Census, "Population Profile of the United States: 1976," *Current Population Reports*, Series p-20, no. 307, Table 6.

45. Data for whites are from the U.S. Bureau of the Census, *Statistical Abstract of the United States, 1977*, Table 217.

46. Ibid.

47. Ibid., Table 219.

48. Ibid., Table 661.

49. Newman, "A Profile of Hispanics," p. 11.

50. For a recent view of the same evolutionary perspective see Nathan Glazer, "Blacks and Ethnic Groups: The Difference and the Political Difference it Makes," *Social Problems* 18 (Spring 1971): 444–461.

51. Everett S. Lee, "A Theory of Migration," *Demography* 3 (1966): 50.

52. Ibid., p. 51.

53. For reviews of the literature on migration, see P. Neal Ritchey, "Explanations of Migration," *Annual Review of Sociology* 2 (1976): 363–404; and William Petersen, "International Migration," *Annual Review of Sociology* 4 (1978): 533–575.

54. Alejandro Portes, "Immigrant Aspirations," *Sociology of Education* 51 (October 1978): 241.

55. See, for example, Robert E. Park, "Human Migration and the Marginal Man," *American Journal of Sociology* 33 (May 1928): 881–893, as well as other writings in *Race and Culture*; William I. Thomas and Florian Znaniecki, *The Polish Peasant in Europe and America*, vol. 2; Marcus L. Hansen, *The Atlantic Migration, 1607–1860: A History of the Continuing Settlement of the United States*; Oscar Handlin, *The Uprooted* and *The Newcomers: Negroes and Puerto Ricans in a Changing Metropolis*; John Higham, *Strangers in the Land: Patterns of American Nativism 1860–1925*; Maldwyn Allen Jones, *American Immigration*; Herbert J. Gans, *The Urban Villagers: Group and Class in the Life of Italian Americans*.

56. Portes, "Immigrant Aspirations," p. 242.

57. Donald L. Noel, "A Theory of the Origin of Ethnic Stratification," *Social Problems* 16 (Fall 1968): 157–172.

58. Edna Bonacich, "A Theory of Ethnic Antagonism: The Split Labor Market," *American Sociological Review* 37 (October 1972): 547–559.

59. Richard A. Schermerhorn, *Comparative Ethnic Relations: A Framework for Theory and Research*, p. 12.

60. As Feagin notes, ethnic groups have been defined in two different senses, one narrow and one broad. The inclusive definition is illustrated by Gordon, who extends it to all groups "set off by race, religion, or national origin . . . in that all of them serve to create, through historical circumstances, a sense of peoplehood. . . ." Gordon, *Assimilation in American Life*, p. 27. The narrow definition is illustrated by Van den Berghe, who omits groups defined by race and limits it to groups defined "on the basis of cultural criteria." Pierre L. Van den Berghe, *Race and Racism: A Comparative Perspective*, p. 10. Feagin reflects that underlying the two definitions are different assumptions as to the similarity of experiences of white and nonwhite groups. See Feagin, *Racial and Ethnic Groups*, pp. 8–10.

61. From personal experience, I am convinced that the adjustment process is the hardest for immigrants who arrive in their adolescence. Adolescents, fully socialized in the values and culture of their country, have to make all their adult choices (courtship, marriage, career goals, and the like) in a culture with totally different values and roles. Immigrants who arrive as children are quickly resocialized; those who arrive as adults have already made their life choices.

62. Portes, "Immigrant Aspirations," p. 242. I stress this point because a great deal of the current work on Mexicans in America fails to distinguish between Mexican Americans properly so (the native-born) and Mexican immigrants. See, for example, Dudley L. Poston, Jr., David Alvírez, and Marta Tienda, "Earnings Differences between Anglo and Mexican American Male Workers in 1960 and 1970: Changes in the 'Cost' of Being Mexican American," *Social Science Quarterly* 57 (December 1976): 618–631; James E. Long, "Productivity, Employment, Discrimination, and the Relative Economic Status of Spanish-Origin Males," *Social Science Quarterly* 58 (December 1977): 357–373; Newman, "A Profile of Hispanics in the U.S. Work Force." Chiswick distinguishes the two analytically and empirically, but ultimately joins them in an unexplained "Mexican ethnic-group effect." Barry R. Chiswick, "The Effect of Americanization on the Earnings of Foreign-Born Men," *Journal of Political Economy* 86 (1978): 914. The study of the Mexican native-born belongs, analytically and empirically, with the study of other native-born ethnic Americans; and the study of Mexican immigrants belongs with the study of other immigrant groups, who experience a cultural and economic life not only in America but also in their own country. The relationship of Mexican immigrants to Chicanos on the basis of their common culture and ethnicity is a question for analysis.

63. Therefore, Puerto Ricans or Hawaiians who migrate to and from the island and the mainland are not immigrants in the same sense as other Latin Americans or Asians. Since they are citizens by birth, part of the nation or commonwealth, their migration is not directed or regulated. Therefore, their migration could be understood analytically as an internal migration. For the changes in immigration law embodied in the 1965 act that overturned the national origins quotas of the 1920s, see Edward M. Kennedy, "The Immigration Act of 1965," *Annals of the American Academy of Political and Social Sciences* 367 (September 1966): 137–149.

64. I use the term "dislocation" to mean, literally, that which happens when one loses one's economic, social, and ideological "place" in a society.

65. Thus the categories "Cuban counterrevolutionary" and "Mexican *bracero*" have meaning. The obverse, "Cuban *bracero*" and "Mexican counterrevolutionary," are ridiculous.

66. The role of the state in deciding whether immigrants are political or economic can be seen once again with respect to the Haitian immigrants in the 1980s.

67. For a detailed history of the Cuban revolution, see Hugh Thomas, *The Cuban Revolution*; for analyses of the first decade, see Carmelo Mesa-Lago, ed., *Revolutionary Change in Cuba*.

68. Richard R. Fagen, Richard A. Brody, and Thomas I. O'Leary, *Cubans in Exile: Disaffection and the Revolution.*

69. U.S. Immigration and Naturalization Service, *Annual Report, 1960*, Table 8; and *1970*, Table 8. The 1970 figures for Cubans most likely correspond to 1968 arrivals since it took about two years to adjust the initial

parolee status to that of immigrant. Data exclude housewives, children, and others with no reported occupation.

70. Alejandro Portes, "Migration and Underdevelopment," *Politics &) Society* 8 (1978): 1–48.

71. The approach derived from Immanuel Wallerstein, *The Modern World-System*. As Wallerstein argues, capitalism is a world economic system. Hence, the problem of migration can easily be reset within the perspective of the modern world system. But doing so merely restates the idea that differences in development promote migration. In addition, the modern world system can explain economic migration very well, but it is helpless to explain political migration. The modern world system is better left to explain uneven development among countries.

72. U.S. Immigration and Naturalization Service, *Annual Report, 1970*, Table 8. Data exclude housewives, children, and others with no reported occupation.

73. Feagin, *Racial and Ethnic Groups*, p. 47.

74. Michael Burawoy, "The Functions and Reproduction of Migrant Labor: Comparative Material from Southern Africa and the United States," *American Journal of Sociology* 81 (March 1976): 1050–1087; Manuel Castells, "Immigrant Workers and Class Struggles in Advanced Capitalism: The Western European Experience," *Politics &) Society* 5 (1975): 33–66; Alejandro Portes, "Structural Causes of Illegal Immigration," (Duke University: Department of Sociology, 1977, mimeographed).

75. See Arthur F. Corwin, *Immigrants—and Immigrants: Perspectives on Mexican Labor Migration to the United States*.

2. Lending Cuban Political Immigrants a Hand

1. The 1976 figure is Lourdes Casal's best estimate. As she says, "The total number of Cuban immigrants since 1959 is impossible to calculate precisely." Since Cuban immigrants entered the United States in a variety of ways (regular flights, boats and rafts, prior residence in other countries) and with a variety of legal statuses ("parolee," "resident," "tourist," "immigrant," and most recently "entrants"), the official immigration figures both undercount them and tend to refer to the year in which they obtained the legal status of permanent residents, often a few years after arrival as "tourists," "parolees," or now "entrants." In addition, the figures of the Cuban Refugee Program include only those who registered with it. See Lourdes Casal, "Cubans in the United States: Their Impact on U.S.–Cuban Relations," in *Revolutionary Cuba in the World Arena*, edited by Martin Weinstein, pp. 109–110. Clark's estimates are that 64.2 percent of the arrivals from 1960 to 1974 came under the parole system, and only 13.9 percent entered as immigrants or residents. Juan M. Clark, "The Exodus from Revolutionary Cuba (1959–1974): A Sociological Analysis," p. 73. For the immigration status of the 1980 refugees from Mariel, see Edward M. Kennedy, "Refugee Act of 1980," *International Migration Review* 15 (Spring 1981): 141–156.

2. Nelson Amaro and Alejandro Portes, "Una sociología del exilio: Situación de los grupos cubanos en Estados Unidos," *Aportes* 23 (January 1972): 6–24; my translation.

3. Casal, "Cubans in the United States," pp. 120–133.

4. José Llanes, *Cuban Americans: Masters of Survival.* To preserve anonymity, Llanes drew 58 composite characters from 187 informants, giving them fictitious names and noncorresponding life histories. He recorded and translated their words faithfully, submitting the composite characters he created to the initial informants from which he drew them. Hence, I use his composite characters for illustration.

5. *Batistianos* means those who had been directly tied to and compromised by Fulgencio Batista's government. In large part, they migrated to Europe, particularly Spain.

6. Amaro and Portes, "Una sociología del exilio," p. 10. See also Maurice Zeitlin, "Cuba: Revolution without a Blueprint," in *Cuban Communism*, edited by Irving Louis Horowitz, pp. 199–210.

7. See Anna P. Schreiber, "Economic Coercion as an Instrument of Foreign Policy: U.S. Economic Measures against Cuba and the Dominican Republic," *World Politics* 25 (April 1973): 387–413. Soon after the United States broke off diplomatic relations with Cuba in January 1961, the U.S. government waived the usual visa required to enter the country, thus facilitating the exodus of Cubans.

8. Llanes, *Cuban Americans*, pp. 53–54.

9. Ibid., p. 64.

10. Amaro and Portes, "Una sociología del exilio," p. 11.

11. Clark, "The Exodus from Revolutionary Cuba," pp. 80–81.

12. Llanes, *Cuban Americans*, pp. 23–24.

13. See Bryan O. Walsh, "Cuban Refugee Children," *Journal of Inter-American Studies and World Affairs* 13 (June 1971): 378–415.

14. Richard R. Fagen, Richard A. Brody, and Thomas J. O'Leary, *Cubans in Exile: Disaffection and the Revolution*, p. 62.

15. Registrations with the Cuban Refugee Emergency Center are always an undercount since they do not include those who first migrated to other countries, or went to friends and family in other parts of the United States. Hence, they are only indicative of the scope of the migration. U.S. Immigration and Naturalization Service estimates of Cubans entering the United States are in Clark, "The Exodus from Revolutionary Cuba," Table 3. The Immigration and Naturalization Service estimates that 248,070 Cubans entered the United States from 1959 to 1962.

16. Fagen, Brody, and O'Leary, *Cubans in Exile*, Table 7.1.

17. Ibid., Table 2.2.

18. Nelson Amaro Victoria, "Mass and Class in the Origins of the Cuban Revolution," in *Cuban Communism*, edited by Horowitz, pp. 155–185.

19. Amaro and Portes, "Una sociología del exilio," p. 11.

20. In Clark, "The Exodus from Revolutionary Cuba," p. 184.

21. Casal, "Cubans in the United States," p. 121.

22. Llanes, *Cuban Americans*, p. 19.

23. For analyses of the militarization of the Cuban revolution, see Marta San Martín and Ramón L. Bonachea, "The Military Dimension of the Cuban Revolution," in *Cuban Communism*, edited by Horowitz, pp. 389–420; and Irving Louis Horowitz, "Military Origins of the Cuban Revolution," and "Military Outcomes of the Cuban Revolution," in *Cuban Communism*, edited by Horowitz, pp. 66–105.

24. Clark, "The Exodus from Revolutionary Cuba," p. 86.

25. See "Cuba: End of the Freedom Flights," *Time*, 13 September 1971.

26. The U.S. Immigration and Naturalization Service estimates that 345,481 Cubans entered the United States from 1965 to 1973. In Clark, "The Exodus from Revolutionary Cuba," Table 3. But these yearly estimates do not correspond to the different phases of the migration. For example, the year 1965 encompassed those who escaped by boats or rafts when nothing else was possible, the Camarioca flotilla exodus in the fall, and the beginning of the airlift in December. The year 1973 saw the end of the air bridge from Varadero to Miami and the start of the arrival of the refugees from Spain.

27. John F. Thomas, "Cuban Refugees in the United States," *International Migration Review* 2 (Spring 1967): 46–57.

28. In Clark, "The Exodus from Revolutionary Cuba," pp. 89–90.

29. Amaro and Portes, "Una sociología del exilio," p. 13.

30. See Schreiber, "Economic Coercion as an Instrument of Foreign Policy."

31. Those who remained in Cuba with the revolution tell the story that these were the years when, watching Nitza Villapol (the Julia Child of Cuban cooking) on television, they nearly expected her to say: "Here is a piece of cardboard. First, fry it in olive oil." Despite the vastness of revolutionary changes in Cuba, Cuban culture and Cuban humor remain intact.

32. Amaro and Portes, "Una sociología del exilio," p. 13.

33. Llanes, *Cuban Americans*, pp. 93–94.

34. Paul Tabori, *The Anatomy of Exile*, p. 348.

35. Casal, "Cubans in the United States," p. 121.

36. Ibid., p. 116.

37. Ibid., p. 118.

38. Jorge I. Domínguez, "La tradición liberal y la emigración cubana," *Areito* 1 (January–March 1975): 4–5; my translation.

39. Alejandro Portes, Juan M. Clark, and Robert L. Bach, "The New Wave: A Statistical Profile of Recent Cuban Exiles to the United States," *Cuban Studies* 7 (January 1977): 1–32.

40. Ibid., p. 15.

41. For more details and a discussion of both its antecedents and consequences, see Carmelo Mesa-Lago, "Ideological Radicalization and Economic Policy in Cuba," in *Cuban Communism*, edited by Horowitz, pp. 211–240.

42. In 1959, the government nationalized all farms of over 1,000 acres; in 1963, of over 165 acres. Ibid., p. 213. For the incremental nature of the collectivization process, see ibid., Table 1.

43. Portes et al., "The New Wave," p. 17.

44. For the five stages of the Cuban revolution, see Carmelo Mesa-Lago, *Cuba in the 1970s: Pragmatism and Institutionalization*, Chapter 1. For a review of the literature on the institutionalization and the debate on its meaning, see Max Azicri, "The Institutionalization of the Cuban Revolution: A Review of the Literature," *Cuban Studies* 9 (July 1979): 63–78; Irving Louis Horowitz, "Institutionalization as Integration: The Cuban Revolution at Age Twenty," *Cuban Studies* 9 (July 1979): 84–90; and Frank T. Fitzgerald, "Reviewing the Literature on the Institutionalization of the Cuban Revolution: A Response to Max Azicri," *Cuban Studies* 11 (January 1981): 87–89. It is important to realize that "socialism" and "communism" have different meanings in different societies. Americans too often use them interchangeably. Where they represent political parties, as in France or Chile, they refer to the specific programmatic vision of those parties. These vary according to the history of the countries. For example, the French Communist Party is analogous to the Chilean Socialist Party in its vision of the good society and its program for radical, revolutionary change; while the French Socialist Party is analogous to the Chilean Communist Party, a more moderate and gradual vision of change often labelled reformist by the other more radical party. In Cuba they do not, of course, represent different political parties with distinct visions. Cubans use socialism to mean the shape of the economy—the income redistribution measures, the provision of health and medical services by the state, and the like; communism is the shape of the political system, the party, and so on. Writing about Cuba, I use them here in the Cuban sense.

45. See also Sergio Roca, "Cuban Economic Policy in the 1970s: The Trodden Paths," in *Cuban Communism*, edited by Horowitz, pp. 265–301; and Robert M. Bernardo, "Moral Stimulation and Labor Allocation in Cuba," in *Cuban Communism*, edited by Horowitz, pp. 338–371.

46. Casal, "Cubans in the United States," p. 128. Casal observes that in the early years of exile the political heterogeneity encompassed the *Batistianos*, who wanted Cuba to be just as it was; the liberal *reformistas*, who felt that the revolution was necessary, but had been betrayed; and the radicals, who supported most policies of the revolution but were against its leaders. The differences among them were obscured by their commitment to the goal of overthrowing Castro. Casal argued that in the 1970s the political heterogeneity was different, ranging from quasi-fascist groups to Marxists, with all kinds of positions in between. Lacking a common goal, they were not united. For more details, see ibid., pp. 124–125.

47. Karl Mannheim, *Essays in the Sociology of Knowledge*.

48. See Maurice Zeitlin, "Political Generations in the Cuban Working Class," *American Journal of Sociology* 71 (March 1966): 493–508.

49. Morris Dickstein, *Gates of Eden: American Culture in the Sixties*,

captures the cultural consciousness of America's youth in the sixties. Arlie Hochschild, "Student Power in Action," in *Cuban Communism*, edited by Horowitz, pp. 372–388, portrays its opposite counterpart in the Cuban youth culture of the sixties, showing that "what it is to be young changes with history."

50. Antonio Maceo was one of the leaders of the Cuban war of independence against Spain. *55 Hermanos* means fifty-five brothers and sisters.

51. With the exception of those who had actively participated in counterrevolutionary activities.

52. Llanes, *Cuban Americans*, p. 142.

53. Casal, "Cubans in the United States"; Jeff Stein, "An Army in Exile," *New York*, 10 September 1979; Dagmaris Cabezas, "You Can Go Home Again," *Nation*, 7 June 1980.

54. Bach's demographic study of the 1980 wave of immigrants who were processed in the three South Florida centers—Coral Gables, Opa Locke, and Eglin—is reported in Robert L. Bach, "The New Cuban Immigrants: Their Background and Prospects," *Monthly Labor Review* 103 (October 1980): 39–46; the demographic study of the immigrants who were processed at the military camps of Fort Eglin, Fort Chaffee, Fort Indiantown Gap, and Fort McCoy is reported in Robert L. Bach, Jennifer B. Bach, and Timothy Triplett, "The Flotilla 'Entrants': Latest and Most Controversial," *Cuban Studies* 11/12 (July 1981/January 1982): 29–48. I have combined both to provide an overall picture of the 1980 wave of immigrants.

55. Calculated from Bach et al., "The Flotilla 'Entrants'." From samples of refugees at the various processing centers, Bach estimates that 90 percent of the South Florida arrivals (N = 1,416) were white, compared to only 50 percent for the camps (N = 4,393).

56. Although many are convinced that this is quite an underestimate. See Benigno E. Aguirre, "Differential Migration of Cuban Social Races," *Latin American Research Review* 11 (1976): 103–124, especially footnote 9.

57. Ibid., p. 105.

58. See Nancy F. Foner, *Jamaica Farewell: Jamaican Migrants in London*, Chapter 2, for the similar meaning of race in Jamaica.

59. Possibly the reason for the undercount of blacks in the Cuban census. As the Brazilians say, "Money bleaches." In Pierre L. Van den Berghe, *Race and Racism: A Comparative Perspective*, p. 69.

60. Lourdes Casal, "Revolution and Race: Blacks in Contemporary Cuba," p. 15.

61. Portes et al., "The New Wave," p. 9. Differences exist also by wave of migration and by region of settlement. Eleanor Rogg's sample of Cubans in West New York was 4 percent black. Eleanor Meyer Rogg, *The Assimilation of Cuban Exiles: The Role of Community and Class*, Table 41. Juan Clark's sample of Cubans that arrived in the United States in the period 1963–1965, in rafts and boats, showed the highest percentage black, 10.2 percent.

62. The process of chain migration often proceeds through kinship ties. See P. Neal Ritchey, "Explanations of Migration," *Annual Review of Sociology* 2 (1976): 389–393.

63. Aguirre, "Differential Migration of Cuban Social Races," pp. 112–114.

64. Of the two types of creolization that Patterson describes for Jamaica and Guyana, segmentary and synthetic, segmentary creolization describes Cuban culture best. There is a tension in segmentary creolization between its two types: Euro–West Indian, almost European in form and bias toward white values and culture; and Afro–West Indian, forged out of the remnants of African culture. Due to the history of Caribbean societies, these overlap with the social classes and races that constituted colonial plantation society. Hence, the middle classes emulate European culture. See Orlando Patterson, "Context and Choice in Ethnic Allegiance: A Theoretical Framework and Caribbean Case Study," in *Ethnicity: Theory and Experience,* edited by Nathan Glazer and Daniel P. Moynihan (Cambridge: Harvard University Press, 1976), pp. 305–349.

65. Maurice Zeitlin, "Economic Insecurity and the Political Attitudes of Cuban Workers," *American Sociological Review* 31 (February 1966): 47.

66. Richard R. Fagen, "Revolution: For Internal Consumption Only," in *Cuban Communism,* edited by Horowitz, p. 188. Also see Irving Louis Horowitz, "Authenticity and Autonomy in Cuban Communism," in *Cuban Communism,* edited by Horowitz, pp. 117–125.

67. Geoffrey E. Fox, "Cuban Workers in Exile," *Trans-Action* 8 (September 1971): 21.

68. Like Casal, I also found that privately many white Cubans express racist opinions. See Lourdes Casal, "Revolution and Race," p. 20.

69. To distinguish among types of discrimination, see Joe R. Feagin and Douglas Lee Eckberg, "Discrimination: Motivation, Action, Effects, and Context," *Annual Review of Sociology* 6 (1980): 1–20.

70. The Cuban movie *Portrait of Teresa* revolves around this very contradiction between Teresa's active participation outside the home and in the revolution, and her husband's sexist attitudes and expectations of her as a wife. The movie ends as she leaves him—in Cuban culture, a remarkable ending.

71. Feagin and Eckberg, "Discrimination," p. 5.

72. Casal, "Revolution and Race," p. 10.

73. See, for example, Constantina Safilios-Rothschild, *Women and Social Policy,* pp. 9–10; Sara Evans, *Personal Politics: The Roots of Women's Liberation in the Civil Rights Movement and the New Left.*

74. Llanes, *Cuban Americans,* pp. 170–171.

75. Bach et al., "The Flotilla 'Entrants'," p. 39.

76. Ibid., p. 44.

77. Llanes, *Cuban Americans,* p. 193.

78. In 1953, 17.9 percent of the economically active labor force had been in commerce; in 1968, it had declined to 11.5 percent. In Joseph Gugler, "A Minimum of Urbanism and a Maximum of Ruralism: The

Cuban Experience," *Studies in Comparative International Development* 15 (Summer 1980): 27–44.

79. Gastón A. Fernández, "The Freedom Flotilla: A Legitimacy Crisis of Cuban Socialism?" *Journal of Interamerican Studies and World Affairs* 24 (May 1982): 183–209.

80. Ibid., p. 200; Bach et al., "The Flotilla 'Entrants'," p. 44.

81. Because the return trips were very expensive—the average in 1979 was $1,000 per person for a two-week stay—they did select from among the more successful Cubans in United States. In addition, when the gap in living standards is very large, as it is between Cuba and the United States, a small item—a Kodak Instamatic camera, a color photograph—is a large difference.

82. Llanes, *Cuban Americans*, p. 145.

83. Although the actual proportion varied among the resettlement camps. Bach's sample of Eglin Air Force Base in South Florida showed 16.4 percent; his sample of the military camps in the Midwest showed 16 percent overall (17.9 percent of all men; 2.9 percent of all women), but Fort McCoy, the last camp to open, held 45.1 percent of all the ex-offenders. Fernández found 28.5 percent of his sample at Fort Chaffee had been in prison. Bach, "The New Cuban Immigrants," p. 43; Bach et al., "The Flotilla 'Entrants'," Table 7 and p. 44; Fernández, "The Freedom Flotilla," p. 189.

84. In Bach et al., "The Flotilla 'Entrants'," p. 46.

85. Bach estimates that at Eglin Air Force Base in South Florida the political prisoners constituted between 9 and 20 percent of those who spent time in jail. Bach, "The New Immigrants," p. 43. No comparable estimate is given for the camps.

86. The U.S. Immigration and Naturalization Service figures are as follows. Of the 124,789 Mariel refugees, 23,970 (or 19.21 percent) had been in jail in Cuba. Of those who had been in prison, 5,486 (22.89 percent) were in jail for political crimes, 16,710 (69.71 percent) for minor crimes or acts that were crimes in Cuba but not here, such as being unemployed or engaging in private enterprise, and only 1,774 (7.4 percent) were considered to be serious criminals. In addition, there were approximately 600 mental patients or mentally retarded persons and about 1,500 homosexuals. See Paul Montgomery, "For Cuban Refugees, Promise of U.S. Fades," *New York Times*, 19 April 1981.

87. Bach, "The New Cuban Immigrants," p. 42; and Bach et al., "The Flotilla 'Entrants'," p. 36.

88. Fernández, "The Freedom Flotilla," p. 194. Fernández also compared the age of the Fort Chaffee refugees to that of the Cuban population. See Table 3.

89. Ibid., pp. 196–197. See also Sergio Díaz-Briquets, "Demographic and Related Determinants of Recent Cuban Emigration," *International Migration Review* 17 (Spring 1983): 95–119.

90. Zeitlin, "Political Generations in the Cuban Working Class," p. 493.

91. Ibid., p. 505.

92. Ibid., p. 508.

93. Llanes, *Cuban Americans*, p. 170.

94. For details, see Montgomery, "For Cuban Refugees, Promise of U.S. Fades." As "entrants," the 1980 immigrants are allowed to stay but do not qualify for the more extensive aid package available to refugees.

95. Bach, "The New Cuban Immigrants," p. 44.

96. Ibid., pp. 44–45.

97. Oscar Handlin, *The Uprooted*, p. 98.

98. For a fuller exposition of those two points of view, see Fernández, "The Freedom Flotilla."

99. This seems equally true in governments that are elected. Under adverse economic conditions, people vote for change, as Americans did in 1980.

100. Therefore, in societies that are democratic in their formal institutions there are some remarkably undemocratic periods. In the fifties, McCarthyism, with its violations of civil liberties, is the most obvious American example.

101. Albert O. Hirschman, *Exit, Voice and Loyalty*.

102. Fagen et al., *Cubans in Exile*, p. 120.

103. Ibid., pp. 116–117.

104. Llanes, *Cuban Americans*, p. 154.

105. Antonio A. Micocci, "A New Life for Cuban Exiles," *American Education* 1 (March 1965): 28.

106. Richard Ferree Smith, "Refugees," *Annals of the American Academy of Political and Social Sciences* 367 (September 1966): 48.

107. John F. Thomas, "Cuban Refugee Program," *Welfare in Review* 1 (September 1963): 1–20. John F. Thomas was the director of the Cuban Refugee Program, Welfare Administration, Department of Health, Education and Welfare.

108. In Rafael J. Prohías and Lourdes Casal, *The Cuban Minority in the U.S.*, p. 102.

109. Based on the differences between the figures of the U.S. Immigration and Naturalization Service for the total number of Cubans admitted in the United States and the registrations at the Cuban Refugee Emergency Center. Clark, "The Exodus from Revolutionary Cuba," p. 116.

110. Thomas, "Cuban Refugees in the United States," p. 50.

111. Prohías and Casal, *The Cuban Minority*, p. 107 and Table 46.

112. Of $100 per family or $60 per individual. Ibid., p. 107.

113. Llanes, *Cuban Americans*, pp. 34–36.

114. See Rogg, *The Assimilation of Cuban Exiles*.

115. Prohías and Casal, *The Cuban Minority*, pp. 119–120.

116. Llanes, *Cuban Americans*, p. 115.

117. In Clark, "The Exodus from Revolutionary Cuba," p. 117.

118. Prohías and Casal, *The Cuban Minority*, p. 110. Prohías and Casal stress that this resettlement program was the determining factor in the present geographic distribution of the Cuban population in the United

States. Certain urban areas were favored due to economic factors, such as the availability of jobs, and social factors, such as the existence of a Cuban community or at least of a Spanish-speaking community.

119. Raúl Moncarz, "A Model of Professional Adaptation of Refugees: The Cuban Case in the U.S. 1959–1970," *International Migration* 11 (1973): 171–183.

120. Thomas, "Cuban Refugees in the United States," p. 51.

121. Herbert Teitelbaum and Richard J. Hiller, "Bilingual Education: The Legal Mandate," *Harvard Educational Review* 47 (May 1977): 138–170.

122. Joe Hall, *The Cuban Refugee in the Public Schools of Dade County, Florida,* Annual Report no. 7, 1967/1968, p. 1.

123. Hall, *The Cuban Refugee in the Public Schools,* Annual Report no. 12, 1972/1973, p. 3. The only other school systems which received funds from the Cuban Refugee Program were Union City and West New York, New Jersey. Since 1970 they received roughly $1 million dollars a year each. In Prohías and Casal, *The Cuban Minority,* p. 142.

124. This financial arrangement remained in effect until the 1968–1969 school year, when a new plan was worked out that ensured that the federal government would not pay for any student who had remained for five years or more in the schools. Thus payment for "old" refugees (those who had arrived before October 3, 1965) stopped beginning with the 1970–1971 school year. Hall, *The Cuban Refugee in the Public Schools,* Annual Report no. 12, 1972/1973.

125. For more details on these various programs of instruction, see Silvia Pedraza-Bailey and Teresa A. Sullivan, "Bilingual Education in the Reception of Political Immigrants: The Case of Cubans in Miami, Florida," in *Bilingual Education and Public Policy in the United States,* edited by Raymond V. Padilla, pp. 376–394.

126. Hall, *The Cuban Refugee in the Public Schools,* Annual Reports no. 1–12, 1961/1962–1972/1973.

127. Hall, *The Cuban Refugee in the Public Schools,* Annual Report no. 3, 1962/1963.

128. Hall, *The Cuban Refugee in the Public Schools,* Annual Report no. 5, 1964/1965.

129. Hall, *The Cuban Refugee in the Public Schools,* Annual Report no. 12, 1972/1973.

130. Thomas, "Cuban Refugee Program," p. 11. From data published by the American Immigration and Citizenship Conference in its "Guide to Occupational Practice Requirements in the U.S.A. for Foreign-Trained Architects, Dentists, Engineers, Lawyers, Librarians, Musicians, Nurses, Physicians, Teachers, Veterinarians," July 1961.

131. Llanes, *Cuban Americans,* p. 131.

132. This summary of the Cuban Teacher Retraining Program draws from Charles V. Sevick, "A History and Evaluation of the Cuban Teacher Retraining Program of the University of Miami 1963–1974."

133. Thomas, "Cuban Refugees in the United States," p. 54.

134. In Sevick, "A History and Evaluation of the Cuban Teacher Retraining Program," p. 21. See also "Iowa Sí!," *Newsweek*, 19 August 1963.

135. Tom Alexander, "Those Amazing Cuban Emigrés," in *The Aliens: A History of Ethnic Minorities in America*, edited by Leonard Dinnerstein and Frederic Cople Jaher, p. 338.

136. This program was instituted when an agreement contract was reached between the federal government and the University of Miami "to provide professional retraining in the American educational system to Cuban refugee teachers to enable them to pursue their careers in the United States" (Department of Health, Education and Welfare Grant No. OE 78-19-0310-105.0). In Sevick, "A History and Evaluation of the Cuban Teacher Retraining Program," p. 25.

137. With the entrance into the program of students with some university credit from Cuban universities, the problem arose of knowing just what credit should be transferred for their former work in Cuba. Henry N. Hardin's study, *Evaluating Cuban Education*, was utilized to solve the problem. Hardin's basic method of evaluation was to examine the transcripts of Cuban students to determine the courses contained in various programs in Cuban universities. He also consulted former Cuban university and school officials. In Cuba, the *escuela normal* program followed elementary school training and was intended strictly as preparation for teaching. In Sevick, "A History and Evaluation of the Cuban Teacher Retraining Program."

138. The Cuban Refugee Program notified the University of Miami that funds would no longer be available after the 1977 fiscal year, and they accepted no new applicants after the spring of 1973.

139. In Sevick, "A History of the Cuban Teacher Retraining Program," p. 17.

140. In Clark, "The Exodus from Revolutionary Cuba," p. 143.

141. "Cuban Doctor's Dilemma," *Time*, 11 June 1973.

142. University of Miami, Center for Advanced International Studies, *The Cuban Immigration 1959–1966 and Its Impact on Miami–Dade County, Florida*, p. 112. Although this program was initiated for Cubans, since its inception physicians from other Latin American countries have also enrolled in it without U.S. government tuition assistance. After 1964, they constituted about 20 percent of the enrollment.

143. "Doctors in Exile," *Time*, 13 April 1962.

144. Thomas, "Cuban Refugees in the United States," p. 54. Moncarz also judged that the Medical Retraining Program definitely helped the effective utilization of former Cuban doctors in the United States. Raúl Moncarz, "Effects of Professional Restrictions on Cuban Refugees in Selected Health Professions in the United States 1959–1969," *International Migration* 8 (1970): 22–28.

145. Information provided to the author by the U.S. Department of Education, Student Financial Assistance, 1981.

146. Clark, "The Exodus from Revolutionary Cuba," p. 120. The author

gratefully acknowledges that she went through college thanks to the Cuban Refugee Loan Program.

147. Thomas, "Cuban Refugees in the United States," p. 55.

148. In Prohías and Casal, *The Cuban Minority*, Table 25. This 1970 peak partly resulted from the 1966 law that facilitated a significant change in the number of Cubans who became permanent residents in 1966.

149. Alexander, "Those Amazing Cuban Emigrés," p. 334.

3. Ignoring Mexican Economic Immigrants

1. So much so that Joe Feagin characterized it as "a roller-coaster immigration pattern." Joe R. Feagin, *Racial and Ethnic Relations*, p. 290.

2. Arthur F. Corwin, "The Study and Interpretation of Mexican Labor Migration: An Introduction," in *Immigrants—and Immigrants: Perspectives on Mexican Labor Migration to the United States*, edited by Arthur F. Corwin, p. 3.

3. Texas, New Mexico, Arizona, California, and parts of Colorado, Nevada, and Utah.

4. Arthur F. Corwin, "Early Mexican Labor Migration: A Frontier Sketch, 1848–1900," in *Immigrants—and Immigrants*, edited by Corwin, pp. 25–37.

5. Ibid., p. 28.

6. Ibid., pp. 29–30.

7. Ibid., Table 1.

8. Ibid., p. 30.

9. Arthur F. Corwin and Lawrence Cardoso, "Vamos al Norte: Causes of Mass Migration to the United States," in *Immigrants—and Immigrants*, edited by Corwin, p. 38.

10. Ernesto Galarza, *Merchants of Labor: The Mexican Bracero Story*, p. 17.

11. Lawrence A. Cardoso, *Mexican Emigration to the United States 1897–1931*, Chapter 1.

12. Corwin and Cardoso, "Vamos al Norte," p. 39. In 1876 the population of Mexico was 9 million; 36 years later, it was almost 15 million.

13. Ibid., pp. 43–44.

14. Carey McWilliams, *North from Mexico: The Spanish-Speaking People of the United States*, p. 144.

15. Corwin and Cardoso, "Vamos al Norte," p. 52. See Table 4 for a comparison of wages.

16. Thus the Alien Contract Labor Law of 1885 was technically not violated. See Corwin and Cardoso, "Vamos al Norte," p. 51.

17. Ibid., p. 45.

18. McWilliams, *North from Mexico*, p. 169.

19. Corwin and Cardoso, "Vamos al Norte," p. 46.

20. Ibid., p. 47.

21. Ibid., p. 50. As were blacks also. See Alan H. Spear, *Black Chicago: The Making of a Negro Ghetto 1890–1920*.

22. McWilliams, *North from Mexico*, pp. 184–185; 221–223. See also Paul S. Taylor, *Mexican Labor in the United States: Chicago and the Calumet Region.*

23. Manuel Gamio, *The Mexican Immigrant: His Life Story*, pp. 21–22.

24. Ibid., p. 72.

25. McWilliams, *North from Mexico*, p. 163.

26. Corwin and Cardoso, "Vamos al Norte," p. 51.

27. McWilliams, *North from Mexico*, p. 111.

28. Gamio, *The Mexican Immigrant*, pp. 31–32.

29. Corwin and Cardoso, "Vamos al Norte," p. 52. See also Julian Samora *Los Mojados: The Wetback Story*, pp. 33–40.

30. Vernon M. Briggs, Jr., *Mexican Migration and the U.S. Labor Market*, p. 14.

31. Arthur F. Corwin, "A Story of Ad Hoc Exemptions: American Immigration Policy toward Mexico," in *Immigrants—and Immigrants*, edited by Corwin, pp. 136–175.

32. N. Ray Gilmore and Gladys W. Gilmore, "The Bracero in California," *Pacific Historical Review* 32 (August 1963): 265–282.

33. Gamio, *The Mexican Immigrant*, pp. 26–27.

34. Carey McWilliams, *Factories in the Fields: The Story of Migratory Farm Labor in California*, p. 266.

35. McWilliams, *Factories in the Fields*, pp. 59–116.

36. Linda C. Majka, "Labor Militancy among Farm Workers and the Strategy of Protest: 1900–1979," *Social Problems* 28 (June 1981): 533–547.

37. McWilliams, *Factories in the Fields*, p. 155.

38. Ibid., pp. 163–166.

39. Ibid., p. 116.

40. Ibid., pp. 132–133.

41. Ibid., p. 127. For the controversy and cleavages that proposals to restrict Mexican immigration occasioned in Texas, see Paul S. Taylor, *An American-Mexican Frontier: Nueces County, Texas.*

42. Corwin and Cardoso, "Vamos al Norte," p. 53.

43. Briggs, *Mexican Migration and the U.S. Labor Market*, p. 6.

44. McWilliams, *Factories in the Fields*, p. 130.

45. Majka, "Labor Militancy among Farm Workers," pp. 538–539.

46. Abraham Hoffman, "Mexican Repatriation Statistics: Some Suggested Alternatives to Carey McWilliams," *Western Historical Quarterly* 3 (October 1972): 391–404. See also Abraham Hoffman, "Mexican Repatriation during the Great Depression: A Reappraisal," in *Immigrants—and Immigrants*, edited by Corwin, pp. 225–247.

47. McWilliams, *North from Mexico*, pp. 186; 177.

48. Corwin and Cardoso, "Vamos al Norte," pp. 53–54.

49. Corwin and Cardoso called the *bracero* program an important "catalyst." Corwin and Cardoso, "Vamos al Norte," p. 53. More than a catalyst, I think it had the strength of a "pull." See also Corwin, "A Story of Ad Hoc Exemptions," in *Immigrants—and Immigrants*, edited by Corwin, pp. 150–154.

50. For the complete legislative history, see Richard B. Craig, *The Bracero Program*; and Gilmore and Gilmore, "The Bracero in California."

51. Samora, *Los Mojados*, p. 19.

52. Galarza, *Merchants of Labor*, p. 32.

53. This analysis of the *bracero* program draws on Galarza's unequalled analysis, *Merchants of Labor*, as well as Craig's *The Bracero Program*.

54. Galarza, *Merchants of Labor*, p. 41.

55. Ibid., pp. 43–45.

56. Ibid., pp. 47–48.

57. Ibid., p. 51; Gilmore and Gilmore, "The Bracero in California," pp. 270–271.

58. For full details on the role of the Farm Placement Service, see Ernesto Galarza, *Farm Workers and Agri-business in California, 1947–1960*, pp. 40–46.

59. Briggs, *Mexican Migration and the U.S. Labor Market*, p. 7.

60. Samora, *Los Mojados*, p. 33. See also Craig, *The Bracero Program*.

61. Corwin and Cardoso, "Vamos al Norte," p. 54.

62. Although, as Samora stresses, these statistics do not necessarily represent separate individuals. An individual *bracero* may have been chosen in five different years, and therefore may be counted five times; an individual wetback may have been apprehended twenty times, and counted each time he was apprehended. Samora, *Los Mojados*, p. 19.

63. Briggs, *Mexican Migration and the U.S. Labor Market*, p. 8.

64. Samora, *Los Mojados*, p. 9.

65. Galarza, *Merchants of Labor*, pp. 56–57.

66. Joan W. Moore, *Mexican Americans*, p. 43.

67. In Galarza, *Merchants of Labor*, p. 70; and Craig, *The Bracero Program*, p. 129.

68. Galarza, *Merchants of Labor*, p. 70.

69. Ibid., pp. 156–157. See Chapter 15 for more details.

70. Ibid., p. 116. See also Chapters 13 and 14.

71. Ibid., p. 159.

72. Ibid., p. 182. See also Chapter 18; and Craig, *The Bracero Program*, pp. 30–31.

73. Galarza, *Merchants of Labor*, p. 216.

74. Its origin was the 1930s Southern Tenant Farmers Union. In California, in 1946, it became the National Farm Labor Union. Renamed the National Agricultural Workers Union in 1951, it lasted until 1960. For an analysis of their history, aims, and difficulties, see Galarza, *Farm Workers and Agri-business*, the basis for this brief discussion.

75. Majka, "Labor Militancy among Farm Workers," p. 541.

76. J. Craig Jenkins and Charles Perrow, "Insurgency of the Powerless: Farm Worker Movements (1946–1972)," *American Sociological Review* 42 (April 1977): 249–268. See also Ernesto Galarza, "Some Comments on the Mexican Migratory Subculture," in *Immigrants—and Immigrants*, edited by Corwin, p. 253.

77. In Mark Day, *Forty Acres: Cesar Chavez and the Farmworkers*,

p. 11. See also Ronald B. Taylor, *Chavez;* and Jacques E. Levy, *Cesar Chavez: Autobiography of La Causa.*

78. Craig, *The Bracero Program,* Chapter 5.

79. Ibid., p. 10.

80. Galarza, *Farm Workers and Agri-business,* pp. 67–68.

81. Craig, *The Bracero Program,* p. 11.

82. Craig, *The Bracero Program,* p. 182.

83. Ibid., p. 153. See also Galarza, *Farm Workers and Agri-business,* for the role Mitchell played supporting the efforts of Galarza and the National Agricultural Workers Union.

84. Craig, *The Bracero Program,* pp. 160–163.

85. Ibid., p. 173.

86. Ibid., p. 200.

87. Ibid., p. 181.

88. Ibid. See pp. 185–195 for details on the pro- and anti-*bracero* positions during congressional hearings.

89. Ibid., p. 196.

90. Ibid., p. 203.

91. U.S. Commission on Civil Rights, *The Tarnished Golden Door: Civil Rights Issues in Immigration,* p. 11.

92. Charles B. Keely, "Effects of the Immigration Act of 1965 on Selected Population Characteristics of Immigrants to the United States," *Demography* 8 (May 1971): 157–169.

93. Douglas S. Massey, "Dimensions of the New Immigration to the United States and the Prospects for Assimilation," *Annual Review of Sociology* 7 (1981): 57–85.

94. U.S. Commission on Civil Rights, *The Tarnished Golden Door,* p. 15.

95. Corwin and Cardoso, "Vamos al Norte," p. 55.

96. For the year 1965, data are in Briggs, *Mexican Migration and the U.S. Labor Market,* Table 2; for the years 1971–1980, data are from the U.S. Immigration and Naturalization Service, Washington, D.C.

97. See Elizabeth Midgley, "Immigrants: Whose Huddled Masses?" *Atlantic Monthly,* April 1978, pp. 6–26. For a rebuttal of the silent invasion thesis that underscores the historical responsibility of the United States in making Mexicans commodity-migrants, see Jorge A. Bustamante, "Commodity-Migrants: Structural Analysis of Mexican Immigration to the United States," in *Views across the Border: The United States and Mexico,* edited by Stanley R. Ross, pp. 183–225.

98. Arthur F. Corwin and Johnny M. McCain, "Wetbackism since 1964: A Catalogue of Factors," in *Immigrants—and Immigrants,* edited by Corwin, pp. 67–107.

99. Ibid., pp. 68–69.

100. Ibid., p. 70.

101. Ibid., p. 71.

102. Ibid., pp. 73–74.

103. Ibid., p. 74.

104. Ibid., p. 79. Until 1976 being the parent of a "citizen child," a child born on American soil, entailed special visa preferences. For some, it was a long-term investment—at age 21 the child could claim his parents under the provisions of family reunification.

105. Ibid., pp. 86–89; Samora, *Los Mojados*, pp. 10–11.

106. For a review of studies and the different methods they used, see Massey, "Dimensions of the New Immigration to the United States," pp. 60–65.

107. David Heer, "What is the Annual Net Flow of Undocumented Mexican Immigrants to the United States?" *Demography* 16 (August 1979): 417–423.

108. Jorge A. Bustamante, "Through the Eyes of a Wetback—A Personal Experience," in Samora, *Los Mojados*, Chapter 7.

109. Charles Hirschman, "Prior U.S. Residence among Mexican Immigrants," *Social Forces* 56 (June 1978): 1179–1202. For the differences between legal and illegal migrants in the size and composition of migrating units, length of stay, and patterns of movement in the United States, see Joshua S. Reichert and Douglas S. Massey, "Patterns of U.S. Migration from a Mexican Sending Community: A Comparison of Legal and Illegal Migrants," *International Migration Review* 13 (Winter 1979): 599–623.

110. Hirschman, "Prior U.S. Residence," p. 1198. See also Alejandro Portes, "Illegal Immigration and the International System, Lessons from Recent Legal Mexican Immigrants to the United States," in *Majority and Minority*, edited by Yetman and Steele, pp. 509–520. For the *net* earnings differential between Mexico and the United States, see Richard W. Cuthbert and Joe B. Stevens, "The Net Economic Incentive for Illegal Mexican Migration: A Case Study," *International Migration Review* 15 (Fall 1981): 543–550.

111. See Portes, "Illegal Immigration and the International System," in *Majority and Minority*, for the characteristics of legal immigrants with prior U.S. residence, residence which indicates that formerly they may have been illegal immigrants.

112. Corwin and Cardoso, "Vamos al Norte," p. 57.

113. Alejandro Portes, "Return of the Wetback," *Society* 11 (March–April 1974): 44.

114. Francisco Alba, "Mexico's International Migration as a Manifestation of Its Development Pattern," *International Migration Review* 12 (Winter 1978): 502–513.

115. Portes, "Illegal Immigration and the International System," p. 517.

116. Portes, "Return of the Wetback," p. 44.

117. Portes, "Illegal Immigration and the International System," pp. 517–518.

118. Bustamante, "Through the Eyes of a Wetback," p. 127.

119. Sidney Weintraub and Stanley R. Ross, *The Illegal Alien from Mexico: Policy Choices for an Intractable Issue*, p. 20. See also Arthur F. Corwin and Walter A. Fogel, "Shadow Labor Force: Mexican Workers in the Ameri-

can Economy," in *Immigrants—and Immigrants*, edited by Corwin, pp. 257–303.

120. Briggs, *Mexican Migration and the U.S. Labor Market*, p. 27.

121. In James Fallows, "Immigration: How It's Affecting Us," *Atlantic Monthly*, November 1983, pp. 56–61.

122. Briggs, *Mexican Migration and the U.S. Labor Market*, p. 15.

4. The Value of Being a Cuban Political Immigrant

1. There are six public use samples from the U.S. 1970 census: two different questionnaires, the 5 percent and the 15 percent questionnaires, are each aggregated at the state, county, or neighborhood levels. In the state samples each state is identified; in the county samples all SMSAs with a population over 250,000 are identified; the neighborhood characteristics samples identified only sections of the country. See U.S. Bureau of the Census, *Public Use Samples of Basic Records from the 1970 Census: Description and Technical Documentation*.

2. Otis Dudley Duncan, "Inheritance of Poverty or Inheritance of Race?" in *On Understanding Poverty: Perspectives from the Social Sciences*, edited by Daniel P. Moynihan, pp. 85–110.

3. Paul M. Siegel, "On the Cost of Being a Negro," *Sociological Inquiry* 35 (Winter 1965): 41–57.

4. Therefore, although the analysis is based on a residual category, it is not atheoretical, as Feagin and Eckberg rightly point out many demographic and statistical studies are. See Joe R. Feagin and Douglas Lee Eckberg, "Discrimination: Motivation, Action, Effects, and Context," *Annual Review of Sociology* 6 (1980): 5–6.

5. U.S. Bureau of the Census, Public Use Sample from the 1970 Census, 5 percent, 1/100.

6. Unfortunately, the census coded the year of immigration variable in five-year intervals. Hence, I had to use 1960–1970 as the period of political immigration rather than 1959–1970, which would have corresponded exactly with the start of the Cuban revolution. Fortunately, however, emigration from Cuba to the United States in 1959 was only a trickle, and the Cuban exodus as such began in the summer of 1960, when the government nationalized the American industries.

7. Peter M. Blau and Otis Dudley Duncan, *The American Occupational Structure*.

8. Erik Olin Wright and Luca Perrone, "Marxist Class Categories and Income Inequality," *American Sociological Review* 42 (February 1977): 32–55.

9. Using the year of immigration in conjunction with age in 1970 yielded how old the immigrant was at the time of immigration. Then the immigrants were split into those who had immigrated at ages 0–24, and at 25 and over. This was expressed as their age in 1970 and cross-tabulated by the highest grade of school completed in order to use the education of adult immigrants as an index for social class origin.

10. See Charles E. Bidwell and John D. Kasarda, "School District Organization and Student Achievement," *American Sociological Review* 40 (February 1975): 55–70, and Duane F. Alwin, "College Effects on Educational and Occupational Attainments," *American Sociological Review* 39 (April 1974): 210–223.

11. Whether an immigrant is legal or illegal is simply not known. But neither is it critical. As we underscored, both the American and Cuban governments organized and concerted the Cuban political exodus. Cuban exiles who arrived without documents received the status of "parolee," which took about two years to change to that of immigrant. Thus illegality is not a criterion in the Cuban political immigration. Cubans arrived largely unrestricted as to numbers or qualifications. This was part of the role of the state regarding political immigrants.

Mexicans, on the other hand, are often illegals. But, as we saw, several studies indicate that a majority of the recently admitted legal immigrants into the United States may have been former undocumented immigrants. By virtue of their previous residence in the United States, they were able to gain legal entry, either by marriage to an American citizen or by the promise of a job from a former employer. This data set, then, does not speak to the issue of illegality. But since illegality is not a criterion in the Cuban migration and since in the Mexican migration legals and illegals are sometimes the same workers on different trips, neither does it have to.

12. Excluded from the analysis are the unemployed and persons not in the labor force, such as housewives, students, and the retired, as well as those for whom data on the independent variables chosen were not available.

13. For an extensive discussion of the U.S. census, see Teresa A. Sullivan, *Marginal Workers, Marginal Jobs: The Underutilization of American Workers*, Appendix A, "Data Adequacy and Methods."

14. It does not include income from social security or railroad retirement, public assistance or welfare, or other sources.

15. See, for example, Gary S. Becker and Barry R. Chiswick, "The Economics of Education: Education and the Distribution of Earnings," *American Economic Review* 56 (May 1966, Supplement): 358–369; Barry R. Chiswick and Jacob Mincer, "Time-Series Changes in Personal Income Inequality in the United States from 1939, with Projections to 1985," *Journal of Political Economy* 80 (May–June 1972): S34–S71; Jacob Mincer, *Schooling, Experience, and Earnings*; Barry R. Chiswick, "The Effect of Americanization on the Earnings of Foreign-Born Men," *Journal of Political Economy* 86 (1978): 897–921; E. M. Beck, Patrick M. Horan, and Charles M. Tolbert II, "Stratification in a Dual Economy: A Sectoral Model of Earnings Determination," *American Sociological Review* 43 (October 1978): 704–720; David L. Featherman and Robert M. Hauser, *Opportunity and Change*. In logging the variable earnings, its meaning is changed from income to relative income, so that it is more suited to an investigation of relative inequality, or the distribution of income. Furthermore, the logged earnings function is related to the measurement of investment in

human capital by years of schooling rather than in terms of dollar investments.

16. This finding deserves attention for its wider implications. Possibly the relationship between educational attainment and earnings or prestige may be different for immigrants or other minority groups in America than for the dominant population. In any case, it should not be assumed a priori that it is the same.

17. Initially developed by Hodge, Siegel, and Rossi. See National Opinion Research Center, *General Social Surveys, 1972–1978; Cumulative Code Book*. N.O.R.C.'s prestige scores differ from Duncan's socioeconomic index mainly in their treatment of farm occupational statuses, which are more highly ranked in the prestige scale. David L. Featherman, F. Lancaster Jones, and Robert M. Hauser, "Assumptions of Social Mobility Research in the U.S.: The Case of Occupational Status," *Social Science Research* 4 (1975): 329–360.

18. Dummy variables mean variables that are dichotomized (for example, not a college graduate = 0; college graduate = 1) so that they become interval variables.

19. I used the general F-ratio test for added explained variance when additional independent variables are incorporated in the analysis. See Jacob Cohen, "Multiple Regression as a General Data-Analytic System," *Psychological Bulletin* 70 (December 1968): 426–443. The reduced model included all independent variables except education; the full model included the two educational measures in addition. Both for all male immigrants and for males who immigrated during 1960–1970, the additional amount of variance in earnings and prestige explained by the addition of the educational measures was significant beyond the .001 level.

20. The 1970 census defines *urban* as localities of over 2,500 persons—far too small to be a meaningful representation of anything that one would really want to call urban. Furthermore, in a rural pocket very near Chicago I saw Mexican workers picking fruit in what was clearly a locality of over 2,500.

21. Chiswick, "The Effect of Americanization on the Earnings of Foreign-Born Men."

22. The states included as southern are Alabama, Arkansas, Delaware, District of Columbia, Florida, Georgia, Kentucky, Louisiana, Maryland, Mississippi, North Carolina, Oklahoma, South Carolina, Tennessee, Texas, Virginia, and West Virginia.

23. It is simply dichotomized as alien vs. naturalized U.S. citizen.

24. The Z-test for the difference in the value of being a Cuban in the two migrations is as follows:

$$Z = \frac{b_{n_{(1960-1970)}} - b_{n_{(1945-1959)}}}{\sqrt{(\text{s.e.}b_{n_{(1960-1970)}})^2 + (\text{s.e.}b_{n_{(1945-1959)}})^2}}$$

b_n = partial coefficient of the variable *nationality*. A one-tail test was used since the direction of the difference was predicted.

25. These perspectives are exemplified by Gary S. Becker, *Human Capital;* Jacob Mincer, *Schooling, Experience and Earnings,* Peter M. Blau and Otis Dudley Duncan, *The American Occupational Structure;* Archibald O. Haller and Alejandro Portes, "Status Attainment Processes," *Sociology of Education* 46 (1973): 51–91; William H. Sewell and Robert M. Hauser, *Education, Occupation and Earnings: Achievement in the Early Career;* Robert M. Hauser and David L. Featherman, *The Process of Stratification: Trends and Analyses.* For a popular version of this perspective, see Thomas Sowell, *Ethnic America: A History.*

26. Becker, *Human Capital,* p. 1.

27. Ibid.

28. For what she calls the political sex appeal of human capital theory, see Alice M. Rivlin, "Income Distribution—Can Economists Help?" in *Problems in Political Economy: An Urban Perspective,* edited by David M. Gordon, pp. 301–306.

29. While separate equations for Cubans and Mexicans in each of the migration periods also make it plausible to compare the returns to the characteristics of Cuban political immigrants with those of Cuban economic immigrants, and of Mexicans who immigrated during the sixties with Mexicans who immigrated before 1960, doing so is not sensible. In effect, it would compare workers whose insertion into the system took place under very different historical periods, as these are defined by the general shape of the economy, political climate and events, changes in immigration law and filters for entry, and the like. Thus, some of the variability in the rates of return would be due to the difference in the historical parameters of the post–World War II era and the sixties in America, and not to the differential incorporation of Cuban and Mexican immigrant workers.

30. Duane F. Alwin and Robert M. Hauser, "The Decomposition of Effects in Path Analysis," *American Sociological Review* 40 (February 1975): 37–47.

31. The Z-test is the following:

$$Z = \frac{b_{i_{Cuban}} - b_{i_{Mexican}}}{\sqrt{(s.e.b_{i_{Cuban}})^2 + (s.e.b_{i_{Mexican}})^2}}$$

32. Portes, "Return of the Wetback," p. 41.

33. Moore, *Mexican Americans,* p. 69.

5. Workers in Labor Markets: Cubans and Mexicans

1. Patrick M. Horan, "Is Status Attainment Research Atheoretical?" *American Sociological Review* 43 (August 1978): 534.

2. Kingsley Davis and Wilbert E. Moore, "Some Principles of Stratification," *American Sociological Review* 10 (April 1945): 242–249.

3. For example, Melvin M. Tumin, "Some Principles of Stratification: A Critical Analysis," *American Sociological Review* 18 (August 1953): 387–394; and Arthur L. Stinchcombe, "Some Empirical Consequences of

the Davis-Moore Theory of Stratification," *American Sociological Review* 28 (October 1963): 805–808.

4. Ross M. Stolzenberg, "Bringing the Boss Back In: Employer Size, Employee Schooling, and Socioeconomic Achievement," *American Sociological Review* 43 (December 1978): 826.

5. Ibid.

6. For a review of the literature, see Glen G. Cain, "The Challenge of Segmented Labor Market Theories to Orthodox Theory: A Survey," *Journal of Economic Literature* 14 (December 1976): 1215–1257.

7. For example, Robert T. Averitt, *The Dual Economy: The Dynamics of American Industry Structure;* David M. Gordon, *Theories of Poverty and Underemployment;* Richard C. Edwards, Michael Reich, and David M. Gordon, eds. *Labor Market Segmentation;* E. M. Beck, Patrick M. Horan, and Charles M. Tolbert II, "Stratification in a Dual Economy: A Sectoral Model of Earnings Determination," *American Sociological Review* 43 (October 1978): 704–720.

8. Variously known as monopoly capitalism, late capitalism, or postindustrial society.

9. Beck, Horan, and Tolbert, "Stratification in a Dual Economy," p. 706.

10. Horan, "Is Status Attainment Research Atheoretical?" p. 540.

11. See Adam Przeworski, "Proletariat into a Class: The Process of Class Formation from Karl Kautsky's *The Class Struggle* to Recent Controversies," *Politics & Society* 7 (1977): 343–401.

12. James N. Baron and William T. Bielby, "Bringing the Firms Back In: Stratification, Segmentation, and the Organization of Work," *American Sociological Review* 45 (October 1980): 738.

13. Ibid., p. 741.

14. Arthur L. Stinchcombe, "Social Mobility in Industrial Labor Markets," *Acta Sociologica* 22 (1979): 217–245.

15. Ibid., p. 220.

16. Ibid., p. 223.

17. Ibid., pp. 224–225.

18. The six labor market dummies are Primary, Small-Skilled, Engineering-based, Petty Bourgeois, Professional, and Bureaucratic. The implicit reference group is Classical Capitalist. See Jacob Cohen, "Multiple Regression as a General Data-Analytic System," *Psychological Bulletin* 70 (December 1968): 426–443.

19. See also Stinchcombe, "Social Mobility in Industrial Labor Markets."

20. The standard deviations are 0.79 and 39.25, respectively.

21. See Przeworski, "Proletariat into a Class."

6. The Functions of Political and Economic Migration

1. Arthur L. Stinchcombe, *Constructing Social Theories*, p. 80.

2. Anthony Giddens, *Sociology: A Brief but Critical Introduction*, p. 78.

3. J. P. Nettl, "The State as a Conceptual Variable," *World Politics* 20 (July 1968): 561.

4. See David A. Gold, Clarence Y. H. Lo, and Erik Olin Wright, "Recent Developments in Marxist Theories of the Capitalist State," *Monthly Review* 27 (October 1975): 29–43.

5. Ralph Miliband, *The State in Capitalist Society.*

6. Nicos Poulantzas, *Political Power and Social Classes.*

7. See Silvia Pedraza-Bailey, "Talcott Parsons and Structural Marxism: Functionalist Theories of Society," *Current Perspectives in Social Theory* 3 (1982): 207–224.

8. Giddens, *Sociology,* p. 175.

9. Charles Tilly, "Western State-Making and Theories of Political Transformation," in *The Formation of National States in Western Europe,* edited by Charles Tilly, pp. 601–638.

10. See, for example, Ronald Cohen and Elman R. Service, *Origins of the State: The Anthropology of Political Evolution;* Lucien W. Pye, "The Concept of Political Development," in *Political Development and Social Change,* edited by Jason L. Finkle and Richard W. Gable.

11. Tilly, "Western State-Making and Theories of Political Transformation," p. 620.

12. James O'Connor, *The Fiscal Crisis of the State,* p. 6.

13. Tilly, "Western State-Making and Theories of Political Transformation," p. 624.

14. André Gunder Frank, "The Development of Underdevelopment," in *The Political Economy of Development and Underdevelopment,* edited by Charles K. Wilber, pp. 103–113; Immanuel Wallerstein, *The Modern-World System.*

15. Only Fernando Henrique Cardoso, "Associated-Dependent Development: Theoretical and Practical Implications," linked dependency to development under authoritarianism. In *Authoritarian Brazil,* edited by Alfred Stepan, pp. 142–176.

16. See Michael Bratton, "Patterns of Development and Underdevelopment," *International Studies Quarterly* 26 (September 1982): 333–372.

17. Charles Tilly, "Historical Sociology," *Current Perspectives in Social Theory* 1 (1980): 59.

18. Nettl, "The State as a Conceptual Variable," p. 563.

19. Ibid., p. 575.

20. For Europe, see Stephen Castles and Godula Kosack, *Immigrant Workers and Class Structure in Western Europe;* for South Africa, see Harold Wolpe, "Industrialism and Race in South Africa," in *Race and Racialism,* edited by Sami Zubaida; for Germany, see Ray C. Rist, "Guestworkers in Germany: Public Policies as the Legitimation of Marginality," *Ethnic and Racial Studies* 2 (October 1979): 401–415.

21. Michael Burawoy, "The Functions and Reproduction of Migrant Labor: Comparative Material from Southern Africa and the United States," *American Journal of Sociology* 81 (March 1976): 1050–1087; Manuel

Castells, "Immigrant Workers and Class Struggles in Advanced Capitalism: The Western European Experience," *Politics & Society* 5 (1975): 33–66; Alejandro Portes, "Structural Causes of Illegal Immigration."

22. Another area of disagreement among them is whether labor migration is a permanent or conjunctural feature of developed capitalist societies. Castells refers to the system of migrant labor as an "organic" part of capitalism at a particular stage of its development (advanced). Its organic nature no doubt derives from his notion that it exists in order to counteract the structural tendency for the rate of profit to fall. For Burawoy, on the other hand, a system of migrant labor is conjunctural—i.e., existing within historically concrete circumstances. As such, it "acts as a functional substitute for other modes of organizing labor under capitalism" (Burawoy, "The Functions and Reproduction of Migrant Labor," p. 1057). Portes finds the view that it is conjunctural "untenable" and instead deems it "central."

23. Castells, "Immigrant Workers and Class Struggles in Advanced Capitalism," p. 49.

24. Portes, "Structural Causes of Illegal Immigration," p. 11.

25. Ibid., p. 29.

26. Ibid., p. 30.

27. Ibid., p. 32.

28. César Chávez's visit to Washington University, St. Louis, Missouri, November 1979. See also Richard Severo, "The Flight of the Wetbacks," *New York Times Magazine,* 10 March 1974.

29. Alejandro Portes, "Illegal Immigration and the International System, Lessons from Recent Legal Mexican Immigrants to the United States," in *Majority and Minority,* edited by Norman R. Yetman and C. Hoy Steele, p. 519.

30. Barry R. Chiswick, "The Effect of Americanization on the Earnings of Foreign-born Men," *Journal of Political Economy* 86 (1978): 897–921.

31. Paul Bullock, "Employment Problems of the Mexican American," in *Mexican-Americans in the United States,* edited by John H. Burma, pp. 147–159.

32. Castells, "Immigrant Workers and Class Struggles in Advanced Capitalism," p. 54.

33. Portes, "Structural Causes of Illegal Immigration," p. 27.

34. Arthur F. Corwin, "Mexican Policy and Ambivalence toward Labor Emigration to the United States," in *Immigrants—and Immigrants: Perspectives on Mexican Labor Migration to the United States,* edited by Corwin, pp. 176–224.

35. Ibid., p. 177.

36. Ibid., 178.

37. Ibid., p. 180.

38. Ibid., p. 184.

39. Ibid., p. 187.

40. Richard B. Craig, *The Bracero Program,* p. 187.

41. Wayne Cornelius, *Mexican Migration to the United States: The*

View from Rural Sending Communities; David S. North and Marion F. Houstoun, *The Characteristics and Role of Illegal Aliens in the U.S. La-* *bor Market: An Exploratory Study.*

42. Sidney Weintraub and Stanley R. Ross, *The Illegal Alien from Mexico: Policy Choices for an Intractable Issue,* p. 17.

43. J. S. Birks and C. A. Sinclair, "Migration and Development: The Changing Perspective of the Poor Arab Countries," *Journal of International Affairs* 33 (Fall/Winter 1979): 285–309.

44. Ibid., pp. 300.

45. My own interviews with Mexican illegal aliens confirmed this.

46. In Corwin, "Mexican Policy and Ambivalence toward Labor Emigration," p. 198.

47. Portes, "Illegal Immigration and the International System," p. 516.

48. Ibid., p. 517.

49. In Corwin, "Mexican Policy and Ambivalence toward Labor Emigration," p. 199.

50. Ibid., p. 204.

51. Ibid., pp. 206–208.

52. Ibid., p. 210.

53. Jorge A. Bustamante and Gerónimo G. Martínez, "Undocumented Immigration from Mexico: Beyond Borders but within Systems," *Journal of International Affairs* 33 (Fall/Winter 1979): 265–284.

54. James Fallows, "Immigration: How It's Affecting Us," *Atlantic Monthly,* November 1983, p. 102.

55. See Paul Tabori, *The Anatomy of Exile.*

56. "Cuba: End of the Freedom Flights," *Time,* 13 September 1971; and *New York Times,* 7 April 1973.

57. For two excellent analyses of the role of the Cuban Communist Party, see Hans Magnus Enzensberger, "Portrait of a Party: Prehistory, Structure and Ideology of the PCC," in *Politics and Crime,* edited by Michael Roloff, pp. 126–155; Jorge I. Domínguez and Cristopher N. Mitchell, "The Roads Not Taken: Institutionalization and Political Parties in Cuba and Bolivia," *Comparative Politics* 9 (January 1977): 173–195.

58. *New York Times,* 7 November 1965. See *New York Times,* 5 February 1968, for a description of the different prisons.

59. Amnesty International, *Amnesty International Report 1977,* p. 135.

60. *New York Times,* 12 June 1976. The Inter-American Human Rights Commission is a branch of the Organization of American States.

61. Amnesty International, *Amnesty International Report 1980,* p. 126.

62. Richard R. Fagen, Richard A. Brody, and Thomas I. O'Leary, *Cubans in Exile: Disaffection and the Revolution,* p. 117; *Granma,* 8 November 1965. Fagen et al. called this the "purification theme" that has tended to dominate both official rhetoric and policy. However, if a purification theme dominated both official rhetoric and policy, it was more than a purification theme.

63. Leo Huberman and Paul M. Sweezy, *Socialism in Cuba,* p. 56.

64. For details and some examples, see *New York Times:* 12 May 1960;

17 May 1960; 2 August 1960; 13 September 1960; 7 November 1960; 14 December 1960; 18 December 1960; 7 January 1961; 14 January 1961; 16 January 1961; 18 January 1961; 19 March 1961. For an article on Huber Matos, see 4 February 1980; and for Matos's letter written from a prison in Havana after fifteen years of imprisonment, see 17 November 1975.

65. *New York Times*, 12 November 1960.

66. *New York Times*, 1 November 1960.

67. See *Revolución*, 5, 10, and 14 November 1960; my translation. See also *New York Times*, 14 November 1960.

68. *Revolución*, 14 April 1961; my translation.

69. *New York Times*, 23 July 1961.

70. *Revolución*, 24 July 1961; my translation.

71. *Revolución*, 7 September 1961; my translation. See also *New York Times*, 7 September 1961.

72. Quoted in Fagen et al., *Cubans in Exile*, p. 119; speech given on 28 September 1961.

73. Enzensberger, "Portrait of a Party," p. 146.

74. In *New York Times*, 30 September 1965.

75. *New York Times*, 1 October 1965, Supplement.

76. In *New York Times*, 7 November 1965.

77. *Granma*, 8 May 1966.

78. In *New York Times*, 8 November 1965.

79. *New York Times*, 24 December 1965.

80. From a speech at the graduation ceremony of the first agronomists and cattle breeders the revolution trained. *Granma*, 25 December 1966.

81. In *New York Times*, 14 and 15 March, 1968.

82. *Granma*, 28 April 1968. Also quoted in Fagen et al., *Cubans in Exile*, pp. 157–158. See also *New York Times*, 5 February 1968.

83. Enzensberger, "Portrait of a Party," p. 153.

84. For Padilla's poem, see Rolando E. Bonachea and Nelson P. Valdés, *Cuba in Revolution*, pp. 527–528.

85. For details, see Carlos Ripoll, "The Cuban Scene: Censors and Dissenters." *Partisan Review* 48 (1981): 574–587; and Lourdes Casal, "Literature and Society," in *Revolutionary Change in Cuba*, edited by Carmelo Mesa-Lago, pp. 447–469.

86. *New York Times*, 6 December 1970.

87. *New York Times*, 18 March 1971. The law made work a social obligation for all able-bodied men between the ages of 17 and 60, and women, 17 to 55. See also *New York Times*, 20 January 1974.

88. For a description of this new period, see Jorge I. Domínguez, "Cuban Foreign Policy," *Foreign Affairs* 57 (Fall 1978): 83–108.

89. *Granma*, 13 April 1980.

90. *Granma*, 22 June 1980.

91. Ibid.

92. Ibid.

93. For the prominent writers and intellectuals, see Carlos Ripoll, "The Cuban Scene." Since 1982, a number of literary magazines edited by Cuban

intellectuals exiled in 1980 have appeared in the United States. See, for example, *Término*, edited by Roberto Madrigal Ecay and Manuel F. Ballagas.

94. In *New York Times*, 8 May 1980.

95. In *New York Times*, 19 January 1961.

96. U.S. Department of State, *Department of State Bulletin*, 9 January 1961. The *Department of State Bulletin* reproduces speeches and pronouncements of major public officials. For example, state of the union addresses, state of the economy addresses, inaugural speeches, and public television and radio interviews.

97. *Department of State Bulletin*, 20 February 1961.

98. *Department of State Bulletin*, 2 June 1975.

99. *Department of State Bulletin*, 26 May 1975.

100. *Department of State Bulletin*, 15 January 1962.

101. Ibid. From Kennedy's letter of 21 July 1961.

102. Arthur M. Schlesinger, Jr., "Introduction," in *Western Europe*, edited by Robert Dallek, vol. 1 of *The Dynamics of World Power: A Documentary History of United States Foreign Policy 1945–1973*, edited by Arthur M. Schlesinger, Jr., p. xlv.

103. *Department of State Bulletin*, 2 April 1962.

104. Zbigniew Brzezinski and Samuel P. Huntington, *Political Power: USA/USSR*, pp. 202–223.

105. Schlesinger, "Introduction," p. xxvii.

106. *Department of State Bulletin*, 29 January 1962.

107. Schlesinger, "Introduction," p. xxx.

108. Robert N. Burr, "United States Latin American Policy 1945–1972," in *Latin America*, edited by Robert N. Burr, vol. 3 of *The Dynamics of World Power*, edited by Schlesinger, pp. xix–li.

109. Schlesinger, "Introduction," p. xxxiii.

110. See John G. Stoessinger, *The Might of Nations*.

111. Schlesinger, "Introduction," pp. xxxiv–xxxv.

112. *Department of State Bulletin*, 21 January 1957.

113. Schlesinger, "Introduction," p. xxxvii. See also Carlos Fuentes, "Three Dates of Change in Latin America," *Harper's*, August 1981.

114. Burr, "United States Latin American Policy," pp. xxxviii–xxxix.

115. Schlesinger, "Introduction," p. xxxviii.

116. *Department of State Bulletin*, 4 February 1957.

117. *Department of State Bulletin*, 24 April 1961.

118. *Department of State Bulletin*, 16 July 1962.

119. *Department of State Bulletin*, 3 September 1962.

120. Dolf Sternberger, "Legitimacy," pp. 244–248 in *International Encyclopedia of the Social Sciences*, vol. 9. See also B. Thomas Trout, "Rhetoric Revisited: Political Legitimation and the Cold War," *International Studies Quarterly* 19 (September 1975): 251–284.

121. Max Weber, *Economy and Society*, edited by Guenther Roth and Claus Wittich, vol. 1, part 1, Chapter 3; and vol. 2, Chapters 10–14. In Weber's analysis, these three types rested on different ultimate principles of legitimation. The personal authority of traditional and charismatic rulers

rested on different sources: traditional legitimation, on the sanction of values handed down by tradition; charismatic legitimation, on the "gift of grace" of a savior, prophet, or hero. The impersonal authority of rational legitimation rested on a system of consciously-made rational rules; the legitimation provided by rules and law and expressed in bureaucracy.

122. Arthur L. Stinchcombe, *Constructing Social Theories*, p. 150; emphasis in original. With his notion of a nesting of reserve sources of power, Stinchcombe's definition of legitimacy answered what Sternberger regarded as the basic question Weber's analysis failed to answer: What is the core of democratic legitimacy? "A power is legitimate," explained Stinchcombe, "to the degree that, by virtue of the doctrines and norms by which it is justified, the power-holder can call upon sufficient other centers of power, as reserves in case of need, to make his power effective" (p. 162).

123. In *New York Times*, 26 July 1961.

124. Ibid.

125. *New York Times*, 28 July 1961.

126. *Department of State Bulletin*, 22 July 1963.

127. *Department of State Bulletin*, 8 May 1961.

128. Ibid.

129. In Eduardo Frei Montalva, "The Alliance That Lost Its Way," in *Latin American Radicalism*, edited by Irving Louis Horowitz, Josué de Castro, and John Gerassi, p. 458.

130. *Department of State Bulletin*, 4 March 1963.

131. Montalva, "The Alliance That Lost Its Way," pp. 457–468.

132. *Department of State Bulletin*, 5 November 1962.

133. Schlesinger, "Introduction," p. xlv.

134. Burr, "United States Latin American Policy," p. xlvi.

135. Schlesinger, "Introduction," p. xlvi.

136. *Department of State Bulletin*, 5 May 1975.

137. *Department of State Bulletin*, 2 June 1975.

138. *Department of State Bulletin*, 16 June 1975.

139. *Revolución*, 24 July 1961; my translation.

140. *Revolución*, 27 July 1961; my translation.

141. *Granma*, 28 April 1968.

142. *Granma*, 9 December 1979.

7. Closing Observations

1. Richard D. Lamm, "America Needs Fewer Immigrants," *New York Times*, 12 July 1981.

2. Select Commission on Immigration and Refugee Policy, *U.S. Immigration Policy and the National Interest*, Table 5.

3. Ibid., Table 4; and p. 91.

4. For the first bill the Senate approved, see Robert Pear, "Senate Votes a Sweeping Revision of the Nation's Immigration Laws," *New York Times*, 18 August 1982. For the latest bill the Senate approved, see Robert Pear, "Senate Approves Immigration Bill with Hiring Curb," *New York Times*, 19 May 1983, and Robert Pear, "Immigration Reform Is Alive and Well,"

New York Times, 22 May 1983. In October 1983, House Speaker Tip O'Neill blocked the bill from reaching the House floor for a vote. See James Fallows, "Immigrant Bill: A Blow," *New York Times,* 9 October 1983. For a brief chronology of events surrounding the immigration reform bills, see "Chronology of Events on the Status of Aliens," *New York Times,* 12 June 1984. For the debate on the House's bill, see Robert Pear, "House to Debate Immigration Bill despite Pleas of Hispanic Groups," *New York Times,* 12 June 1984. For the bill the House approved, see Robert Pear, "House, by 216–211, Approves Aliens Bill after Retaining Amnesty Plan in Final Test," *New York Times,* 21 June 1984. For the similarities and differences between the bills approved by the Senate and the House, see "The Immigration Bills: A Comparison," *New York Times,* 21 June 1984. For the conference committee's failure to reach an agreement, see Robert Pear, "Conference on Immigration Bill Stalls," *New York Times,* 26 September 1984; Robert Pear, "Ambitious Immigration Bill Fails As Charges of Blame Are Traded," *New York Times,* 12 October 1984.

    5. Thomas F. Gossett, *Race: The History of an Idea in America,* p. 383.

    6. For examples, see Robert Pear, "Reagan Aides Draft a Plan to Let Mexicans Work in U.S. as Guests," *New York Times,* 11 May 1981; James Kelly, "Closing the Golden Door," *Time,* 18 May 1981; Robert Pear, "Bill on Aliens a Divisive Issue for Democrats," *New York Times,* 22 April 1984; Estevan T. Flores, "1982 Simpson-Mazzoli Immigration Reform and the Hispanic Community," *La Red/The Net* (newsletter of the National Chicano Council on Higher Education), February 1983, pp. 14–16; "Bill on Immigration: Diversity in House's Debate," *New York Times,* 17 June 1984; Robert Pear, "Aliens Bill Nears Reality," *New York Times,* 18 June 1984; Robert Pear, "House Backs Plan Legalizing Aliens in U.S. before 1982," *New York Times,* 18 June 1984; Robert Pear, "The Immigration Bill's Melting Pot," *New York Times,* 2 July 1984.

    7. Michael S. Teitelbaum, "Right versus Right: Immigration and Refugee Policy in the United States," *Foreign Affairs* 59 (Fall 1980): 51.

    8. Ricardo Otheguy, "Language Rights and Linguistic Minorities: The United States Case," in *International Human Rights: Contemporary Issues,* edited by Jack L. Nelson and Vera M. Green, pp. 159–167. Nathan Glazer undertook a similar comparison between blacks and the early European immigrants. The arguments that follow apply equally to that comparison. See Nathan Glazer, "Blacks and Ethnic Groups: The Difference, and the Political Difference It Makes," *Social Problems* 18 (Spring 1971): 444–461.

    9. Otheguy, "Language Rights and Linguistic Minorities," p. 163.

    10. Vernon M. Briggs, Jr., *Mexican Migration and the U.S. Labor Market,* p. 33.

Bibliography

Aguirre, Benigno E. "Differential Migration of Cuban Social Races." *Latin American Research Review* 11 (1976): 103–124.

Alba, Francisco. "Mexico's International Migration as a Manifestation of Its Development Pattern." *International Migration Review* 12 (Winter 1978): 502–513.

Alexander, Tom. "Those Amazing Cuban Emigrés." In *The Aliens: A History of Ethnic Minorities in America*, edited by Leonard Dinnerstein and Frederic Cople Jaher. New York: Meredith, 1970.

Alwin, Duane F. "College Effects on Educational and Occupational Attainments." *American Sociological Review* 39 (April 1974): 210–223.

Alwin, Duane F., and Robert M. Hauser. "The Decomposition of Effects in Path Analysis." *American Sociological Review* 40 (February 1975): 37–47.

Amaro, Nelson, and Alejandro Portes. "Una sociología del exilio: Situación de los grupos cubanos en los Estados Unidos," *Aportes* 23 (January 1972): 6–24.

Amaro Victoria, Nelson. "Mass and Class in the Origins of the Cuban Revolution." In *Cuban Communism*, edited by Irving Louis Horowitz. New Brunswick, N.J.: Transaction, 1977.

Amnesty International. *Amnesty International Report 1975–1976*. London: Amnesty International Publications, 1976.

———. *Amnesty International Report 1977*. London: Amnesty International Publications, 1977.

———. *Amnesty International Report 1980*. London: Amnesty International Publications, 1980.

Averitt, Robert T. *The Dual Economy: The Dynamics of American Industry Structure*. New York: Norton, 1968.

Azicri, Max. "The Institutionalization of the Cuban Revolution: A Review of the Literature." *Cuban Studies* 9 (July 1979): 63–78.

Bach, Robert L. "The New Cuban Exodus." *Caribbean Review* 11 (Winter 1982).

———. "The New Cuban Immigrants: Their Background and Prospects." *Monthly Labor Review* 103 (October 1980): 39–46.

Bach, Robert L., Jennifer B. Bach, and Timothy Triplett. "The Flotilla 'Entrants': Latest and Most Controversial." *Cuban Studies* 11/12 (July 1981/January 1982): 29–48.

Baron, James N., and William T. Bielby. "Bringing the Firms Back In: Stratification, Segmentation, and the Organization of Work." *American Sociological Review* 45 (October 1980): 737–765.

Beck, E. M., Patrick M. Horan, and Charles M. Tolbert II. "Stratification in a Dual Economy: A Sectoral Model of Earnings Determination." *American Sociological Review* 43 (October 1978): 704–720.

Becker, Gary S. *Human Capital*. New York: National Bureau of Economic Research, 1964.

Becker, Gary S., and Barry R. Chiswick. "The Economics of Education: Education and the Distribution of Earnings." *American Economic Review* 56 (May 1966, Supplement): 358–369.

Bernardo, Robert M. "Moral Stimulation and Labor Allocation in Cuba." In *Cuban Communism*, edited by Irving Louis Horowitz. New Brunswick, N.J.: Transaction, 1977.

Bidwell, Charles E., and John D. Kasarda. "School District Organization and Student Achievement." *American Sociological Review* 40 (February 1975): 55–70.

"Bill on Immigration: Diversity in House's Debate." *New York Times*, 17 June 1984.

Birks, J. S., and C. A. Sinclair. "Migration and Development: The Changing Perspective of the Poor Arab Countries." *Journal of International Affairs* 33 (Fall/Winter 1979): 285–309.

Blau, Peter M., and Otis Dudley Duncan. *The American Occupational Structure*. New York: Wiley, 1967.

Bonachea, Rolando E., and Nelson P. Valdés. *Cuba in Revolution*. New York: Anchor, 1972.

Bonacich, Edna. "A Theory of Ethnic Antagonism: The Split Labor Market." *American Sociological Review* 37 (October 1972): 547–559.

Bratton, Michael. "Patterns of Development and Underdevelopment." *International Studies Quarterly* 26 (September 1982): 333–372.

Briggs, Vernon M., Jr. *Mexican Migration and the U.S. Labor Market*. Austin: University of Texas, Center for the Study of Human Resources and the Bureau of Business Research, Studies in Human Resource Development, no. 3, 1975.

Brinton, Crane. *The Anatomy of Revolution*. New York: Vintage, 1965.

Brzezinski, Zbigniew, and Samuel P. Huntington. *Political Power: USA/ USSR*. New York: Viking, 1964.

Bullock, Paul. "Employment Problems of the Mexican American." In *Mexican-Americans in the United States*, edited by John H. Burma. Cambridge, Schenkman, 1970.

Burawoy, Michael. "The Functions and Reproduction of Migrant Labor: Comparative Material from Southern Africa and the United States." *American Journal of Sociology* 81 (March 1976): 1050–1087.

Burr, Robert N. "United States Latin American Policy 1945–1972." In *Latin America*, edited by Robert N. Burr. Vol. 3 of *The Dynamics of*

World Power: A Documentary History of United States Foreign Policy 1945–1973. Edited by Arthur M. Schlesinger, Jr. New York: Chelsea House, 1973.

Bustamante, Jorge A. "Commodity-Migrants: Structural Analysis of Mexican Immigration to the United States." In *Views across the Border: The United States and Mexico,* edited by Stanley R. Ross. Albuquerque: University of New Mexico Press, 1978.

———. "Through the Eyes of a Wetback—A Personal Experience." In Julian Samora, *Los Mojados: The Wetback Story.* Notre Dame: University of Notre Dame Press, 1971.

Bustamante, Jorge A., and Gerónimo G. Martínez. "Undocumented Immigration from Mexico: Beyond Borders but within Systems." *Journal of International Affairs* 33 (Fall/Winter 1979): 265–284.

Cabezas, Dagmaris. "You Can Go Home Again." *Nation,* 7 June 1980.

Cain, Glen G. "The Challenge of Segmented Labor Market Theories to Orthodox Theory: A Survey. *Journal of Economic Literature* 14 (December 1976): 1215–1257.

"California Tries to Dam the Alien Tide." *Business Week,* 12 February 1972.

"California: What Help for the Harvest?" *Newsweek,* 2 November 1964.

Cardoso, Fernando Henrique. "Associated-Dependent Development: Theoretical and Practical Implications." In *Authoritarian Brazil,* edited by Alfred Stepan. New Haven: Yale University Press, 1976.

Cardoso, Lawrence A. *Mexican Emigration to the United States 1897–1931.* Tucson: University of Arizona Press, 1980.

Casal, Lourdes. "Cubans in the United States: Their Impact on U.S.–Cuban Relations." In *Revolutionary Cuba in the World Arena,* edited by Martin Weinstein. Philadelphia: Ishi, 1979.

———. "Literature and Society." In *Revolutionary Change in Cuba,* edited by Carmelo Mesa-Lago. Pittsburgh: University of Pittsburgh Press, 1971.

———. "Revolution and Race: Blacks in Contemporary Cuba." Washington, D.C.: Woodrow Wilson International Center for Scholars, 1980.

Castells, Manuel. "Immigrant Workers and Class Struggles in Advanced Capitalism: The Western European Experience." *Politics & Society* 5 (1975): 33–66.

Castles, Stephen, and Godula Kosack. *Immigrant Workers and Class Structure in Western Europe.* London: Oxford University Press, 1973.

Chapman, Leonard F. " 'Silent Invasion' That Takes Millions of American Jobs." *U.S. News & World Report,* 9 December 1974.

Chiswick, Barry R. "The Effect of Americanization on the Earnings of Foreign-born Men." *Journal of Political Economy* 86 (1978): 897–921.

Chiswick, Barry R., and Jacob Mincer. "Time-Series Changes in Personal Income Inequality in the United States from 1939, with Projections to 1985." *Journal of Political Economy* 80 (May–June 1972): S34–S71.

"Chronology of Events on the Status of Aliens." *New York Times,* 12 June 1984.

Clark, Juan M. "The Exodus from Revolutionary Cuba (1959–1974): A Sociological Analysis." Ph.D. diss., University of Florida, 1975.

Cohen, Jacob. "Multiple Regression as a General Data-Analytic System." *Psychological Bulletin* 70 (December 1968): 426–443.

Cohen, Ronald, and Elman R. Service. *Origins of the State: The Anthropology of Political Evolution.* Philadelphia: ISHI, 1978.

Cornelius, Wayne. *Mexican Migration to the United States: The View from Rural Sending Communities.* Cambridge, Mass.: Migration and Development Study Group, Massachusetts Institute of Technology, 1976.

Corwin, Arthur F., ed. *Immigrants—and Immigrants: Perspectives on Mexican Labor Migration to the United States.* Westport, Conn.: Greenwood, 1978.

Craig, Richard B. *The Bracero Program.* Austin: University of Texas Press, 1971.

Cuba. Oficina Nacional de los Censos Demográfico y Electoral. *Censos de Población, Viviendas y Electoral,* Informe General. Havana: P. Fernández, 1955.

"Cuba: End of the Freedom Flights." *Time,* 13 September 1971.

"Cuban Doctor's Dilemma." *Time,* 11 June 1973.

"A Cuban Success Story—in the United States." *U.S. News & World Report,* 20 March 1967.

Cuthbert, Richard W., and Joe B. Stevens. "The Net Economic Incentive for Illegal Mexican Migration: A Case Study." *International Migration Review* 15 (Fall 1981): 543–550.

Davis, Kingsley, and Wilbert E. Moore. "Some Principles of Stratification." *American Sociological Review* 10 (April 1945): 242–249.

Day, Mark. *Forty Acres: Cesar Chavez and the Farmworkers.* New York: Praeger, 1971.

"Deathtrap for Wetbacks." *Time,* 11 October 1968.

Díaz-Briquets, Sergio. "Demographic and Related Determinants of Recent Cuban Emigration." *International Migration Review* 17 (Spring 1983): 95–119.

Dickstein, Morris. *Gates of Eden: American Culture in the Sixties.* New York: Basic, 1977.

"Doctors in Exile." *Time,* 13 April 1962.

Domínguez, Jorge I. "Cuban Foreign Policy." *Foreign Affairs* 57 (Fall 1978): 83–108.

———. "La tradición liberal y la emigración cubana." *Areito* 1 (January–March 1975): 4–5.

Domínguez, Jorge I., and Christopher N. Mitchell. "The Roads Not Taken: Institutionalization and Political Parties in Cuba and Bolivia." *Comparative Politics* 9 (January 1977): 173–195.

Duncan, Otis Dudley. "Inheritance of Poverty or Inheritance of Race?" In *On Understanding Poverty: Perspectives from the Social Sciences,* edited by Daniel P. Moynihan. New York: Basic, 1968.

———. "A Socioeconomic Index for All Occupations." In *Occupations and Social Status,* edited by Albert J. Reiss, Jr. New York: Free Press of Glencoe, 1961.

Edwards, Richard C., Michael Reich, and David M. Gordon, eds. *Labor Market Segmentation.* Lexington, Mass.: D. C. Heath, 1975.

Enzensberger, Hans Magnus. "Portrait of a Party: Prehistory, Structure and Ideology of the PCC." In *Politics and Crime,* edited by Michael Roloff. New York: Seabury, 1974.

Evans, Sara. *Personal Politics: The Roots of Women's Liberation in the Civil Rights Movement and the New Left.* New York: Vintage, 1980.

Fagen, Richard R. "Revolution: For Internal Consumption Only." In *Cuban Communism,* edited by Irving Louis Horowitz. New Brunswick, N.J.: Transaction, 1977.

Fagen, Richard R., Richard A. Brody, and Thomas J. O'Leary. *Cubans in Exile: Disaffection and the Revolution.* Palo Alto, Calif.: Stanford University Press, 1968.

Fallows, James. "Immigrant Bill: A Blow." *New York Times,* 9 October 1983.
———. "Immigration: How It's Affecting Us." *Atlantic Monthly,* November 1983.

Feagin, Joe R. *Racial and Ethnic Relations.* Englewood Cliffs, N.J.: Prentice-Hall, 1978.

Feagin, Joe R., and Douglas Lee Eckberg. "Discrimination: Motivation, Action, Effects, and Context." *Annual Review of Sociology* 6 (1980): 1–20.

Featherman, David L., and Robert M. Hauser. *Opportunity and Change.* New York: Academic Press, 1978.

Featherman, David L., F. Lancaster Jones, and Robert M. Hauser. "Assumptions of Social Mobility Research in the U.S.: The Case of Occupational Status." *Social Science Research* 4 (1975): 329–360.

Fernández, Gastón A. "The Freedom Flotilla: A Legitimacy Crisis of Cuban Socialism? *Journal of Interamerican Studies and World Affairs* 24 (May 1982): 183–209.

Fitzgerald, Frank T. "Reviewing the Literature on the Institutionalization of the Cuban Revolution: A Response to Max Azicri." *Cuban Studies* 11 (January 1981): 87–89.

"Flight from Cuba—Castro's Loss Is U.S. Gain," *U.S. News & World Report,* 31 May 1971.

Flores, Estevan T. "1982 Simpson-Mazzoli Immigration Reform and the Hispanic Community." *La Red/The Net* (newsletter of the National Chicano Council on Higher Education), February 1983, pp. 14–16.

Foner, Nancy E. *Jamaica Farewell: Jamaican Migrants in London.* Berkeley: University of California Press, 1978.

Fox, Geoffrey E. "Cuban Workers in Exile." *Trans-Action* 8 (September 1971): 21–30.

Fuentes, Carlos. "Three Dates of Change in Latin America." *Harper's,* August 1981.

Galarza, Ernesto. *Farm Workers and Agri-business in California, 1947–1960.* Notre Dame: University of Notre Dame, 1977.

————. *Merchants of Labor: The Mexican Bracero Story.* Santa Barbara, Calif.: McNally & Loftin, 1964.

————. "Some Comments on the Mexican Migratory Subculture." In *Immigrants—and Immigrants,* edited by Arthur F. Corwin. Westport, Conn.: Greenwood, 1978.

Gamio, Manual. *The Mexican Immigrant: His Life Story.* Chicago: University of Chicago Press, 1931.

Gans, Herbert J. *The Urban Villagers: Group and Class in the Life of Italian Americans.* New York: Free Press, 1962.

Giddens, Anthony. *Sociology: A Brief but Critical Introduction.* New York: Harcourt Brace Jovanovich, 1982.

Gilmore, N. Ray, and Gladys W. Gilmore. "The Bracero in California." *Pacific Historical Review* 32 (August 1963): 265–282.

Glazer, Nathan. "Blacks and Ethnic Groups: The Difference, and the Political Difference It Makes." *Social Problems* 18 (Spring 1971): 444–461.

Gold, David A., Clarence Y. H. Lo, and Erik Olin Wright. "Recent Developments in Marxist Theories of the Capitalist State." *Monthly Review* 27 (October 1975): 29–43.

Gordon, David M. *Theories of Poverty and Underemployment.* Lexington, Mass.: D. C. Heath, 1972.

Gordon, Milton M. "Assimilation in America: Theory and Reality." In *Majority and Minority,* edited by Norman R. Yetman and C. Hoy Steele. Boston: Allyn and Bacon, 1982.

————. *Assimilation in American Life.* New York: Oxford University Press, 1964.

Gossett, Thomas F. *Race: The History of an Idea in America.* New York: Schocken, 1971.

Greeley, Andrew M. *Ethnicity in the United States: A Preliminary Reconnaissance.* New York: Wiley, 1974.

"Growers Face Loss of Braceros." *Business Week,* 22 August 1964.

Gugler, Joseph. "A Minimum of Urbanism and a Maximum of Ruralism: The Cuban Experience." *Studies in Comparative International Development* 15 (Summer 1980): 27–44.

Gunder Frank, André. "The Development of Underdevelopment." In *The Political Economy of Development and Underdevelopment,* edited by Charles K. Wilber. New York: Random House, 1979.

Hall, Joe. *The Cuban Refugee in the Public Schools of Dade County, Florida.* Annual Reports no. 1–12. Dade County, Florida: Board of Public Instruction, Department of Administrative Research, 1960/1961–1972/1973.

Haller, Archibald O., and Alejandro Portes. "Status Attainment Processes." *Sociology of Education* 46 (1973): 51–91.

Handlin, Oscar. *The Newcomers: Negroes and Puerto Ricans in a Changing Metropolis.* Cambridge: Harvard University Press, 1959.

————. *The Uprooted.* Boston: Little, Brown, 1973.

Hansen, Marcus L. *The Atlantic Migration, 1607–1860: A History of the*

Continuing Settlement of the United States. Cambridge: Harvard University Press, 1940.

Hardin, Henry N. *Evaluating Cuban Education*. Miami: University of Miami Press, 1965.

Hauser, Robert M., and David L. Featherman. *The Process of Stratification: Trends and Analyses*. New York: Academic Press, 1977.

Heer, David M. "What Is the Annual Net Flow of Undocumented Mexican Immigrants to the United States?" *Demography* 16 (August 1979): 417–423.

Herberg, Will. *Protestant-Catholic-Jew*. Garden City, N.Y.: Doubleday, 1955.

Higham, John. *Strangers in the Land: Patterns of American Nativism 1860–1925*. New Jersey: Rutgers University Press, 1955.

Hirschman, Albert O. *Exit, Voice and Loyalty*. Cambridge: Harvard University Press, 1970.

Hirschman, Charles. "Prior U.S. Residence among Mexican Immigrants." *Social Forces* 56 (June 1978): 1179–1202.

Hochschild, Arlie. "Student Power in Action." In *Cuban Communism*, edited by Irving Louis Horowitz. New Brunswick, N.J.: Transaction, 1977.

Hodge, Robert W., Paul M. Siegel, and Peter H. Rossi. "Occupational Prestige in the United States, 1925–63." *American Journal of Sociology* 70 (November 1964): 286–302.

Hoffman, Abraham. "Mexican Repatriation during the Great Depression: A Reappraisal." In *Immigrants—and Immigrants*, edited by Arthur F. Corwin. Westport, Conn.: Greenwood, 1978.

———. "Mexican Repatriation Statistics: Some Suggested Alternatives to Carey McWilliams." *Western Historical Quarterly* 3 (October 1972): 391–404.

Horan, Patrick M. "Is Status Attainment Research Atheoretical?" *American Sociological Review* 43 (August 1978): 534–541.

Horowitz, Irving Louis. "Authenticity and Autonomy in Cuban Communism." In *Cuban Communism*, edited by Irving Louis Horowitz. New Brunswick, N.J.: Transaction, 1977.

———. "Institutionalization as Integration: The Cuban Revolution at Age Twenty." *Cuban Studies* 9 (July 1979): 84–90.

———. "Military Origins of the Cuban Revolution." In *Cuban Communism*, edited by Irving Louis Horowitz. New Brunswick, N.J.: Transaction, 1977.

"How the Immigrants Made It in Miami." *Business Week*, 1 May 1977.

Huberman, Leo, and Paul M. Sweezy. *Socialism in Cuba*. New York: Monthly Review Press, 1969.

"The Immigration Bills: A Comparison." *New York Times*, 21 June 1984.

"'Invasion' by Illegal Aliens, and the Problems They Create." *U.S. News & World Report*, 23 July 1973.

"Iowa Sí!" *Newsweek*, 19 August 1963.

"It's Your Turn in the Sun." *Time*, 16 October 1978.

222   *Bibliography*

Jenkins, J. Craig, and Charles Perrow. "Insurgency of the Powerless: Farm Worker Movements (1946–1972)." *American Sociological Review* 42 (April 1977): 249–268.

Jones, Maldwyn Allen. *American Immigration.* Chicago: University of Chicago Press, 1960.

Keely, Charles B. "Effects of the Immigration Act of 1965 on Selected Population Characteristics of Immigrants to the United States." *Demography* 8 (May 1971): 157–169.

Kelly, James. "Closing the Golden Door." *Time,* 18 May 1981.

Kennedy, Edward M. "The Immigration Act of 1965." *Annals of the American Academy of Political and Social Sciences* 367 (September 1966): 137–149.

———. "Refugee Act of 1980." *International Migration Review* 15 (Spring 1981): 141–156.

Kennedy, Ruby Jo Reeves. "Single or Triple Melting-Pot? Intermarriage Trends in New Haven, 1870–1940." *American Journal of Sociology* 49 (January 1944): 331–339.

———. "Single or Triple Melting-Pot? Intermarriage in New Haven, 1870–1950." *American Journal of Sociology* 58 (July 1952): 56–59.

Lamm, Richard D. "America Needs Fewer Immigrants." *New York Times,* 12 July 1981.

Lee, Everett S. "A Theory of Migration." *Demography* 3 (1966): 47–57.

Levy, Jacques E. *Cesar Chavez: Autobiography of La Causa.* New York: W. W. Norton, 1975.

Linehan, Edward J. "Cuba's Exiles Bring New Life to Miami." *National Geographic* 144 (July 1973): 68–95.

"The Little Strike That Grew to La Causa." *Time,* 4 July 1969.

Llanes, José. *Cuban Americans: Masters of Survival.* Cambridge, Mass.: ABT, 1982.

Long, James E. "Productivity, Employment, Discrimination, and the Relative Economic Status of Spanish-Origin Males." *Social Science Quarterly* 58 (December 1977): 357–373.

Majka, Linda C. "Labor Militancy among Farm Workers and the Strategy of Protest: 1900–1979." *Social Problems* 28 (June 1981): 533–547.

Mannheim, Karl. *Essays in the Sociology of Knowledge.* New York: Oxford University Press, 1952.

Massey, Douglas S. "Dimensions of the New Immigration to the United States and the Prospects for Assimilation." *Annual Review of Sociology* 7 (1981): 57–85.

McWilliams, Carey. *Factories in the Field: The Story of Migratory Farm Labor in California.* Boston, Mass.: Little, Brown, 1939.

———. *North from Mexico: The Spanish-Speaking People of the United States.* New York: Greenwood, 1968.

Mesa-Lago, Carmelo. *Cuba in the 1970s: Pragmatism and Institutionalization.* Albuquerque: University of New Mexico Press, 1978.

———. "Ideological Radicalization and Economic Policy in Cuba." In

Cuban Communism, edited by Irving Louis Horowitz. New Brunswick, N.J.: Transaction, 1977.

————, ed. *Revolutionary Change in Cuba*. Pittsburgh: University of Pittsburgh Press, 1971.

México. Dirección General de Estadística. *VIII Censo General de Población, 1960:* Resumen General. Mexico, D.F., 1963.

Micocci, Antonio A. "A New Life for Cuban Exiles." *American Education* 1 (March 1965); 28–32.

Midgley, Elizabeth. "Immigrants: Whose Huddled Masses?" *Atlantic Monthly*, April 1978.

"Migrants and Machines." *New Republic*, 24 July 1961.

"Migrant Workers' Plight." *Fortune*, November 1959. '

Miliband, Ralph. *The State in Capitalist Society*. London: Quartet, 1973.

Mills, C. Wright. *The Sociological Imagination*. New York: Grove Press, 1961.

Mincer, Jacob. *Schooling, Experience, and Earnings*. New York: National Bureau of Economic Research, 1974.

Mittelbach, Frank G., and Joan W. Moore. "Ethnic Endogamy—The Case of Mexican Americans." *American Journal of Sociology* 74 (July 1968): 50–62.

Moncarz, Raúl. "Effects of Professional Restrictions on Cuban Refugees in Selected Health Professions in the United States 1959–1969." *International Migration* 8 (1970): 22–28.

————. "A Model of Professional Adaptation of Refugees: The Cuban Case in the U.S. 1959–1970." *International Migration* 11 (1973): 171–183.

————. "Professional Adaptation of the Cuban Teachers in the United States, 1959–1969." *International Migration* 8 (1970): 110–115.

Montalva, Eduardo Frei. "The Alliance That Lost Its Way." In *Latin American Radicalism*, edited by Irving Louis Horowitz, Josué de Castro, and John Gerassi. New York: Vintage, 1969.

Montgomery, Paul. "For Cuban Refugees, Promise of U.S. Fades." *New York Times*, 19 April 1981.

Moore, Joan W. *Mexican Americans*. Englewood Cliffs, N.J.: Prentice-Hall, 1976.

National Opinion Research Center. *General Social Surveys, 1972–1978: Cumulative Code Book*. Chicago: NORC, 1977.

Nettl, J. P. "The State as a Conceptual Variable." *World Politics* 20 (July 1968): 559–592.

Newman, Morris J. "A Profile of Hispanics in the U.S. Work Force." *Monthly Labor Review* 101 (December 1978): 3–14.

Noel, Donald L. "A Theory of the Origin of Ethnic Stratification." *Social Problems* 16 (Fall 1968): 157–172.

North, David S., and Marion F. Houstoun. *The Characteristics and Role of Illegal Aliens in the U.S. Labor Market: An Exploratory Study*. Washington, D.C.: Linton, 1976.

O'Connor, James. *The Fiscal Crisis of the State*. New York: St. Martin's, 1973.

Otheguy, Ricardo. "Language Rights and Linguistic Minorities: The United
  States Case." In *International Human Rights: Contemporary Issues,*
  edited by Jack L. Nelson and Vera M. Green. New York: Earl M.
  Coleman, 1980.
Park, Robert E. "Human Migration and the Marginal Man." *American Jour-
  nal of Sociology* 33 (May 1928): 881–893.
———. *Race and Culture.* New York: Free Press, 1950.
Patterson, Orlando. "Context and Choice in Ethnic Allegiance: A Theo-
  retical Framework and Caribbean Case Study." In *Ethnicity: Theory
  and Experience,* edited by Nathan Glazer and Daniel P. Moynihan.
  Cambridge: Harvard University Press, 1976.
Pear, Robert. "Aliens Bill Nears Reality." *New York Times,* 18 June 1984.
———. "Ambitious Immigration Bill Fails As Charges of Blame Are Traded."
  New York Times, 12 October 1984.
———. "Bill on Aliens a Divisive Issue for Democrats." *New York Times,*
  22 April 1984.
———. "Conference on Immigration Bill Stalls." *New York Times,* 26 Sep-
  tember 1984.
———. "House Backs Plan Legalizing Aliens in U.S. before 1982. *New
  York Times,* 18 June 1984.
———. "House, by 216–211, Approves Aliens Bill after Retaining Am-
  nesty Plan in Final Test." *New York Times,* 21 June 1984.
———. "House to Debate Immigration Bill despite Pleas of Hispanic
  Groups." *New York Times,* 12 June 1984.
———. "The Immigration Bill's Melting Pot." *New York Times,* 2 July 1984.
———. "Immigration Reform Is Alive and Well." *New York Times,* 22 May
  1983.
———. "Reagan Aides Draft a Plan to Let Mexicans Work in U.S. as Guests."
  New York Times, 11 May 1981.
———. "Senate Approves Immigration Bill with Hiring Curb." *New York
  Times,* 19 May 1983.
———. "Senate Votes a Sweeping Revision of the Nation's Immigration
  Laws." *New York Times,* 18 August 1982.
Pedraza-Bailey, Silvia. "Talcott Parsons and Structural Marxism: Func-
  tionalist Theories of Society." *Current Perspectives in Social Theory* 3
  (1982): 207–224.
Pedraza-Bailey, Silvia, and Teresa A. Sullivan. "Bilingual Education in the
  Reception of Political Immigrants: The Case of Cubans in Miami,
  Florida." In *Bilingual Education and Public Policy in the United
  States,* edited by Raymond V. Padilla. Ypsilanti: Eastern Michigan Uni-
  versity, 1979.
Petersen, William. "International Migration." *Annual Review of Sociology*
  4 (1978): 533–575.
Portes, Alejandro. "Illegal Immigration and the International System,
  Lessons from Recent Legal Mexican Immigrants to the United States."
  In *Majority and Minority,* edited by Norman R. Yetman and C. Hoy
  Steele. Boston, Mass.: Allyn and Bacon, 1982.

———. "Immigrant Aspirations." *Sociology of Education* 51 (October 1978): 241–260.

———. "Migration and Underdevelopment." *Politics & Society* 8 (1978): 1–48.

———. "Return of the Wetback." *Society* 11 (March–April 1974): 40–46.

———. "Structural Causes of Illegal Immigration." Duke University: Department of Sociology, 1977. Mimeographed.

Portes, Alejandro, Juan M. Clark, and Robert L. Bach. "The New Wave: A Statistical Profile of Recent Cuban Exiles to the United States." *Cuban Studies* 7 (January 1977): 1–32.

Poston, Dudley L., Jr., and David Alvírez. "On the Cost of Being a Mexican American Worker." *Social Science Quarterly* 53 (March 1973): 697–709.

Poston, Dudley L., Jr., David Alvírez, and Marta Tienda. "Earnings Differences between Anglo and Mexican American Male Workers in 1960 and 1970: Changes in the 'Cost' of Being Mexican American." *Social Science Quarterly* 57 (December 1976): 618–631.

Poston, Dudley L., Jr., Walter T. Martin, and Jerry D. Goodman. "The Socioeconomic Patterns of the New Immigrants to the U.S.: Does Increased Visibility Mean Decreased Opportunities?" Austin: University of Texas, Department of Sociology, 1978.

Poulantzas, Nicos. *Political Power and Social Classes.* London: NLB, 1973.

Prohías, Rafael J., and Lourdes Casal. *The Cuban Minority in the U.S.: Preliminary Report on Need Identification and Program Evaluation.* Washington, D.C.: Cuban National Planning Council, 1974.

Przeworski, Adam. "Proletariat into a Class: The Process of Class Formation from Karl Kautsky's *The Class Struggle* to Recent Controversies." *Politics & Society* 7 (1977): 343–401.

Pye, Lucien W. "The Concept of Political Development." In *Political Development and Social Change*, edited by Jason L. Finkle and Richard W. Gable. New York: Wiley, 1971.

Reichert, Joshua S., and Douglas S. Massey, "Patterns of U.S. Migration from a Mexican Sending Community: A Comparison of Legal and Illegal Migrants." *International Migration Review* 13 (Winter 1979): 599–623.

Ripoll, Carlos. "The Cuban Scene: Censors and Dissenters." *Partisan Review* 48 (1981): 574–587.

Rist, Ray C. "Guestworkers in Germany: Public Policies as the Legitimation of Marginality." *Ethnic and Racial Studies* 2 (October 1979): 401–415.

Ritchey, P. Neal. "Explanations of Migration." *Annual Review of Sociology* 2 (1976): 363–404.

Rivlin, Alice M. "Income Distribution—Can Economists Help?" In *Problems in Political Economy: An Urban Perspective*, edited by David M. Gordon. Lexington, Mass.: D. C. Heath, 1977.

Roca, Sergio. "Cuban Economic Policy in the 1970s: The Trodden Paths." In *Cuban Communism*, edited by Irving Louis Horowitz. New Brunswick, N.J.: Transaction, 1977.

Rogg, Eleanor Meyer. *The Assimilation of Cuban Exiles: The Role of Community and Class.* New York: Aberdeen, 1974.

Safilios-Rothschild, Constantina. *Women and Social Policy.* Englewood Cliffs, N.J.: Prentice-Hall, 1974.

Samora, Julian. *Los Mojados: The Wetback Story.* Notre Dame: University of Notre Dame Press, 1971.

San Martín, Marta, and Ramón L. Bonachea. "The Military Dimension of the Cuban Revolution." In *Cuban Communism,* edited by Irving Louis Horowitz. New Brunswick, N.J.: Transaction, 1977.

Schermerhorn, Richard A. *Comparative Ethnic Relations: A Framework for Theory and Research.* Chicago: University of Chicago Press, 1978.

Schlesinger, Arthur M., Jr., ed. *The Dynamics of World Power: A Documentary History of United States Foreign Policy 1945−1973.* 5 vols. New York: Chelsea House, 1973.

Schoen, Robert, and Lawrence E. Cohen. "Ethnic Endogamy among Mexican American Grooms: A Reanalysis of Generational and Occupational Effects." *American Journal of Sociology* 86 (September 1980): 359−366.

Schoen, Robert, and Verne E. Nelson. "Intermarriage among Spanish Surnamed Californians, 1962−1974." *International Migration Review* 12 (Fall 1978): 359−369.

Schreiber, Anna P. "Economic Coercion as an Instrument of Foreign Policy: U.S. Economic Measures against Cuba and the Dominican Republic." *World Politics* 25 (April 1973): 387−413.

Select Commission on Immigration and Refugee Policy. *U.S. Immigration Policy and the National Interest.* Final Report and Recommendations of the Select Commission on Immigration and Refugee Policy to the Congress and the President of the United States, March 1, 1981.

Severo, Richard. "The Flight of the Wetbacks." *New York Times Magazine,* 10 March 1974.

Sevick, Charles V. "A History and Evaluation of the Cuban Teacher Retraining Program of the University of Miami 1963−1974." Ph.D. diss., University of Miami, 1974.

Sewell, William H., and Robert M. Hauser. *Education, Occupation and Earnings: Achievement in the Early Career.* New York: Academic Press, 1975.

Siegel, Paul M. "On the Cost of Being a Negro." *Sociological Inquiry* 35 (Winter 1965): 41−57.

Smith, Richard Ferree. "Refugees." *Annals of the American Academy of Political and Social Sciences* 367 (September 1966): 43−52.

Sowell, Thomas. *Ethnic America: A History.* New York: Basic, 1981.

Spear, Allan H. *Black Chicago: The Making of a Negro Ghetto 1890−1920.* Chicago: University of Chicago Press, 1969.

Stein, Jeff. "An Army in Exile." *New York,* 10 September 1979.

Sternberger, Dolf. "Legitimacy." *International Encyclopedia of the Social Sciences.* Vol. 9. New York: Macmillan, 1968.

Stinchcombe, Arthur L. *Constructing Social Theories.* New York: Harcourt, Brace & World, 1968.

———. "Social Mobility in Industrial Labor Markets." *Acta Sociologica* 22 (1979): 217–245.

———. "Some Empirical Consequences of the Davis-Moore Theory of Stratification." *American Sociological Review* 28 (October 1963): 805–808.

Stoessinger, John G. *The Might of Nations.* New York: Random House, 1982.

Stolzenberg, Ross M. "Bringing the Boss Back In: Employer Size, Employee Schooling, and Socioeconomic Achievement." *American Sociological Review* 43 (December 1978): 813–828.

Sullivan, Teresa A. *Marginal Workers, Marginal Jobs: The Underutilization of American Workers.* Austin: University of Texas Press, 1978.

Tabori, Paul. *The Anatomy of Exile.* London: Harrap, 1972.

Taylor, Paul S. *An American-Mexican Frontier: Nueces County, Texas.* New York: Russell & Russell, 1971.

———. *Mexican Labor in the United States: Chicago and the Calumet Region.* Berkeley: University of California Press, 1932.

Taylor, Ronald B. *Chavez.* Boston: Beacon, 1975.

Teitelbaum, Herbert, and Richard J. Hiller. "Bilingual Education: The Legal Mandate." *Harvard Educational Review* 47 (May 1977): 138–170.

Teitelbaum, Michael S. "Right versus Right: Immigration and Refugee Policy in the United States." *Foreign Affairs* 59 (Fall 1980): 21–59.

Thomas, Brinley. *Migration and Economic Growth.* Cambridge: Cambridge University Press, 1954.

Thomas, Hugh. *The Cuban Revolution.* New York: Harper & Row, 1977.

Thomas, John F. "Cuban Refugee Program." *Welfare in Review* 1 (September 1963): 1–20.

———. "Cuban Refugees in the United States." *International Migration Review* 2 (Spring 1967): 46–57.

Thomas, William I., and Florian Znaniecki. *The Polish Peasant in Europe and America.* Vol. 2. New York: Alfred A. Knopf, 1927.

Tienda, Marta. "A Socioeconomic Profile of Hispanic-American Male Workers: Perspectives on Labor Utilization and Earnings." In *National Symposium on Hispanics and CETA 1980,* edited by Antonio Furino. San Antonio: University of Texas at San Antonio, Human Resources Management and Development Program, 1980.

Tilly, Charles. "Historical Sociology." *Current Perspectives in Social Theory* 1 (1980): 55–59.

———. "Western State-Making and Theories of Political Transformation." In *The Formation of National States in Western Europe,* edited by Charles Tilly. Princeton, N.J.: Princeton University Press, 1975.

"Tossed Salad." *Newsweek,* 20 February 1961.

Trout, B. Thomas. "Rhetoric Revisited: Political Legitimation and the Cold War." *International Studies Quarterly* 19 (September 1975): 251–284.

Tumin, Melvin M. "Some Principles of Stratification: A Critical Analysis." *American Sociological Review* 18 (August 1953): 387–394.

U.S. Bureau of the Census. *Census of Population: 1970.* Vol. 1, *Characteristics of the Population,* Part 1, United States Summary—Section 1. Washington, D.C.: U.S. Government Printing Office, 1973.

———. *Census of Population, 1970. Subject Reports: Earnings by Occupation and Education.* Final Report PC(2)-8B. Washington, D.C.: U.S. Government Printing Office, 1973.

———. *Census of Population, 1970. Subject Reports: Educational Attainment.* Final Report PC(2)-5B. Washington, D.C.: U.S. Government Printing Office, 1973.

———. *Current Population Reports.* Series P-20, no. 99. "Literacy and Educational Attainment: March 1959." Washington, D.C.: U.S. Government Printing Office, 1960.

———. *Current Population Reports.* Series P-20, no. 307. "Population Profile of the United States: 1976." Washington, D.C.: U.S. Government Printing Office, 1977.

———. *Current Population Reports.* Series P-20, no. 354. "Persons of Spanish Origin in the United States: March 1979." Washington, D.C.: U.S. Government Printing Office, 1980.

———. *Public Use Samples of Basic Records from the 1970 Census: Description and Technical Documentation.* Washington, D.C.: U.S. Government Printing Office, 1972.

———. *Statistical Abstract of the U.S.: 1973.* 94th ed. Washington, D.C.: U.S. Government Printing Office, 1973.

———. *Statistical Abstract of the U.S.: 1977.* 98th ed. Washington, D.C.: U.S. Government Printing Office, 1977.

U.S. Commission on Civil Rights. *Social Indicators of Equality for Minorities and Women.* Washington, D.C.: U.S. Government Printing Office, 1978.

———. *The Tarnished Golden Door: Civil Rights Issues in Immigration.* Washington, D.C.: U.S. Government Printing Office, 1980.

U.S. Department of State. *Department of State Bulletin,* weekly, 1955–1978.

U.S. Immigration and Naturalization Service. *1960 Annual Report of the Immigration and Naturalization Service.* Washington, D.C.: U.S. Government Printing Office, 1960.

———. *1970 Annual Report of the Immigration and Naturalization Service.* Washington, D.C.: U.S. Government Printing Office, 1971.

———. *1980 Statistical Yearbook of the Immigration and Naturalization Service.* Washington, D.C.: U.S. Government Printing Office, 1983.

University of Miami, Center for Advanced International Studies. *The Cuban Immigration 1959–1966 and Its Impact on Miami–Dade County, Florida.* Coral Gables: University of Miami, 1967.

Van den Berghe, Pierre L. *Race and Racism: A Comparative Perspective.* New York: Wiley, 1978.

"Violence in the Oasis." *Time,* 17 February 1961.

Wallerstein, Immanuel. *The Modern-World System*. New York: Academic Press, 1974.

Walsh, Bryan O. "Cuban Refugee Children." *Journal of Inter-American Studies and World Affairs* 13 (June 1971): 378–415.

Weber, Max. *Economy and Society*. Edited by Guenther Roth and Claus Wittich. 2 vols. Berkeley: University of California Press, 1978.

Weintraub, Sidney, and Stanley R. Ross. *The Illegal Alien from Mexico: Policy Choices for an Intractable Issue*. Austin: University of Texas Press, 1980.

"Where Braceros Once Worked." *Business Week*, 16 January 1965.

Wilson, William J. *The Declining Significance of Race*. Chicago: University of Chicago Press, 1978.

Wolpe, Harold. "Industrialism and Race in South Africa." In *Race and Racialism*, edited by Sami Zubaida. London: Tavistock, 1970.

Wright, Erik Olin, and Luca Perrone. "Marxist Class Categories and Income Inequality." *American Sociological Review* 42 (February 1977): 32–55.

Yetman, Norman R., and C. Hoy Steele, eds. *Majority and Minority*. Boston: Allyn and Bacon, 1982.

Zeitlin, Maurice. "Cuba: Revolution without a Blueprint." In *Cuban Communism*, edited by Irving Louis Horowitz. New Brunswick, N.J.: Transaction, 1977.

———. "Economic Insecurity and the Political Attitudes of Cuban Workers." *American Sociological Review* 31 (February 1966): 35–51.

———. "Political Generations in the Cuban Working Class." *American Journal of Sociology* 71 (March 1966): 493–508.

Index